DATE DUE

NOV 14 '80			
APR 3 0			
MAY 2 7			
JUN 10			
FEB 10			
APR 1 9 1988			
JUL 1 4 1988			
MAY 20 '91			
MAY 1 7 1994			
DEC 1 1994			
OCT 1 8 1995			
NOV 2 1 1995			
DEC 1 3 1995			
APR 0 1 2002			
APR 2 4 2002			

DEMCO 38-297

INSTITUTE OF PSYCHIATRY
Maudsley Monographs

ALCOHOLISM

INSTITUTE OF PSYCHIATRY

MAUDSLEY MONOGRAPHS

Number Twenty-Six

ALCOHOLISM

A comparison of treatment and advice,
with a study of the influence of marriage

By

JIM ORFORD

M.A., DIP. PSYCH., PH.D.
Senior Lecturer in Clinical Psychology
University of Exeter
Principal Clinical Psychologist
Exe Vale Hospital, Exeter
previously Senior Lecturer and Research Worker
Institute of Psychiatry

and

GRIFFITH EDWARDS

M.A., D.M., F.R.C.P., F.R.C. PSYCH., D.P.M.
Reader in Drug Dependence
University of London
Institute of Psychiatry
Honorary Consultant
Bethlem Royal Hospital and the Maudsley Hospital
Honorary Director, Addiction Research Unit, Institute of Psychiatry

OXFORD UNIVERSITY PRESS
1977

Oxford University Press, Walton Steet, Oxford OX2 6DP

OXFORD LONDON GLASGOW NEW YORK
TORONTO MELBOURNE WELLINGTON CAPE TOWN
IBADAN NAIROBI DAR ES SALAAM LUSAKA ADDIS ABABA
KUALA LUMPUR SINGAPORE JAKARTA HONG KONG TOKYO
DELHI BOMBAY CALCUTTA MADRAS KARACHI

British Library Cataloguing in Publication Data

Edwards, Griffith
    Alcoholism. – (Maudsley monographs; no. 26).
    1. Alcoholism – Treatment – Great Britain
    2. Marriage – Great Britain
    I. Title   II. Orford, Jim   III. Series
    362.2'92   HV5275   ·77–30166

ISBN 0–19–712148–9

*Printed in Great Britain
by Richard Clay (The Chaucer Press), Ltd,
Bungay, Suffolk*

CONTENTS

MAUDSLEY MONOGRAPHS

HENRY MAUDSLEY, from whom the series of monographs takes its name, was the founder of The Maudsley Hospital and the most prominent English psychiatrist of his generation. The Maudsley Hospital was united with the Bethlem Royal Hospital in 1948, and its medical school, renamed the Institute of Psychiatry at the same time, became a constituent part of the British Postgraduate Medical Federation. It is entrusted by the University of London with the duty to advance psychiatry by teaching and research.

The monograph series reports work carried out in the Institute and in the associated Hospital. Some of the monographs are directly concerned with clinical problems; others, less obviously relevant, are in scientific fields that are cultivated for the furtherance of psychiatry.

Joint Editors

PROFESSOR SIR DENIS HILL   PROFESSOR G. S. BRINDLEY
F.R.C.P., F.R.C.PSYCH., D.P.M.   M.D., F.R.C.P., F.R.S.

with the assistance of

MISS S. E. HAGUE, B.SC. (ECON.), M.A.

ACKNOWLEDGEMENTS

WE would like to thank Professor Sir Denis Hill in whose Department this research was conducted for his constant support and encouragement of the work of the Addiction Research Unit. This study was very much a team effort and we would like to thank our collaborators: Mrs. Stella Egert, Miss Celia Hensman, Mrs. Sally Guthrie, Dr. Martin Mitcheson, Mr. Peter Nicholls, Miss Edna Oppenheimer, Mr. Upendra Patel, and Mr. Colin Taylor. Dr. A. N. Oppenheim played a major part in the design of this study and we are grateful for his generous help. Assistance with coding was given by Miss Christina Kells. Mrs. Joyce Oliphant and Miss Beryl Skinner were project secretaries. The preparation of this report involved a great deal of expert secretarial work which was undertaken with unfailing patience by Mrs. Julia Polglaze. Staff of the Bethlem Royal and Maudsley Hospitals helped in the treatment programme.

Some previously published material has been reprinted by permission in modified form, as follows. From the *Journal of Studies on Alcohol*, Vol. 36, pp 1254–67, 1975; Vol. 36, pp 1537–63, 1975; and Vol. 38, pp 1004–31, 1977 (Copyright by Journal of Studies on Alcohol, Inc., New Brunswick, NJ 08903). From the *Journal of Consulting and Clinical Psychology*, Vol. 44, pp 534–45, 1976 (Copyright, 1976, by the American Psychological, Association). From *Behaviour Research and Therapy*, Vol. 14, pp 409–18, 1976. From the *British Journal of Psychiatry*, Vol. 128, pp 318–39, 1976. From the *Proceedings of the Royal Society of Medicine*, Vol. 70, 1977, and from the *International Journal of the Addictions*. The DHSS, Home Office, and Customs and Excise provided the official statistics which are quoted in CHAPTER I.

The study was initially supported by the Nuffield Foundation, and later jointly by the MRC and the DHSS.

J.O
G.E.

London
1977

SUMMARY

INTRODUCTION

(1) Any research which can speak to the more effective design of alcoholism treatment services will bear on an important issue of health planning. Over £4 million is a conservative estimate of the amount being spent by the NHS annually on in-patient and out-patient care of alcoholics. If treatment is less effective than assumed, then the need for prevention becomes the more urgent: treatment is one element in the *national response* to drinking.

CHAPTER I THE EVOLUTION OF PRESENT TREATMENT SERVICES

(2) The evolution of Britain's present pattern of services for treatment of alcoholism is discussed, with particular emphasis on the last twenty-five years. In 1962 the Ministry of Health advised the setting up of small specialized in-patient units with an emphasis on group therapy, but there has since been a shift toward a more community-based treatment model, and a greater acceptance of an out-patient approach. The influence of research on policy developments is considered.

(3) NHS admissions to mental illness hospitals for treatment of alcoholism and alcoholic psychosis have increased about twentyfold in the last twenty-five years. True increase in prevalence of alcoholism contributed, but a greater willingness to accept help has probably been substantially important also. It therefore becomes a crucial question whether this growing investment in the treatment element of the national response is effective. A brief review of the international literature reveals little evidence that any particular treatment regime is better than any other, or that intensive help gives better results than a less intensive approach.

CHAPTER II ALCOHOLISM AND MARRIAGE

(4) A number of disparate approaches are evident in the literature on alcoholism and marriage. One line of thought views the behaviour of the alcoholic's spouse as crisis reaction, and is concerned with such matters as altered marriage roles and family coping responses. Another line stresses the personality disturbance of spouses, and is concerned with such matters as abnormal mate choice and 'decompensation' by wives when their husbands recover. Other notable research has examined interperson perception and marriage.

(5) This literature is criticized on two grounds. Firstly, there is an absence of an overall social psychological theory which would serve to integrate the various separate approaches. Secondly, the field is over-specialized, with too little reference to the wider field of marriage research. Few previous investigations have looked specifically at factors within marriage which influence alcoholism treatment outcome. This was part of the purpose of the present research.

CHAPTER III BASIC RESEARCH DESIGN

(6) The sample consisted of 100 marriages in which the husband was an alcoholic. After comprehensive out-patient assessment which included measures of marital interaction, and with independent information from husband and wife, families were randomized between Treatment and Advice groups. *Advice group families* were immediately given an initial session of counselling and were then left with the responsibility for working towards stated goals. They were given no further appointments but were of course quite free to seek help elsewhere. *Treatment group families* were offered a comprehensive programme of psychiatric and social work care. The

treatment model is seen as generally congruent with present views of what should constitute a reasonable standard of specialized help for the alcoholic.

(7) For twelve months after initial assessment, four-weekly follow-up assessments were obtained from wives only in both groups. At the end of the twelve months a full follow-up assessment was made involving both husbands and wives. During the second year no attempt was made to maintain a distinction between the treatment experience of the two groups, but patients were followed up to twenty-four months particularly with a view to examining variations in drinking behaviour and evidence for controlled drinking.

Chapter IV   Results of the Trial at Twelve Months

(8) The two groups were satisfactorily matched. Full follow-up information was obtained on 46/50 Advice and 48/50 Treatment patients. A variety of treatment outcome measures, including abstinence, drinking level, symptoms, wife's hardship, perceived improvement, and employment, showed no significant between-group differences.

(9) There was conclusive evidence that the treatment experience of the two groups remained sharply contrasted during the study year, with Advice group patients engaging in relatively little compensatory help-seeking. In the Treatment group about one-third of patients had rather minimal therapeutic contact despite what was offered (0–6 out-patient visits in the year), about one-third had medium intensity contact (7–12 visits), and the remaining third had more intensive contact (13 + visits). In addition, one quarter of the Treatment patients were admitted to a specialized alcoholism treatment unit for four weeks or longer. By and large, within neither group was greater engagement in help-seeking related to better outcome, except that the minority of Advice group patients who were frequent AA attenders was larger for those with a good outcome than for those with a bad outcome, and improved Treatment group patients had more frequently attended GPs and general hospitals.

(10) At the end of twelve months, each patient completed a check list of factors which might have aided in improvement. In rank order, and for both groups, the four items given the highest rating did not include in-patient care, out-patient care, AA, or other helping agency contact. Changes in external reality (especially occupation and housing), intra-psychic change, and change in the marital relationship were rated more highly. The single session of advice which had been given at the start of the year was valued by both groups. Advice group patients were significantly more likely than Treatment group patients to see change in external reality as helpful.

(11) There was no evidence at twelve months of a significant treatment/patient interaction effect: it was not the 'more ill' patients (those with more 'symptoms' or 'troubles') who had done better with treatment than advice.

(12) Due note should be taken of methodological limitations (which are discussed), but it may fairly be concluded from the treatment trial aspect of this study that at *twelve months the offer of a much more intensive as opposed to a much less intensive therapeutic approach had produced no effect on outcome*, but had succeeded in engaging patients in therapy and to an extent restructuring their appraisal of what had helped.

Chapter V   Marital and Other Social–environmental Factors and Treatment Outcome

(13) The 100 marriages displayed great heterogeneity in terms of a variety of marital variables including reported levels of marital affection; husband participation in

family tasks; wife favourability of perception of husband when sober; optimism about the future of the marriage; warm, hostile, and dominant behaviour in a standardized joint interview; and reported frequency of marital sexual behaviour. Variables under the first four of these headings (affection, task-participation, wife perception, and optimism) defined a factor ('marital cohesion') which significantly predicted a good drinking outcome for the husband. The meaning of the marital cohesion factor is discussed and, in view of broadly similar findings in other fields (particularly research on relapse and schizophrenia), the following general hypothesis is put forward: *That a breakdown in the mutual rewardingness of marital or other family relationships is predictive of a relatively unfavourable outcome following treatment or counselling for any psychological disorder.*

(14) Marital variables were not independent of other variables: cohesion tended to be high when occupational status and husband's self-esteem were high and when drink-related hardship for wives was low. Higher rating at intake of husband's occupational status was strongly associated with a better outcome; a higher level of wife's hardship at intake was significantly associated with a worse outcome; as were lower scores on a scale of husband's intake self-esteem. By combining occupational status, hardship, and husband's self-esteem, predictive power was increased: of twenty-two couples with extreme negative characteristics only one husband had a good outcome, while of eleven with extreme positive characteristics, only one had a bad outcome. Marital cohesion was not predictive of outcome for sub-groups of higher occupational status or higher self-esteem but remained predictive for other sub-groups. Difficulties of attributing causal significance are discussed.

(15) Stability and change in marital interaction were studied by comparing various scores at intake and twelve-month follow-up. There was considerable evidence of stability on all measures despite changes in drinking, but more evidence of changes in expected directions for some measures than for others. Wives' descriptions of their husbands when sober did not show significant change but there was significant evidence of shift toward greater husband task participation with good outcome. Affection scales were intermediate in this respect. These results are difficult to incorporate into any simple model of alcoholism and marriage.

(16) At intake each wife was asked whether she had used each of fifty-six forms of coping behaviour. Wives who reported more hardship, and wives who obtained higher scores on a scale of 'neuroticism', generally reported more coping, and wives whose husbands had higher status jobs generally reported less coping. Most forms of coping carried a relatively poor prognosis especially if they implied avoidance or withdrawal. Wives who do most 'coping' may have more to cope with, and having to cope is probably to be seen as part of a deteriorated family environment. It is hypothesized that forms of coping that display engagement and discrimination may be more adaptive.

CHAPTER VI PERSONALITY AND ALCOHOLISM–COMPLICATED MARRIAGES

(17) The Eysenck Personality Inventory was administered to all husbands and wives at intake and at twelve-month follow-up. Comparison of intake scores with EPI norms showed highly significantly raised N (neuroticism) scores for husbands but normal E (extraversion) and L (lie) scores. Wives showed highly significantly raised N scores (but less than husbands), a tendency toward low E scores, and highly significantly raised L scores. There was a significant inverse relationship between duration of marriage and wives' N scores but no such relationship for husbands. Overall, husbands' N scores ($r = 0.52$) and E scores ($r = 0.50$) showed considerable

twelve-month stability. For wives also there was a considerable twelve-month stability in N scores (r = 0·75) but not E scores (r = 0·25). Husbands with better outcome showed a highly significant decrease in N scores at twelve months: at intake there was a borderline tendency for those with subsequent good outcome to show a lower N and higher E score. There was also a non-significant tendency for all wives to shift toward higher N scores and the tendency was strongest for those whose husbands had a good outcome. Alternative explanations for these findings are discussed.

(18) Adjective check list descriptions of husband sober, husband drinking, and ideal spouse showed that, overall, both spouses saw the effect of drinking as involving an increase in husbands' dominance which brought them closer to the ideal, but also as involving a decrease in affection which took behaviour further from the ideal. Socially, drinking may be both functional and malfunctional at the same time. Overall, husbands and wives agreed about the level of husbands' (sober) and wives' affection, and about husbands' dominance. A significant discrepancy, indicating an important possible source of marital conflict, existed for wives' dominance, with husbands attributing more dominance to their wives than the latter did to themselves.

CHAPTER VII ABSTINENCE OR CONTROL:
SOME FINDINGS AT TWENTY-FOUR MONTHS

(19) An attempt was made to follow-up all couples again two years after intake, but because of marital separation and other reasons it was only possible to obtain independent information from both husband and wife for sixty-five couples (whose data form the major basis of this chapter), although information from one or other spouse only was available for nineteen further couples.

(20) According to their wives all but ten of ninety-five men had drunk within the first four months after intake, by the first anniversary all but eight, and by the second anniversary all but two. Not all drinking was of a type 'unacceptable to wives' however—for instance, by twenty-four months eighteen men had still not drunk 'unacceptably'. The relapse curve is markedly negatively accelerated: similar curves have previously been described for relapse into other addictions.

(21) Comparison was made between drinking outcome at one and two years: a rather high level of stability was apparent. The same initial factors tended to be predictive at two years as at one year, but the actual predictive power of individual factors was attenuated—only wife's initial hardship remained significantly related (negatively) to good outcome.

(22) Scrutiny was then made of the second year drinking histories of twenty-six men whose second year outcome was 'good' according to stated criteria: eleven of these men were found to have been totally or virtually totally abstinent during the second twelve months, while ten men had continued to drink but in a relatively controlled and acceptable fashion—eight of this latter group had in fact been drinking in a controlled fashion from the early part of the first year. Initially, patients who became controlled drinkers were, in comparison to those who became abstainers, likely to have had lower symptom (trouble) scores, not to have been diagnosed initially as gamma alcoholics, and to have been *more* confident about abstaining.

(23) Contrary therefore to commonly held expectations, 'controlled drinking' was not a 'rare phenomenon' at two years—it was no more rare than abstinence. But if it was generally true that controlled drinkers are more usually 'non-gamma', the contention that those who 'return to normal drinking' are unlikely to be 'real alcoholics' might have some meaning.

CHAPTER VIII IMPLICATIONS FOR TREATMENT AND RESEARCH

(24) Limitations which must attach to the interpretation of this study are discussed. In particular, clinical applications have to be construed on the evidence of equal efficacy of Treatment and Advice, without an additional No Treatment control. What can though be concluded is that the approach to alcoholism treatment should *in general* be less interventionist than has been the fashion.

(25) Proposals for a basic treatment scheme are than outlined, but with many of the underlying assumptions admittedly untested. This scheme envisages (*a*) comprehensive assessment, (*b*) a single, detailed counselling session for the patient and, when the patient is married, the spouse, and (*c*) some follow-up system to check on progress. Common reasons for perhaps going beyond this basic approach in some cases are then outlined.

(26) Implications for the future organization of treatment services which would stem from such a revision in the basic treatment model are briefly noted. It becomes, for instance, an open question whether the specialism of in-patient units needs to be retained at all.

(27) Any reappraisal of the efficacy of treatment must also have implications for the relative balance of investment in treatment and prevention, within the total strategy of national response to alcohol problems. The preventive element in that response has over recent decades been much neglected.

(28) Implications for alcoholism research are considered. In so far as specific therapies are to be investigated, research would only seem worth while if radically new approaches are to be tested, rather than minor modifications of traditional regimes. Research on the influence of setting different *treatment goals*, is at present much needed. Study of the impact of *general and non-specific elements* in treatment deserves more attention. Research on *family and other natural influences* should certainly also be given priority. Study of the influence of a variety of *individual differences* which may interact with treatment should be taken further.

(29) The plea is finally repeated that alcoholism studies should not be allowed to become too isolated. Such isolation carries with it the danger of too unchallenged an investment of the therapist in his own activities, too confident pronouncements on treatment effectiveness, and too great a ritualization of therapeutic methods.

26
11
10
8
___
55

INTRODUCTION

THE treatment of alcoholism is today a considerable NHS undertaking. Data which will be presented in CHAPTER I suggest that over £4 million is being spent annually on in-patient care alone. Twenty-one special units have been established, representing a significant allocation of scarce professional manpower.

Any research which can speak to the more effective design of alcoholism treatment services will bear therefore on an important issue in health planning. It is part of the concern of this book to relate present research findings and previously reported studies very directly to the questions of how treatment services may best be developed, and the place which treatment should be accorded within the total national strategy of response to the nation's drinking problems:

The problems associated with drug dependence evoke a wide variety of responses at national and other levels. These responses often appear to be the result of quite contradictory objectives. In many countries, the situation with respect to alcohol is illustrative. The constellation of responses at national and other levels constitutes an inter-reacting system. Changes in one type of response will have an influence on others; new conditions will also affect the entire system (WHO, 1970).

Over recent years the treatment element has been much to the fore in the development of official policies on alcoholism. There has been a belief that treatment *works*, and that the proper way to grapple with the national alcoholism problem is to set up services to treat or rehabilitate even greater numbers of patients, and to bring these patients into treatment earlier. Faith in treatment has been matched by a general lack of confidence in the availability of any effective methods of prevention, and there has been little official effort directed toward planning or implementing relevant preventive strategies. The idea of changes in one type of response having possible influences on others therefore becomes real. Treatment research should not only have an influence on the design of treatments, but any consequent reappraisal of the value of treatment must surely influence thinking on the necessity for prevention. If treatment is less effective than is assumed, the need for prevention becomes the more urgent.

Before going any further with discussion of alcoholism it is necessary to find some way of meeting the semantic problems with which the word 'alcoholism' is notoriously surrounded. The term has never had any precise scientific meaning and this state of affairs is hardly likely to be repaired. Rather than try to force any new and stricter meaning on the word it is best simply to note that different research reports, different clinicians, and different government documents have all used the same word in more-or-less different ways; when interpreting any statement on alcoholism one has to try to form an idea of the way in which the word was being used in that particular setting. If there is any common core to these many meanings it is *drinking behaviour which brings serious and persistent risk of adverse consequences to physical or mental health or social adjustment*—what is to be deemed 'serious' or 'persistent', is open to many idiosyncratic assessments. Such a notion comes near to a definition put forward some time ago by the World Health Organisation (WHO, 1952). In the present book the word alcoholism will be used in this very general and inclusive manner. For the purposes of case selection, it was however necessary to set up an operational definition (p. 39), and the drinking symptomatology and other characteristics of the sample will be precisely described (pp. 43, 44).

That one should have to admit such loose usage of a key word is unsatisfactory but inevitable—perhaps more positively one should accept that this term's looseness of meaning is in accord with society's need for a very elastic word to describe such extremely variable happenings, and clusters of happenings, as may constitute the adverse consequences of excessive drinking. Stricter terminology has recently been suggested by a WHO scientific group (Edwards, Gross *et al.*, 1976): differentiation is made between a *dependence syndrome* (Edwards and Gross, 1976) and varieties of *alcohol-related disability*.

The epidemiology of alcoholism sets many questions which need not here be pursued in detail. Prevalence estimates depend on what is to count as alcoholism (Clark, 1966; Edwards, 1975), and as noted above, the meanings given to that term have been varied. Broadly speaking two distinct approaches to prevalence estimation have been used. 'Indirect estimates' take some recorded statistic (e.g. cirrhosis death rate) and calculate alcoholism prevalence on the basis of a formula which takes account of the proportion of the population experiencing the recorded event over given time, and other necessary correction factors. One indirect estimate method—the Jellinek formula, based indeed on cirrhosis death rate—suggested a figure of 86,000 alcoholics 'with complications' in England and Wales, and perhaps three times as many alcoholics 'without complications' (WHO, 1951): the terms employed are rather imprecise, but the prevalence of subjects 'with or without complications' was given as 11 per 1,000 adults. A later indirect estimate based on reported deaths from alcoholism gave a figure of 76,000 persons sufficiently severely affected to be typical of a hospital population, although not all would necessarily at any time be hospitalized (Nicholls *et al.*, 1974): the calculation related to the years 1956–60. An alternative approach is the direct community survey (with questions asked either of a sample of the population or comprehensively of relevant medical and social agencies in a given area). A household survey conducted in Camberwell in 1966 gave a prevalence rate of 31·3 'problem drinkers' per 1,000 population aged eighteen or over (Edwards, Hawker *et al.*, 1973), while a survey conducted in the same area in 1974 gave an estimate of 56 'alcohol abusers' per 1,000 population aged over sixteen (Cartwright *et al.*, 1975). A number of other British estimates have been reviewed (Edwards, 1973). The recent government White Paper (DHSS, 1975) accepted as 'a fairly conservative estimate . . . that in a health district with a population of 250,000 there might be 2,000 persons with a serious drinking problem': this estimate may well be very conservative. If, instead of categories of persons (alcoholics, problem drinkers, alcohol abusers, etc.) who are labelled as 'cases', all the bits and pieces and gradations of ways in which excessive drinking may adversely affect the individual, his family, or society were counted, a more complete and subtle picture would emerge. Such a count would have to cover the contribution of drinking to family unhappiness and family breakdown, to cycles of deviance and poverty, to unemployment, absenteeism, industrial and home accidents, to road traffic casualties, to crime, to great varieties of physical ill-health, to suicide and attempted suicide, and to much else besides. In the midst of conflicting prevalence estimates of 'cases', what is uncontentious is that the abnormal use of alcohol sets in this country a worryingly large problem, and a pressing challenge to design of effective health policies.

The present project sought to determine whether a conventional alcoholism treatment regime, of an intensity resembling that which is generally believed to be necessary and appropriate for helping people with this condition, had any objective advantage over a very much simpler and less costly approach. In a controlled trial 100 marriages in which the husband was an alcoholic, were randomized between two contrasting regimes—'Treatment' and 'Advice'. Opportunity was at the same time taken to study certain aspects of marital interaction, and the influence on treatment outcome of qualities in the patient's marriage. The marital aspect of the work is seen as of importance in its ability to illuminate some of the immediate environmental influences and processes which bear on the possibility of behaviour change. We believe that the way ahead in alcoholism treatment research should increasingly embrace the closer study of 'natural' forces which can be captured and exploited by planned therapeutic intervention.

This study was also much concerned with the development of methodology. There are many problems in applying the strategy of the controlled trial to anything so complex and various as alcoholism. Case description, measurement of outcome, measurement of the dimensions of marital interaction, all demand the development of multiple measures.

Although this book has, as its immediate focus, alcoholism treatment and the marriages of alcoholics, it certainly borrows from a wider literature. In turn it might be hoped that the alcoholism research reported here could give something back to the general business of research on psycho-social problems. We would make a strong plea against the enclosed specialism which has sometimes been a mark of the alcoholism literature.

The general shape of the book will be as follows. The first two chapters provide background reviews—a review of the development of alcoholism treatment services and of research on treatment efficacy (CHAPTER I), and a review of the literature on marriages complicated by alcoholism (CHAPTER

II). Then follows a short section (CHAPTER III) on the general design of the study. The bulk of the results on the treatment trial are given in CHAPTER IV and the following two results sections (CHAPTERS V and VI) present the work on marriage. Two-year follow-up results are given in CHAPTER VII. A final section (CHAPTER VIII) brings together the main practical and scientific implications of this study, and considers the bearing of its findings on future research strategies.

REVIEWS

CHAPTER I

THE EVOLUTION OF PRESENT TREATMENT SERVICES

In this chapter the evolution of Britain's present pattern of services for treatment of alcoholism will be discussed, with emphasis on the events of the last twenty-five years or so. The concern is both with the way in which treatment is organized, and with the actual content of treatment. The bearing of various influences and assumptions which have shaped this evolution will be examined, and in particular the degree to which policies have taken cognizance of available research results. Again, although the immediate focus of discussion is alcoholism, what is being discussed is a particular example of a much more general problem—the relationship between science and policy (Hawks, 1976).

BEFORE THE NATIONAL HEALTH SERVICE

The first major British contribution to the literature on the treatment of alcoholism was Thomas Trotter's 'essay on drunkenness' (Trotter, 1804). As an exposition of the sensitive and informed approach to the individual patient it has not been bettered. For instance, Trotter saw the importance of involving the patient's wife in the helping process. In the earlier part of the nineteenth century a number of physicians took an interest in alcoholism, but the predominant response was to view drinking as a social rather than medical problem. Buckingham's Select Committee on Intoxication (Select Committee, 1834) had no medical doctors among its members, and its proposed solutions were entirely social (Edwards, 1970). Drunkenness was a 'social evil' and the nineteenth-century Temperance movement was fundamentally a movement of social reform—the individual drunkard was to be saved, but the real target was society's acceptance of drinking and the drunkenness of the nation. But during the course of that century the emphasis was gradually to change toward greater focus on the individual casualty (or troublesome person). The Habitual Drunkards Act of 1879 established inebriates' homes which sought to treat or contain the individual alcoholic. In 1884 the foundation in London of the Society for the Study of Inebriety, witnessed the new seriousness of medical interest, and the journal of that society (today the *British Journal of Addiction*), thenceforward carried many medical contributions to the study of alcoholism. By the early part of the twentieth century there were a number of well-established private nursing homes for the treatment of inebriety, and specialists in this subject had come on the scene.

The impact of drunkenness on national productivity caused a reawakening of interest in social solutions during the First World War, and rigorous licensing laws and other control measures were introduced (Wilson, 1940; Smart, 1974). Between the two wars there was relatively little interest in alcoholism treatment in this country—a number of private nursing homes remained in operation, alcoholics were being admitted to the public mental institutions, but alcoholism was certainly not accorded high national priority on either the medical or social agendas.

It is after the Second World War that the beginnings of the evolution of present patterns of services can be identified. There were some new ideas in the air, and the treatment of alcoholism began to look more hopeful. Aversion treatment, which was pioneered at the Shadell Sanatorium in California (Voegtlin and Broz, 1949) had begun to be used in Britain; Alcoholics Anonymous, which had been founded in America in the 1930s, became established in Britain after the second war; and disulfiram which had been first used clinically in Denmark (Hald *et al.*, 1948), seemed to offer a promising new treatment. The influence of certain private practitioners (particularly Dr. Lincoln Williams, and Dr. Yerbury Dent), and of the forum provided by the Society for the Study of Addiction, should be acknowledged.

But if alcoholism treatment in post-war Britain was fully to join in the mainstream of psychiatric advance, the National Health Service (set up in 1948), had to take an interest in a subject which had up to then been seen as the province of a few enthusiastic private practitioners, or as a minor and rather unwelcome sector of asylum practice.

THE EVOLUTION OF NHS INVOLVEMENT 1948–75

The initial response by the NHS was tepid. When in 1951 an NHS consultant applied for nomination to attend a WHO scientific meeting on alcoholism in Copenhagen which was being organized by E. M. Jellinek, he states that he was told by the Ministry of Health that 'there was no alcoholism in England and Wales, and that the subject hardly merited the time of a consultant psychiatrist in the NHS' (Moss and Davies, 1967).

However, during the 1950s two NHS centres began to take a major interest in alcoholism, and their respective contributions were to be important to the evolution of NHS treatment services. A group at the Maudsley published a report on the two-year outcome for alcoholics treated in general psychiatric wards (Davies *et al.*, 1956). Therapeutic emphasis was on the patient's immediate realities and social adjustment: the social worker was an important member of the team. Disulfiram was given to most patients, and introduction effected to AA. A wide range of social factors and personality assessments were related to prognosis. The results were impressive and were taken to support a more optimistic view of alcoholism treatment than had often previously existed. The second NHS centre which at much the same time made very important contributions, was Warlingham Park (Glatt, 1955; 1961a; 1961b; 1975). The model here was sharply different from the Maudsley approach to alcoholism and was certainly for the immediate future to be more influential. The emphasis was on group therapy in the setting of a specialized and self-contained in-patient unit. Patients were expected to stay for about twelve weeks. There was close liaison with AA. The results claimed were again good.

In 1961 a joint report on alcoholism was published by the British Medical Association and the Magistrates' Association which recommended the setting up of specialized alcoholism in-patient units. This report was available to the Ministry of Health, when shortly afterwards issuing a memorandum entitled *Hospital Treatment of Alcoholism* (Ministry of Health, 1962). This was the first important evidence of major official NHS commitment to development of alcoholism treatment services. The situation which the Ministry sought to meet was described as follows:

The majority of alcoholics who receive hospital treatment . . . are admitted to psychiatric hospitals, and admissions to such hospitals for alcoholism and alcoholic psychosis increased from 775 in 1953 to 2044 in 1959. Few psychiatric hospitals have provision specifically for alcoholism. In 1959 over half the patients admitted to psychiatric hospitals were scattered throughout 100 hospitals, the number admitted to each hospital varying from 1 to 19. The remaining patients were admitted to 22 hospitals, but of these only 5 (all situated in the Metropolitan Regions) admitted 40 or more patients during the year.

The policy which this memorandum then proposed for the development of NHS treatment services was essentially the setting up of more specialized in-patient units, with emphasis on group therapy:

It is therefore recommended that treatment for alcoholism and alcoholic psychosis should, as far as possible, be given in specialised units. It is suggested that Boards which have not already done so should establish such units, aiming initially at one per region and increasing the provision if the scale of demand makes it necessary . . . . It is suggested that the units should have between 8 and 16 beds. This would be a convenient size for group therapy, which the Advisory Committee regarded as often being a valuable form of treatment . . . . It will be necessary for the special units to run out-patient clinics and to co-operate in after-care with Alcoholics Anonymous (who have a very important contribution to make).

The treatment model favoured by this memorandum clearly owed much to the Warlingham experience. Although out-patient care received a mention, this was ancillary to the Unit as in-patient centre. There was certainly here no recipe for the development of alcoholism treatment in terms of contemporarily evolving notions of community psychiatry. The Ministry's recommendations were based on the Standing Mental Health Advisory Committee's assessment of the evidence, but it is to be noted that important policies were being formulated in the absence of any very certain relevant data—specialized units, group therapy, and Alcoholics Anonymous were all commended, without any scientifically acceptable evidence being available which bore on these judgements. To make this point is not to criticize the initiative which the Ministry took in 1962—an initiative was much needed, and policy could only be formulated on the basis of information and experience then to hand.

A Ministry memorandum of this kind could advise hospital authorities throughout the country on what was officially seen as the desirable line of development, but the responsibility for deciding whether there should be implementation lay entirely with the Regional Boards. In the event, this memorandum appears to have had real impact. Up to 1961 there existed perhaps two or three units of the kind envisaged. By 1968 there were thirteen such units in existence, and by the beginning of 1975 there were twenty-one special treatment units providing a total of 434 beds, and a further three units were being planned.

It seems likely that the majority of the units still operate rather within the 1962 model, with emphasis on group therapy and in-patient care, although a second memorandum issued in 1968 (Ministry of Health, 1968) had taken a broader view of treatment. This latter document showed greater awareness of the need to involve the patient's family and to give attention to 'all the social, occupational, cultural, environmental and individual factors which have played their part in the development of dependence'. There was emphasis on the need to give the special unit its context in community services (both statutory and voluntary). In-patient care was still accorded priority of mention, but out-patient care received more note than previously:

Treatment will frequently involve an initial admission to hospital as an in-patient and more than one admission to hospital may be necessary because of relapse. In-patient treatment can best be undertaken in small specialised hospital units. . . . In the view of some experts energetic out-patient care alone will sometimes give as good results. An in-patient may come to rely on the supports of hospital life and their removal when he leaves hospital may present difficulties.
. . . Out-patient treatment has the general advantage of enabling the patient to retain his job and thus remain in the community. . . . Clinical trials are needed to investigate specific indications for in-patient and out-patient care.

This last sentence quoted from the 1968 document introduced a type of thinking which had been absent from the earlier memorandum—the idea that the design of alcoholism treatment might be influenced by the research evidence. The 1968 memorandum seems therefore to have moved toward a position where planning of alcoholism services was to acknowledge two of the major contemporary developments of general psychiatry—the stress on community or social psychiatry, and the notion that treatment efficacy should be assessed by rigorous clinical experiment.

The latter assumption (and the discussion of the potential for out-patient care), may have been influenced by the publication of a controlled trial on out-patient versus in-patient care (Edwards and Guthrie, 1966; 1967). Forty alcoholic men, who had no other severe physical or mental illness and who agreed to accept either treatment, were randomized to in-patient or out-patient therapy. The average stay in hospital was 8·9 weeks for in-patients; out-patients on average spent 7·7 weeks in 'intensive treatment'. All patients were followed to one year, with monthly assessment of progress made by independent raters. At the end of twelve months, the two groups showed remarkably similar outcome.

A circular sent in May 1973 by the DHSS to all Directors of Social Services (DHSS, 1973a), was entitled *Community Services for Alcoholics*. It blueprinted in considerable detail the community care element in the total approach, but the special focus was on the needs of the homeless alcoholic— the reason for this circular was DHSS acceptance of responsibility for implementing certain recommendations made by the Home Office Working Party on Habitual Drunken Offenders (Home Office, 1971). This acceptance of responsibility was immediately to draw the Department into the planning of community alcoholism services to a much greater extent than had ever previously been approached, but fuller note of this circular is more appropriately deferred to discussion on special services for the vagrant alcoholic (p. 13).

Another important official document to discuss planning of alcoholism treatment services, was issued in November 1973 (DHSS, 1973b): it was a paper prepared by the Standing Medical Advisory Committee of the Central Health Services Council as information for doctors. The paper boldly declared that 'the treatment for alcoholics is improving all the time'. It generally reinforced previous recommendations:

Many patients require treatment in hospital for their physical and psychological dependence. Withdrawal of alcohol from dependent patients may best be carried out as an in-patient procedure. . . . The treatment of the factors which underlie addiction rests mainly on the skilled use of discussion, whether individually or in groups, based on a doctor-patient relationship arising out of extensive history taking.

The document went on to express some fairly definitive views on special techniques:

Specialised techniques such as behaviour therapy or aversion therapy . . . have a limited role to play in treatment and are not yet fully evaluated . . . there is no reason at present to think that they offer greater hope of success than more conventional treatments. . . . Disulfiram . . . and citrated calcium carbimide . . . have an adjuvant role to play, and their use is best initiated in hospital.

The relevance of research to service planning was thus again implicitly acknowledged, although evaluations of treatment methods put forward by the memorandum itself were not particularly well related to then available research information. It would have been difficult, for instance, to find any research which supported the notion that 'the treatment for alcoholics is improving all the time'; statements made on criteria for in-patient admission would have found no validation in the research literature; the literature would certainly have given rather negative evaluation of aversion therapy, but not much more favourable estimates of the clinical usefulness of deterrent drugs. The correctness of the central assumption that 'the skilled use of discussion' was an effective treatment for alcoholism, had not been proved, and if new treatments were being compared against 'more conventional treatments', a new product was being compared with a largely untested old product. What were being taken as the givens were not properly givens at all. This document also gave greater attention than had previous government memoranda, to 'the special role' of the general practitioner and to a community psychiatry perspective in rehabilitation and after-care. Indeed, community approaches in this document received quite heavy emphasis, and thinking here was complementary to that expressed in the document sent earlier in the same year to Local Authorities.

'BETTER SERVICES FOR THE MENTALLY ILL': DHSS FORWARD THINKING IN 1975

The most recent document outlining government thoughts on development of alcoholism treatment services comes in a White Paper which discusses the whole spectrum of plans for the country's psychiatric services—*Better Services for the Mentally Ill* (DHSS, 1975). To a consideration of alcohol (and drug dependence) was devoted one of the nine chapters of a paper described by the Secretary of State as 'a long-term strategic document against which we should take decisions'. Alcoholism was thus in 1975 accorded a degree of recognition as a health planning problem strikingly greater than a quarter of a century previously when 'the subject hardly merited the time of a consultant psychiatrist in the NHS'.

The 1975 document contains ideas which are, in some respects, a product of the natural and continuous evolution of ideas in the 1962, 1968, and two 1973 papers, but some of the suggestions now made represent a rather sharper break with previous policies. Discussion of the special units seems to have moved toward a re-definition of their role, with even greater emphasis on community approaches:

The majority of identified alcoholics who are admitted to hospital for psychiatric treatment are treated in the general psychiatric wards of mental illness hospitals or in psychiatric departments in general hospitals. A minority—estimated at 35 per cent—are admitted to special units. . . . These specialist units were not developed to replace the facilities offered by the existing psychiatric services . . . but so that they might serve as a local focus of expertise, training and research for all the services concerned with alcoholics in their region. . . . The emphasis in provision should perhaps turn towards a more locally based treatment service with much of the work done in the community or in an out-patient or day hospital setting, supplemented by in-patient facilities, whether these are specialised or part of the local psychiatric service.

It is interesting to put the 1975 statement that the special units were not developed to replace other services for the alcoholic, against the statement in the 1962 memorandum that 'treatment for alcoholism and alcoholic psychosis should, as far as possible, be given in specialised units'. The wheel seems to have turned full circle. In 1962 the problem was seen as that of alcoholics being admitted too widely to general psychiatric services—'over half the patients admitted to psychiatric hospitals were scattered throughout 100 hospitals'. Whereas in 1975 there is no problem remarked in the fact that only 35 per cent of patients go to special units, and the emphasis is on 'increasing the effectiveness and skill with which primary health care teams, social workers and others, deal with the drinking problems they encounter among their patients or clients'. The idea of the specialized unit has changed from that of a largely in-patient unit with ambitions to monopolize alcoholism treatment, to a centre which activates, offers advice, shows others how to help the alcoholic, and which is part of a service 'with much of the work done in the community'.

This shift of emphasis from 1962 to 1975 requires explanation. No doubt thinking on alcoholism services had, to an important extent, simply been carried forward by the general tide of ideas (and fashions) on the organization of mental health services—the stress on community care, team work, and the development of the district service. There had also been a stretch of years during which practical experience had been gained in the running of alcoholism services. This had led both to an awareness of the inadequate contribution which specialized units made if they worked in isolation, and on the positive side there had been experience in some centres of the practical possibilities of a community treatment approach to alcoholism. Hostels for alcoholics had been developed (Edwards, Hawker and Hensman, 1966; Cook et al., 1968), counselling bureaux run by lay staff had made their mark (Edwards, Kellog-Fisher et al., 1967), and out-patient treatment was becoming more accepted. For instance, by 1975 the specialized alcoholism treatment service of the Maudsley admitted only about one quarter of its case-load to in-patient care: in the 1950s at the same hospital in-patient care would have been seen as almost mandatory. The emphasis of the 1975 document on development of alcoholism treatment in terms of relatively low-cost community services and the training and activation of the non-specialist also accorded with the realities of the country's economic plight. In a general situation where spending was having to be frozen or cut back, any formula which saw the development of services in terms of the setting up of further expensive in-patient units would not be much of a runner.

This 1975 White Paper also showed an awareness of the need to evaluate and to keep options open:

Most services are in some sense experimental. . . . There are gaps in our knowledge of the existing services and their effectiveness: more evaluation is needed of different methods and settings of treatment. . . . New patterns of provision may emerge and we should not yet draw up a definitive policy for future services.

Although the Paper thus took what might be called a research perspective, as with previous planning documents the research data on which policy recommendations could be based inevitably was far from complete.

Thus there was no research information available which would conclusively favour a community based rather than institutional approach to alcoholism as regards treatment efficacy. Tangible evidence of the failure of the present pattern of services to reach the majority of persons in need of help had however been given in a report of a community survey in Camberwell (Edwards, Hawker *et al.*, 1973). Two parallel epidemiological investigations into prevalence of abnormal drinking had been conducted in the same London borough. The first inquired of a wide spectrum of 'reporting agencies' (e.g. courts, newspapers, casualty departments, probation service, clergy, employers, statutory and voluntary welfare agencies, AA, general practitioners, psychiatric and general hospitals), the number of cases coming to their notice over a twelve month period. The second phase of the study involved house-to-house interviewing and elicitation of the subjects' own reports of troubles experienced with drinking over the previous twelve months. The reporting agency survey revealed a 'labelled prevalence' per 1,000 adults aged over sixteen of 8·6 for men, 1·3 for women, and 4·7 overall. About half these cases were known to a medical agency. The sample survey gave a prevalence of 'problem drinking' per 1,000 adults aged eighteen or over of 61·3 for men, 7·7 for women, and 31·3 overall. The likely ratio of 'needful cases' to cases in contact with an 'apposite agency' was thought to lie between 4 : 1 and 9 : 1— there could be no doubt that the majority of people in the community who were experiencing severe drinking problems were not in contact with any appropriate agency.

On the basis of these findings this research report had concluded:

If these results were confirmed, it would be difficult to believe that sufficient psychiatric manpower could be found to meet the problem by setting up more specialised hospital services operating simply within the present model. . . . A strategy which the epidemiological findings might seem to suggest as worth consideration would be the setting up of local agencies (situated either within or outside the hospital), which would have in essence the following twin responsibilities: (1) the integration, activation, and support of those who are to help the alcoholic. . . . (2) Responsibility for seeking out the person who is indeed in need of special help. . . .

A plea for a more community oriented model had been made earlier by Evans (1970). By 1975 there had in fact been such an accumulation of epidemiological evidence, showing the prevalence of alcohol problems in the general population and in special groups, as to make it obvious that the specialized unit operating within the old formula no longer by itself offered a credible solution (Moss and Davies, 1967; Edwards, Williamson *et al.*, 1968; Gath *et al.*, 1968; Edwards, Hensman, and Peto, 1971 and 1972; Edwards, Chandler *et al.*, 1972; Edwards, Hawker *et al.*, 1973; Wilkins, 1974). Detailed proposals for a community model for alcoholism treatment have recently been given by Cartwright *et al.* (1975), who have developed their ideas on the basis of surveys in Camberwell of drinking problem prevalence, and community and professional attitudes to such problems. These authors still saw a place for specialism but concluded that 'problems from drinking are much too varied and extensive to be solved by expanding "alcoholism services" '. This important document provides the most thorough analysis to date of the types of training and support, and kind of organization, which would in practice be needed, if community services were indeed to carry the larger part of the responsibility for people in trouble with drink.

The White Paper referred to 'gaps in our knowledge of the existing services and their effectiveness'. What is still lacking is not just data bearing on the extremely difficult question of whether the treatment given actually works (a matter which will be returned to later in this chapter), but even simple monitoring information on the characteristics of case loads and the treatments given. Edwards, Kyle, and Nicholls (1974) provided some information on type of patients admitted to four mental illness hospitals in or near London between 1953 and 1957, and showed that over that particular period different hospitals were recruiting case loads with very varying characteristics— Warlingham Park for instance had 48 per cent of its alcoholic patients drawn from social class I, II, and only 21 per cent from IV, V, while St. Francis observation ward drew 23 per cent of its alcoholics from I, II, and 47 per cent from social class IV, V. At that date, therefore, there was more than a hint that a specialized unit might be operating a selective class bias, but that particular study was of course dealing with the system's operation twenty or more years ago.

The only recent survey of the case loads of specialized alcoholism units was reported by Hore and Smith (1975). They obtained data on 334 patients attending fifteen alcoholism units in England and Wales. Forty-three per cent of these patients were drawn from Social Class I, II, suggesting that the sort of bias of which there was a hint in the earlier study was still perpetuated. There were between-hospital and between-region variations: the one special unit sampled from Wales, for example, had 53 per cent of its patients from class I, II (about 20 per cent of the general population from that region would have been in class I, II). Social class is only one of many variables on which the characteristics of a patient population might be described, but bias in class selection may be a fair indicator that the special unit typically emphasizes the selection of more socially stable and more verbally fluent patients, of a type thought suitable for the preferred group-therapy regime. Such an argument has though to be qualified by the admission that rather little is still reliably known about the class distribution of the total alcoholic population which would be found in the community—the base on which representativeness of any hospital alcoholic sample ought really to be judged.

SERVICES FOR THE VAGRANT ALCOHOLIC

Rather separate from the evolution of hospital services has been the development of services for the vagrant alcoholic, or drunkenness offender. Traditionally the business of helping the down-and-out alcoholic has been left largely to voluntary organizations, and often those with religious motivation.

At a time when the NHS was doing little to provide services for the generality of alcoholics, resistance to involvement with the homeless sector of the problem was likely to be marked. Even when the special centres came into being, this resistance continued, and these centres often were reluctant to admit a type of patient who might be seen as 'a drunk' rather than a real alcoholic, as presenting a social rather than a medical problem, and as certainly not a natural candidate for group therapy.

A number of factors contributed to the awakening of official interest. Glatt and Whitely (1956) provided the first substantial description in Britain of this population, and a series of papers then described the social and clinical characteristics of London's skid row (Edwards, Hawker et al., 1966), alcoholism in a Reception Centre (Edwards, Williamson et al., 1968), the contribution of alcoholism to a prison population (Edwards, Hensman, and Peto, 1971), and the characteristics of 150 drunkenness offenders appearing before two London magistrates courts (Gath et al., 1968). These researches between them revised the notion that such men were outside the remit of official health and social agencies. The consistent finding was that the homeless drunk or public inebriate typically displayed a drinking problem in no way distinguishable from what, in anyone's terms, would constitute 'alcoholism'. The presentation of his problem was however coloured and complicated by his lack of social resources. He was penniless, jobless, homeless, and often out of contact with any remaining family—alcoholism and social breakdown each exacerbated the other, and made a way out of the situation for the individual almost impossible.

The response to this problem had therefore to be in terms of restoring social stability as well as any specific emphasis on alcoholism. The specialized alcoholism hostel began to hold the centre of attention, rather than in this instance the specialized in-patient unit. It was the Home Office rather than the Ministry of Health which took the initiative in framing new policy, and the report of the Home Office Working Party on the Drunkenness Offender (Home Office, 1971) put forward a series of proposals which were very much within a model of community care. Following the publication of this report there was a protracted debate as to which government department should bear responsibility for implementing the recommendations, with the decision finally being that responsibility would be taken by the DHSS. Reference has already been made (p. 9) to the DHSS circular (1973a) which then gave detailed advice to local authorities on the establishment of community services concerned with implementing recommendations of this Home Office report. Alcoholics other than those in the drunkenness offender group might of course benefit from the proposed community facilities, but it was the problem of the drunkenness offender which was forcing the pace. The circular discussed the role of information centres and 'shop front' consultation bureaux in making contact with the alcoholic, detoxification centres as a substitute for the police cells, the role of the social worker, and the special importance of hostels.

A grant scheme was outlined which would operate for a period of five years and which would provide central funds to supplement local authority provisions. Progress was not, however, rapid. By 1976 there was the prospect of two or three detoxification centres being opened on an experimental basis and there had been a gradual expansion of hostels and other community facilities.

Research in this instance seems largely to have had an impact on policy in terms of its drawing attention to the nature and size of a problem. Descriptions of one particular skid-row hostel and its associated projects, also did much to remedy the previously very pessimistic appraisal of the skid-row alcoholic's chances of recovery (Cook et al., 1968; Cook and Pollak, 1970; Cook, 1975). A recent series of socio-psychological investigations has looked specifically at the mode of functioning of alcoholism hostels, and the sort of results which are achieved in the short term (Orford and Hawker, 1974; Orford et al., 1974 and 1975a, b; Otto and Orford, 1977): although the authors were by no means negative in their conclusions, they made it clear that the majority of residents would be drinking when they left the hostels.

STATISTICS ON NHS ADMISSION FOR TREATMENT OF
ALCOHOLISM, AND OTHER DATA

Figures are available from the DHSS on annual admissions to NHS in-patient mental illness facilities in England and Wales (mental illness hospitals and units under Regional Hospital Boards and Teaching Hospitals). Data for the years 1949 to 1974 are reproduced in TABLE I. The limitations of this information should be noted. The criteria employed for diagnosis are varied and uncertain, and there may be shifts in diagnostic habits over time. Figures relate to a count of admissions and not a count of patients—if the same patient is admitted twice during the year, he will be counted twice. Only in-patients are recorded, and there appear to be no national data available for out-patient registrations. As the footnote to the table makes clear, a change in the official basis for differentiating 'primary' from 'secondary diagnosis' took place in 1970. All these matters, together with absence of any data on secondary diagnosis of alcoholism before 1964, and a total breakdown in data collection both in 1950 and for the years 1961–63, must mean that the central monitoring of the NHS investment in alcoholism treatment services has not yielded any long run of data such as to repay very detailed analysis. Despite all the difficulties which attach to interpretation of the recordings, the simple fact does undoubtedly emerge that, over a quarter century, NHS admissions with a diagnosis of alcoholism and alcoholic psychosis have increased by a considerable order of magnitude—from perhaps about 600 in 1949 (making a guess at the figure which should be added for secondary diagnosis), to about 12,000 twenty-five years later, or a twentyfold increase.

The relative contribution to that increase made by changes in diagnostic habits as opposed to true change in number of alcoholics admitted, cannot be determined, but there is no obvious reason for supposing that diagnostic practice could have undergone a sufficiently radical alteration to account for most of the observed twentyfold change. Trends for the primary category 'Alcoholic psychosis' did not at all consistently follow change under the primary diagnosis of 'alcoholism' over the run of years 1949–69, but this in no way adds to the ease of interpretation.

Some light may be shed on the question of whether the large increase in hospitalized alcoholism is likely to be fact or diagnostic artefact, by looking at other official statistics on alcohol related problems, or at national alcohol consumption figures. Figures for drunkenness arrest in England and Wales from 1950 to 1974, are given in TABLE 2. The changes have by no means been smooth and continuous, and there have been years in which the total arrests have fallen, as well as years in which there has been an increase. Even as there may be changes in medical diagnostic habits, there may be changes in police arrest practices. And here again one is dealing with a count of incidents rather than a count of persons. Whatever the underlying explanations, the immediate fact is that between 1950 and 1974 there was rather over a twofold increase in drunkenness arrests. This would support the expectation of a real increase over the same years in people seeking treatment for alcoholism, but there is nothing comparable to the twentyfold rise. There is however no reason why trends for drunkenness arrests and hospital admissions for alcoholism should strictly follow one another. Public drunkenness is a phenomenon particularly associated with homelessness, social disintegration, and lower occupational status (Gath et al., 1968). The pool of homeless people who would largely generate the total of drunkenness arrests may not have had the same 'growth potential' as the prevalence of alcoholism in the more settled sector of the community, but such an argument is only conjectural.

Figures for cirrhosis death rates are shown in TABLE 3. There are other causes of cirrhosis than alcoholism but there is considerable support for the assertion that *changes* in cirrhosis over a period of years are largely caused by changes in alcoholic cirrhosis mortality. The table shows that from 1950 to 1974, there was a 70 per cent increase in cirrhosis deaths. This might at first be viewed as unexpectedly small when set against alcoholism admissions or drunkenness arrests, but as only a fraction of the 1950 total is likely to represent alcoholic cirrhotic deaths, the percentage increase in alcoholic deaths over twenty-five years may in fact be quite large. It could also be argued that death by cirrhosis is an event which is only likely to take place after many years of heavy alcohol consumption, and a cohort effect is therefore likely to operate: increase in alcoholism prevalence in one decade may not be fully reflected in cirrhosis deaths until some years later. But as with the other statistics, it must be evident that interpretation is difficult.

Another statistic which must be examined here is national alcohol consumption. TABLE 4 shows national consumption separately for different beverage types (beer, spirits, and wine) for the years 1950 to 1974, and gives in the last column an estimate of annual *per capita* consumption in terms of litres of absolute alcohol. Over twenty-five years, *per capita* consumption can be seen to have increased by 81 per cent. The change which this may imply in number of heavy drinkers must depend on the shape of the population distribution curve for alcohol consumption. There is evidence that this curve approximates to a log-normal form (Ledermann, 1956), and any increase in *per capita* consumption would be expected to result in a greater percentage increase in proportion of the population drinking heavily, e.g. drinking more than 150 g absolute alcohol per day. There is empirical evidence to support this expectation: on average if the mean consumption is doubled, prevalence of what might reasonably be considered heavy drinking, will go up four times (Bruun *et al.*, 1975).

Thus, if one compares data on trends in hospital admissions for alcoholism against trends in drunkenness arrests, cirrhosis death rates, or *per capita* alcohol consumption, it is evident that the very greatest caution would be needed in interpreting any covariance. Data beset by uncertainties are being put against data beset with yet other uncertainties. But without in any way discarding caution, it can be said that drunkenness arrests, cirrhosis death rates, and alcohol consumption have all shown upward trends over the last quarter century: and hence it is not unexpected that there should have been a coincidental increase in alcoholism admissions. However, none of the first three variables has shown a large enough change to make it likely that a twentyfold increase in admissions can be accounted for entirely by an increased prevalence of alcoholism—there is really no support for the belief that over twenty-five years there has been such an explosive increase in drinking as would result in there being twenty alcoholics down a street where there had previously been only one. Neither an explosion in alcoholism nor a change in diagnostic habits (nor a combination of the two), seems sufficient to account for the rise in diagnosed admissions. It is necessary to invoke a third factor: an increased expectation that the NHS is in business to treat alcoholism, increasing the demand for admission. Although only a minority of alcoholics are in touch with treatment services, the trend over recent years may well be towards an increased public willingness to see alcoholism as an illness, together with an increased likelihood of various agents an agencies making a hospital referral—a referral which in most regions can be made to a specialized treatment centre. In short, the increased supply of services may have generated an increased demand for service. The degree to which this factor has contributed to the twentyfold increase in admissions cannot be exactly determined but the possibility exists that this factor alone might account for a large part of the recorded change.

If what is being seen is indeed an increase in alcoholism admissions as a consequence of greater consumer demand, the constructive response would be to interpret this as a triumph for health service organization—for 'health care delivery'. We might have here an important illustration of what may happen when a particular condition is at least partially de-stigmatized—there can be no doubt that especially over the last ten years the notion that 'alcoholism is a treatable illness' has been propagated by the media, by organizations such as the National Council on Alcoholism and the Medical Council on Alcoholism, and by activists in the medical profession.

A more pessimistic response to this probable evidence of increased consumer demand would be to note that bringing more people into hospital for treatment of alcoholism is not an advantage, unless there is at the same time evidence that hospital treatment actually helps—a question to be taken up in the final section of this chapter.

It is only possible to give a very rough estimate of what in-patient services for alcoholism are costing the NHS each year. The maintenance of twenty-one specialized treatment centres must alone constitute a considerable investment both in terms of cash and man-power. These units provide between them 434 beds. The cost per bed per week might currently be taken as about £50, and on this basis the annual in-patient cost of the special units would come to more than £1,100,000. This may be an under-estimate, for some of these units are probably staffed on a more generous basis than the ordinary psychiatric ward. The only way of estimating the total cost of alcoholism in-patient care (special units and general psychiatric facilities together) is on the basis of the census of patients in mental illness hospitals and units conducted by the DHSS at the end of 1971. This showed that there were 556 in-patients with a primary diagnosis of alcoholic psychosis and 1,092 with primary diagnosis of alcoholism on a given date, giving a total of 1,548 patients (DHSS, 1976). If this were taken as the usual weekly level of occupancy, then at 1976 prices the annual cost of in-patient care for alcoholics would be £52 × 1,548 × 50, i.e. over £4,000,000.

THE RESEARCH CONTRIBUTION AND A CRUCIAL QUESTION

At various points in this chapter reference has been made to the relevance of particular pieces of research to the evolution of policies. Without being privy to the intimate processes of decision making, or knowing what was in the mind of a particular committee or official draftsman at a particular date, it must be evident that the business of policy making has gone ahead as best it may and often without much available help from research. Now and then the research reports have seemed however to speak very directly to the policy concerns and, when the data have really had something to say, research seems eventually to have been influential in shaping policy. The revision of the original official notion of the form which the special unit should take appears in particular to have been influenced by the hard evidence that out-patient care can be as effective as the expensive in-patient programme, and by the epidemiological evidence that as a delivery system a model centred on the enclosed and specialized treatment centre cannot effectively get the help out to the people in need.

What has finally to be asked is whether, if review is made of the international literature on alcoholism treatment, there is at present any persuasive evidence that one treatment is better than another—or indeed that treatment is better than no treatment at all. This is a crucial question, and one which must now briefly be considered. Is the whole treatment business a bad case of the Emperor's new clothes?

There have been a number of excellent reviews of the alcoholism treatment literature (Hill and Blane, 1966; Gillespie, 1967; Pattison, 1968; Emrick, 1974 and 1975; Hamburg, 1975; Baekland et al., 1975). The number of relevant research publications is now extremely large, and in the confines of the present monograph it is neither possible nor necessary to go over again in detail the same ground as has been covered by these previous extensive reviews.

The starting point might rather be to examine some of the conclusions drawn by Emrick (1975), who, in the most recent major review, compared reports of 'no or minimal' treatment with papers dealing with 'more than minimal' treatment. On this basis he felt able to state that 'treatment seems to increase an alcoholic's chances of at least reducing his drinking problem', and he then went on less guardedly to conclude that 'Clearly the sizable expenditure of human and financial resources for alcoholism treatment have not been in vain.' Regrettably no such clear or comforting deduction can safely be drawn from comparing, on the one hand, untreated or minimally treated patients, many of whom may have refused treatment or been considered unsuitable for treatment, against on the other hand, patients who have accepted formal treatment—the bias induced by selective patient recruitment must vitiate Emrick's interpretation.

A further aspect of Emrick's review then deserves scrutiny. He was able to list five controlled trials which matched up to his critical standards, and which appeared to show that one particular regime gave better results than another, often less intensive, approach. Even if the majority of controlled trials gave negative results, the presence of only five well supported instances of a positive result would certainly give pause for thought. In fact Emrick felt that these studies had a confounding factor in common. In each instance results for the control group may have been depressed by these subjects responding negatively to the disappointment and deprivation of being in the control, rather than experimental group. This hypothesis is interesting but cannot be substantiated. A close scrutiny of these papers also suggests that in several instances further caution is needed in their interpretation. For example, a study of patients allocated to four different group therapy regimes does not make it clear whether the allocation was random, and only fifty-eight of an original ninety-six patients were available to follow-up (Ends and Page, 1957). In a trial of electrical aversion treatment, randomization was unsatisfactory, and only fifty-one of seventy-three patients were followed-up (Vogler et al., 1970). Losses to one-year follow-up were 38 per cent, 42 per cent, and 37 per cent for, respectively, a treatment and two control groups, in a trial of L.S.D.

therapy for alcoholics (Tomsovic and Edwards, 1970). Three of Emrick's five references to positive findings must therefore be seen as providing far from conclusive evidence. The fourth reference is to a paper by Pittman and Tate (1972), which is of particular interest because it reports a positive finding on randomization of men of rather low social stability (e.g. 77 per cent single, 70 per cent unemployed) between three and six weeks in-patient care followed by intensive after-care (n = 177), as opposed to ten days in-patient care and no after-care (n = 78). Improvement was greater (but not always significantly so), in the first group, at nine to thirty-two months follow-up. Perhaps equally important as the between-group difference in the small total abstaining category (12 per cent v. 4 per cent), was the remarkable group similarity for self-report of improvement in drinking (60 per cent v. 55 per cent)—the between-group outcome differences on drinking behaviour in fact do not appear to have been very great. The final paper in this series of five, is one by Sobell and Sobell (1973) which reported on randomization of seventy patients between four groups who were followed up for one year. It would seem to provide fairly convincing evidence that at twelve months a broad-spectrum behaviour therapy approach gave better results than a conventional regime, and this whether the treatment goal was abstinence or controlled drinking. Even as regards interpretation of this paper there are some reservations: the authors used multiple information sources for outcome reporting, and do not describe how possibly conflicting reports were weighted or amalgamated; their outcome measures, in terms of 'majority days' drinking status, were difficult to interpret; and Emrick's 'control group disappointment' criticisms may well be pertinent (see p. 19).

There is therefore in the previous literature no very substantial evidence that any intensive conventional treatment is of proven superiority to a less intensive approach. Nor, with the possible exception of the Sobells' behavioural package, is there convincing evidence that any specific modality has the edge on more conventional regimes. Not only is the research literature poor in reports which suggest that any particular treatment is advantageous; it is rich in reports which demonstrate that a given treatment is no better than another. Emrick (1975) in his extensive literature review, found thirty-one negatives to set against the five claimed positives which have just been discussed. These thirty-one papers cannot be re-analysed in detail here, but it is fair to note that in some instances the methodology may have been as questionable as was the case with some of the claimed positives. One paper does however deserve note for its particular relevance. Levinson and Sereny (1969) randomized sixty alcoholics between a conventional in-patient treatment regime, and an in-patient regime which was a pale shadow of the conventional approach. In the conventional regime:

The staff was trained in a team approach and the patients were involved in a well-structured and fully-planned treatment program which occupied their whole day. The program included a didactic lecture series, selected films about addictions, regular group psychotherapy sessions, community meetings, occupational therapy periods and recreational activities. Beyond this each patient was assessed and assigned to a therapist for individual treatment.

In the control group 'all formal aspects of the treatment program were discontinued', and 'the onus for seeking further help was placed upon the patient'. The report unfortunately did not include any precise count of therapeutic hours offered to the two groups but stated that for the control group 'the number of professional hours devoted to "formal therapy" was reduced to a minimum'. At one-year follow-up there was no difference in outcome between the intensively treated patients and those who had been offered the much attenuated regime.

One may therefore conclude that whatever the pattern of services which delivers the care, there remains a very important question as to whether the type of care which is being delivered is of much effect. It is to this question that we return in CHAPTER IV, when the results of the present trial are presented.

CHAPTER II

ALCOHOLISM AND MARRIAGE

A MAJOR focus of the project which will be reported in this book was marriage complicated by alcoholism—the influence of marital interactions on treatment outcome and, reciprocally, of outcome on change in the marriage. This chapter is devoted therefore to a review of the literature bearing on these matters.

Marriages selected because of the presence of alcoholism or problem drinking are still all too often studied and discussed as if the problems experienced within them, and the abnormalities displayed by them are unique, and there is too little recognition of the possibility that these abnormalities might be more general. Such short-sightedness is all the more striking when, as this chapter will attempt to demonstrate, a comparison of the alcohol-specific literature and parts of the more general literature on marriage reveal abundant evidence of the generality of the problems described by students of alcoholism and marriage. The literature will be discussed under a number of separate headings. In each case attention will be drawn to writings on marriage in general which suggest either that the concepts employed in the more specialized alcoholism literature have been over-simple or that parallels between events occurring in alcoholism-complicated marriages and other marriages have been neglected.

ALCOHOLISM AS CRISIS OR SOURCE OF STRESS

Jackson's contribution (1954) has been highly influential. She saw the behaviour of alcoholics' wives in terms of crisis reactions precipitated by the stress imposed by the presence in the family of the alcoholic. She emphasized the unpredictability of the wife's situation as well as the lack of clear directions which her reactions might take: individual wives were forced to evolve techniques of adjustment by a process of trial and error. Jackson went on to outline seven successive stages of family adjustment to this crisis. Lemert (1960) tested this idea by interviewing relatives (mostly wives) of alcoholics and asking about the sequence of the first occurrences of eleven events relating to the family's perception of, and reaction to, the drinking problem. The major conclusion was that the sequence of events showed a great deal of inconsistency and unevenness. At best Lemert's data suggested two broad, and fairly distinct, stages.

James and Goldman (1971) have more recently reported a study which also belongs in the 'stress reaction' tradition. Each of eighty-five wives was asked twenty-five questions concerning their methods of 'coping' during four stages of their husband's drinking: social drinking, excessive drinking, 'alcoholismic' drinking, and abstinence. The wives reported a progressive increase in all types of coping from the first to the third of these stages. In addition, wives who reported that their husband had become violent and aggressive were those who were most likely to report that they had reacted with quarrelling, avoidance, anger and helplessness, pretending to be drunk themselves, locking the husband out of the house, and seeking a separation.

Alcoholism in one partner is, however, only one among a number of circumstances which have been construed as crises to which marriages must adjust. Other such circumstances which have been studied include economic depression and unemployment (e.g. Angell, 1936), bereavement (Eliot, 1948), war separation and reunion (Hill, 1949) and mental illness (Clausen and Yarrow, 1955). These so-called crises differ in the suddenness or gradualness of onset of the stresses involved, and also in the degree to which they are likely to be seen as having their origin outside or within the family. These may be among the factors which make it relatively easy or difficult for family members to blame one another for the crisis (Hansen and Hill, 1964) or to make use of relatively blameless constructions such as 'mental disorder' (Clausen and Yarrow, 1955) or 'alcoholism'.

That marriages complicated by alcoholism should not be thought of as unique is shown by Hansen and Hill's review (1964) of the problems faced by families in other sorts of crisis. For example, they report that the frequency and patterning of sexual behaviour may change, and may even cease altogether for some couples in crisis. It may be noted here that one study of sexual adjustment of alcoholics and their wives (Burton and Kaplan, 1968) found these marriages to be indistinguishable as a group, in this regard, from a group of maritally-counselled couples whose marriages were not complicated by alcoholism. It seems unlikely therefore that the changes in sexual behaviour noted by Jackson (1954) and Lemert (1960) are in any way specific to alcoholism. Heightened anxiety and insecurity, and other 'personality changes', are also noted among the reactions of family members to crises or stressful circumstances. This serves as a reminder that 'disturbance' in the non-alcoholic spouses of alcoholics (Bailey et al., 1962; Kogan et al., 1963; Lewis, 1954) can be partly attributed to non-specific stress or crisis factors. Hansen and Hill (1964) even make mention of the likelihood of emotional disturbance being displayed by family members (often 'in turn' rather than together) when the crisis is alleviated. This is reminiscent of the frequent suggestion that spouses of alcoholics are likely to become disturbed when the alcoholic gets better. Role transfer from alcoholic husband to non-alcoholic wife, noted by Jackson (1954) and Lemert (1960) for example, and the subsequent difficulties in returning to the original role arrangement after the husband's 'recovery', have been remarked by those who have studied the effects of such things as economic depression and unemployment and war separation on families (e.g. Hill, 1949), and by those who have studied the impact of mental illness on the family (e.g. Clausen and Yarrow, 1955).

Social isolation is part of the family reaction noted by students of alcoholism and marriage and again this has been noted in other contexts, particularly when shame is part of the family reaction (e.g. Clausen and Yarrow, 1955). Finally, it can be said that uncertainty about the interpretation of a husband's behaviour as 'normal', 'a problem', or an 'illness', and the absence of clear guidelines for reactions, all of which were noted by Jackson (1954), were also given great prominence by Clausen and Yarrow (1955) in their account of the impact of the mental illness and hospitalization of thirty-three husbands on their families.

Despite the 'progressive stages of reaction' theme in the alcoholism and marriage literature, no advantage has been taken of parallel developments in other fields. For example the 'profile' model, showing the 'ups and downs' of family organization graphically, is one that has provided a framework for analysing family reactions to crisis. Hill (1949) made use of this method in his study of war separation and reunion and showed notable individual differences in parameters such as initial level of organization, level of disorganization, 'angle of recovery' (i.e. steep and rapid or gradual and prolonged), and new level of reorganization. Mention should be made too of the 'family development' framework (Broderick, 1971) which has given rise to various classifications of families based on length of marriage and the presence and ages of children. The overall level and precise nature of 'marital satisfaction' varies from stage to stage (e.g. Burr, 1970). It is clear that the 'state of a marriage' should be judged in relation to developmental stage.

Whatever the specific factors involved, it is therefore possible to begin to see alcoholism in marriage not as a unique set of circumstances but as a set of circumstances which can be placed within a spectrum of events associated with marriage.

MARRIAGE ROLES

The under-involvement of alcoholic husbands in the tasks and decision-making of the family is a feature of alcoholism-complicated marriage which is often noted clinically. Lemert (1962) confirmed a higher frequency of 'wife-dominance of the family' in comparison with two control samples, although the adequacy of the latter as suitable controls is disputable. Results to be reported in CHAPTER V of this book show that 52 of 100 alcoholic husbands and their wives reported a pattern of family task and decision-making involvement which departs, in a 'wife-dominated' direction, from the relatively egalitarian ideal of marriage roles to which they subscribed. The probable limitations of the 'reaction to crisis or stress' view of alcoholism and marriage are apparent from the findings of both Lemert and the present study that many couples reported a 'wife-dominated' pattern in the early years of their marriages and that about half the couples were of the opinion that the husband's drinking problem predated the marriage.

Studies of marriage roles occupy a prominent position in the general literature on marriage and a traditional questionnaire methodology has grown up (e.g. Blood and Wolfe, 1960) which would enable comparisons of alcoholism-complicated and other marriages to be made. More recently, however, the limitations of this methodology have been pointed out and attention has been drawn to the complex and multidimensional nature of family task and de-cision-making participation (e.g. Olson and Rabunsky, 1972; Turk and Bell, 1972). The perceived locus of authority within a family, and who actually makes decisions, are not necessarily the same thing. Furthermore, predictions, actual behaviour, and recall may not be congruent. The distinction between 'decision-making' and 'task performance' has long been made and this dis-tinction should be made in discussions of roles in alcoholism-complicated marriages. The present study found overall husband under-involvement in family 'tasks' but no under-involvement (indeed, in one area slight over-involvement) in 'social and sexual decision-making' (see p. 63).

Of particular relevance is the conceptual framework of Herbst (1954) in a study of Australian children's perceptions of family roles. He proposed a 'pathfield' along which the husband's activities progress, one way or the other, depending on whether his participation in family activities is on the increase or on the decrease. The same exercise was carried out for wives with very different results. While husbands had a relatively lengthy pathway represent-ing different degrees of engagement or disengagement in family activities, along which they might move while still remaining a member of the family, wives had relatively little room for manoeuvre. A further conceptual point concerns discrepancies between role performance and role expectations. To clinicians involved in marital therapy (e.g. Dicks, 1967), and to many re-searchers (e.g. Hicks and Platt, 1970; Hurvitz, 1965; Ort, 1950), it is this discrepancy, rather than role performance *per se*, which often appears to be of the greatest importance.

Quite apart from the failure of the 'alcoholism and marriage' specialists to take advantage of conceptual and methodological developments in the more general literature, there is no reason to suppose that substantive findings will be very different for alcoholism-complicated and other problem- or crisis-facing families. For example, Collins *et al.* (1971) found that husbands diag-nosed 'neurotic' contributed significantly less than control husbands to housework and child care. They concluded that neurosis in husbands was associated with 'minimal co-operation' in marriage and that deviant role patterns produced conflict. However, the importance of the distinction between task performance and decision-making is shown by their finding that decision-making was dominated by the husband in more patient than control marriages. Another dimension of potential relevance to alcoholism studies is suggested by their finding that, even in the absence of conflict, there were more 'segregated' than 'co-operative' patterns of decision-making among the patient families than among the controls. Ovenstone (1973) confirmed a high rate of 'segregated' and 'dominated' role patterns in the marriages of a further sample of 'neurotic' men. The severity of the husband's neurosis was associated with the number of 'divided' roles in her sample.

Clausen and Yarrow (1955) refer to changes in family roles, particularly when husband-patients are hospitalized, as being an important part of the impact of mental illness upon families; and Merrill (1969), referring to the reactions of men to their wives' hospitalizations for schizophrenia, comments on the 'remarkable extent of . . . adaptation of some husbands to include their wives' roles'. Indeed in a manner reminiscent of some who have written of the wives of alcoholics, he questions 'whether the husband's willingness . . . may not have contributed in some cases to the development or exacerbation of the wife's illness'. Hansen and Hill (1964) refer to the usurping by other family members of the father's role as breadwinner which has been reported in studies of the effects of economic depression and unemployment on families. Again, Hill (1949), in reporting his own study of war separation and subsequent family reunion, mentions that among the various patterns of reaction observed was one in which a relatively good adjustment was made to separation, but a relatively poor subsequent adjustment to reunion.

MARITAL SATISFACTION

High levels of conflict have frequently been noted in alcoholism-complicated marriages (e.g. Bullock and Mudd, 1959; Gorad, 1971), and various sources of 'hardship' or 'deviance' to which non-alcoholic spouses of alcoholics may be exposed have also been examined (e.g. Bailey et al., 1962; Jackson and Kogan, 1963). These sources include loss of family earnings, infidelity, involvement with police, rowing, and physical violence. Research findings have suggested that spouses of alcoholics are more likely to seek outside help, and are more likely to take action which leads to the termination of their marriage, if the level of hardship or deviance experienced is relatively high (Haberman, 1965; Jackson and Kogan, 1963).

Surprisingly, little use has been made in the specialist alcoholism literature of unifying concepts such as those of marital happiness, satisfaction, or cohesiveness. In the general marriage literature, on the other hand, such concepts have a long history although the use of global concepts has been criticized of late (e.g. Lively, 1969). One of the criticisms concerns the subjective nature of marital satisfaction; it is argued that marriage may be happy for one partner but not for the other. However, a review of several relevant studies suggests that this criticism may not be wholly warranted: although they are variable, correlations of husband and wife reported marital satisfaction are invariably positive and usually substantial.

Nor is it entirely clear why marital happiness should be considered, by some critics, an atheoretical concept. It might be thought, for example, to have some affinity with the more general concept of interpersonal attraction. There have been a number of attempts (e.g. Hawkins, 1968; Kirkpatrick, 1967) to view marital happiness in terms of a balance between positive aspects (degree of companionship, amount of affection, number of sources of mutual satisfaction, etc.) and negative aspects (amount of hostility, number of sources of tension, etc.). It is not difficult to conceive of the hardship and deviance to which spouses of alcoholics are exposed (spouses are nearly always wives in the relevant studies and far less is known about the hardship of being a husband married to an alcoholic wife) as negative forces tipping the balance in the direction of marital unhappiness or dissatisfaction. Indeed, analyses of divorce court testimonies have found 'drinking' to be a frequent source of marital dissatisfaction and complaint (e.g. Kephart, 1954; Levinger, 1966), and the early large-scale studies of marital satisfaction make mention of drinking as a source of marital unhappiness or maladjustment (e.g. Burgess and Cottrell, 1939; Terman, 1938). While these studies were North American in origin, Slater and Woodside (1951) found that a sample of English soldiers (diagnosed 'neurotic') and their wives gave 'drink' as the most frequent cause of discord in their parents' marriages.

The gains to be had from putting the study of alcoholism and marriage within more general ground are also to be seen if marital happiness is viewed not from a dyadic perspective but rather from the monadic perspective of a study of the individual personalities of marital partners. On the basis of studies which claimed to find 'predictors' of marital happiness (although such studies rarely employed the necessary prospective research design), Burgess and Wallin (1943) listed the following characteristics as the most decisive in differentiating happily married from unhappily married individuals: emotionally stable; considerate as opposed to critical of others; yielding as opposed to dominating; companionable as opposed to isolated; self-confident; emotionally dependent as opposed to emotionally self-sufficient. Other reviewers (e.g. Tharp, 1963) are convinced of the association between marital satisfaction and general behaviour characteristics ('personality') of the partners. It seems that the impression which unhappily married men and women have made on general investigators of personality and marriage is very similar to the impression which alcoholics sometimes make, relatively late in life, on the clinicians who treat them (e.g. Gliedman et al., 1956) and even, prior to the development of their alcoholism, on those who observe them as adolescents (Jones, 1968; McCord et al., 1960; Robins, 1966). The latter prospective studies of personality and alcoholism have each recorded an association between later alcoholism and early personality traits which have a 'competitive–exploitive', 'blunt–aggressive', and 'skeptical–distrustful' ring to them—to use the nomenclature of Leary's system (1957) and the adjective check-list derived from that system which has been used in several studies of alcoholism and marriage (e.g. Kogan and Jackson, 1963b; and in the present study—see p. 61).

INTERPERSON PERCEPTION AND MARRIAGE

Kogan and Jackson (1963b) reported that Alcoholics Anonymous wives, in comparison with wives in a 'friends and neighbours' control group, described their husbands as relatively 'skeptical–distrustful', as possessing few socially desirable characteristics, and as failing to fulfil the expressive marital role. In many cases perceptions were 'atypical' in this way whether the wives were describing their husbands 'sober' or 'drunk' (Kogan and Jackson, 1964). In another report (1963a) the same researchers provided data on wives' perceptions of themselves: wives of alcoholics, again in comparison with controls, described themselves in unusually hyperfeminine terms. Drewery and Rae (1969) have reported a very similar finding concerning wives of alcoholics in Scotland.

Mitchell (1959) contributed a relatively early paper using the now fashionable analytic technique of computing discrepancy scores in an attempt to capture aspects of interpersonal sensitivity, understanding, and communication. For example, how a wife described her husband was compared with how the husband described himself and the size of the discrepancy between these two perceptions was taken to indicate the degree of lack of sensitivity on the wife's part. Essentially Mitchell found that his sample of alcoholic husbands and their wives were no less sensitive to each other than a non-alcoholic comparison group of husbands and wives who were attending a marriage council. However, Mitchell took relatively little account of the many possibilities of artefactual findings in interperson data analysis (Cronbach, 1955; Wright, 1968) and the conclusions are probably unwarranted.

More note was taken of the possibility of artefact in a later more sophisticated series of studies by Drewery and Rae (1969) and Rae and Drewery (1972). They found a number of significantly larger discrepancies in interperson perception among alcoholic husbands and their wives than among a control group of 'normal' couples. Larger discrepancies in the former group were apparent in comparisons of spouse perceptions and meta-perceptions (e.g. a comparison of what H thinks of W with what W thinks H thinks about her) as well as at simpler levels. However, by a detailed but relatively straightforward analysis Drewery and Rae were able to show that these results were largely attributable to the stronger operation of a masculine 'stereotype response set' in the control group, and not necessarily to any greater sensitivity or understanding of 'normal' husbands and wives in their own marriages. There appeared to be a much clearer stereotype for describing normal males than females and the largest between-group differences concerned perceptions of husbands. In the general literature, both Luckey (1964) and Corsini (1956) found an association between marital satisfaction and aspects of marital person perception but again only when husbands were the objects of perception.

Corsini was also able to show, by a method of analysis similar in its effect to that used by Drewery and Rae, that these results were due not to interpersonal sensitivity within marriage but rather to the stronger operation of a perceptual stereotype of males among happy than among unhappy couples. In elegant fashion, Corsini 'reshuffled' the data so that the description of her husband provided by one wife was being compared with the description of himself provided, not by her own husband, but by a randomly drawn husband. It turned out that happily married wives were just as sensitive to men who were happily married to other women as they were to their own husbands.

The problems associated with the computing of discrepancy scores have led some general investigators to examine the content of simple self- or spouse-perceptions in much the same way as Kogan and Jackson (1963b) examined wives' perceptions of their alcoholic husbands. For example, Luckey (1964) reported a purely monadic analysis of the same data which she had reported earlier (1960) in terms of dyadic indices. Husbands and wives who were dissatisfied with their marriages were much more likely to use phrases in the 'skeptical–distrustful' and 'blunt–aggressive' categories than were satisfied couples, whether they were describing themselves or their spouses. Items of self- or spouse-perception which were positively correlated with satisfaction were predominantly in the 'responsible–overgenerous', the 'co-operative–overconventional' and the 'docile–dependent' categories. Murstein and Glaudin (1966) obtained very similar results.

The conclusions which can be drawn from this section of the general literature appear to be fairly clear-cut. Husbands and wives who take the view that their marriages are happy, adjusted or compatible (whether or not this view is realistic) describe themselves and their spouses in favourable terms. Furthermore, if further elements of an approved sex role are fairly widely shared, as is perhaps the case for assertiveness or dominance in the male role in industrial English-speaking countries, then the same subjects will describe the husband in these terms also. This has consequences for dyadic indices or discrepancies. The happily married, as a consequence, appear to be more perceptive, understanding, or sensitive. This puts alcoholism-and-marriage findings, such as those of Drewery and Rae, into clearer perspective. It would appear that they have demonstrated nothing very unique in the marriages of alcoholics but rather that alcoholic marriages in general tend to resemble marriages which are self-admittedly unhappy, whether or not complicated by alcoholism.

MATE CHOICE

Many writers on the subject (e.g. Futterman, 1953; Whalen, 1953) have stressed the personality disturbance of the non-alcoholic spouses of alcoholics. They have stated that the deviance, or potential deviance, of the alcoholic spouse is often a conscious or unconscious attraction, that the non-alcoholic spouse often has an 'investment' in the alcoholic's continued drinking, and that should the latter's deviance cease the non-alcoholic spouse may attempt to engineer his return to deviance or may herself break down. Prominent among these ideas is that of non-accidental mate choice along complementary lines. In particular the theme of the attraction of opposites along the dominance–submissiveness axis is repeatedly to be found. The strong-assertive woman attracted to the weak-submissive man is a recurring story. None the less it is a fact that the subject of mate selection processes in the specific context of alcoholism has received next to no scientific attention. While impressionistic accounts from the alcoholism and marriage field have stressed the attraction of opposites, the relevant general sociological and psychological literature has stressed husband–wife similarities. This literature has been reviewed or summarized on many occasions (e.g. Burgess and Wallin, 1943; Richardson, 1939) and there appears to be overwhelming evidence for assortative mating along homogamous lines (likes marrying likes). The degree of husband–wife similarity is far greater for variables such as race, age, religion, education, social class, attitudes, and interests than for personality and temperament.

However, a variety of more complex models of mate selection have been developed. Winch (1958) proposed a two-phase process. Only within a relatively small 'field of eligibles', defined for any individual on the basis of similarity, might selection take place on the basis of heterogamy or complementarity. His findings in apparent support of this theory, however, have been disputed by many writers since (e.g. Tharp, 1963). The 'filter' theory of Kerckhoff and Davis (1962) is another variety of two-stage theory. This theory proposed that selection takes place in terms of values, attitudes, and interests at a relatively early stage, and is influenced by the complementariness of psychological needs only at a later stage. In accordance with this theory they found that value-consensus within couples was predictive of relationships coming 'closer' when the relationship was of relatively short duration at the beginning of the study, while need-complementarity was predictive of closer relationships when these were already relatively long-standing. A similar but rather more elaborate theory involving three stages ('stimulus', 'value', and 'role') has been presented by Murstein (1970). Social exchange theory is used to organize findings relevant to each of these stages, the process of mate selection being likened to an economic one in which goods are exchanged and each partner is motivated to make a good 'buy'. Consistent with this theory are findings that partners are similar in terms of variables such as physical attractiveness and level of self-acceptance. For Murstein the concept of 'settling' for a partner is substituted for the concept of 'choosing'; those with greatest liabilities and least assets having the least choice. Several other models of mate selection (e.g. Karp et al., 1970) have attempted to reconcile the principles of homogamy and heterogamy.

Complementariness as opposed to similarity may conceivably be more frequent in marriages complicated by some type of psychological disorder in one or both partners (Cattell and Nesselroade, 1967) but once again, in the psychiatric literature, it is similarity which is most apparent. The findings include above-chance levels of husband–wife concordance for mental disorder (e.g. Gregory, 1959; Hagnell and Kreitman, 1974) and significant positive husband–wife correlations on tests or scales of psychological ill-health or 'neuroticism' (e.g. Coppen *et al.*, 1965; Hare and Shaw, 1965). Needless to say, assortative mating is not the only possible explanation for these modest but rather consistent husband–wife similarities.

Thus it may fairly be claimed that discussions of mate selection in the specialist alcoholism and marriage literature have been over-simplified and insufficiently informed by the general literature. Not that this is the only specialist literature at which this criticism can be levelled. Similar assumptions about complementary mate choice prevail in regard to spouses of opiate addicts (Taylor *et al.*, 1966) and compulsive gamblers (Boyd and Bolen, 1970), for example.

DISTURBANCE AND DECOMPENSATION IN WIVES

Relatively few studies have attempted to back up that part of the 'wife as villain rather than victim' model which speaks of the psychopathology of the non-alcoholic spouse married to an alcoholic, and of her tendency to break down or 'decompensate' if his deviance diminishes. Kogan *et al.* (1963) did find that significantly more Alcoholics Anonymous wives produced MMPI responses indicating psychopathology than did control wives, but abnormality was by no means limited to the former group and only a minority of them gave abnormal responses. Clearly such results offer no greater support for the 'wife's psychopathology' position than for the 'reaction to stress' view.

Most frequently referred to as providing evidence in support of 'decompensation' is a paper by Macdonald (1956), who screened a large number of women admitted to a state mental hospital and recruited those who had alcoholic husbands. In eleven of the eighteen cases Macdonald believed that the wife's mental disorder had its onset following a decrease in the husband's drinking. In several of the eleven cases which appeared to support the 'decompensation' view the evidence does not seem to have been strong. Macdonald's claims are in fact rather more modest than many have subsequently supposed. He stated that, 'In at least three instances the onset . . . coincided almost exactly with cessation. . . .' Even in some of these cases the events of note occurred several years prior to the investigation and the co-occurrence of events must have been difficult to establish.

A number of other studies have cast serious doubt on the general application of the 'decompensation' hypothesis. For example, Bailey and her colleagues (Bailey, 1967; Bailey *et al.*, 1962; Haberman, 1964) made use of a series of questions on psychophysiological symptoms which had been employed in the Midtown community mental health survey. Of all Midtown married women (controls) 35 per cent appeared to be moderately disturbed. In comparison, 43 per cent of the 'living with abstinent husband' group and 65 per cent of the 'living with still actively alcoholic husband' group were moderately disturbed (Bailey et al., 1962). Wives who were no longer living with drinking husbands (either because the husband had stopped drinking or because they were separated) reported less disturbance the longer the time since they were last living with a 'drinking husband' (Bailey, 1967). More than 80 per cent of wives who could contrast periods when they were living with a drinking husband and when they were not, reported a higher level of disturbance during the former period, and only a very small proportion (6 to 9 per cent) reported the reverse (Haberman, 1964). There is a strong suggestion that this small percentage could be accounted for by the statistical artefact of 'regression to the mean'.

These studies are seriously limited by the over-simplicity, and apparent opposition, of the two 'positions' which underlie this and other aspects of the alcoholism and marriage literature (spouse as victim and spouse as villain). A glance at some of the findings on extra-alcoholism marriage highlights these weaknesses. For one thing, the possibility that married couples may encounter disturbing problems when they reunite, or when the deviance of one partner has diminished or has been cured, is fairly widely recognized (e.g. Hill, 1949; Merrill, 1969), but it is not necessarily assumed that this implies that the non-deviant spouse is really a long-standing deviant in her own right, or that she necessarily has an 'investment' in her partner's continued deviance. An interesting alternative hypothesis suggests that there is only a limited amount of 'emotional room' for illness within a family at any one time, and that following a crisis family members may take it in turn to display emotional disturbance (Hansen and Hill, 1964). Again this suggests that 'decompensation', if it were to occur, could be explained without resorting to a full-scale 'wife's psychopathology' explanation.

In work on families complicated by psychological disorder of other types, for example in studies of 'neurosis' in husbands or wives (Kreitman, 1964), a range of possible explanations has been considered for the increased rate of disturbance to be found in the 'well' spouses. Among these are assortative mating, some sort of 'infection' (Nielsen, 1964) or 'contagion' (Ehrenwald, 1963), direct stress occasioned by the 'ill' partner's behaviour, and non-specific stress related to illness (e.g. hospitalization of a family member). The assumption seems to be that a variety of factors operate in most cases.

Even in the specific alcoholism and marriage literature it is not clear that anyone would seriously propose that all spouses of alcoholics are thoroughly 'psychopathological' themselves or that they want their partners to remain alcoholics. In fact no one universal type of personality among wives of alcoholics has been proposed. It is variety that has been emphasized. Nor have even the strongest proponents of the 'wives' psychopathology' position, such as Whalen (1953), supposed that problematic features of personality were exclusive to spouses of alcoholics. There is therefore a danger of setting up an extreme, and universal, 'villainous alcoholic's wife' theory as a straw man which can only too easily be knocked down. A variation of this theory had been suggested by Rae and Forbes (1966), who found evidence, in the MMPI responses of a sample of wives of in-patient alcoholics, for a sub-division of the wives into two types. The majority, if they showed abnormality at all, were likely to describe themselves as unusually depressed and anxious. But there was a minority, who Rae and Forbes admit made the strongest clinical impact, who were hostile, uncooperative, apparently cold and indifferent, and who had relatively high scores on the psychopathic deviate (Pd) scale of the MMPI. They suggest that wives in the former group may be essentially 'normal' people reacting to stress, while the latter are 'character disordered'.

A related attempt at sub-division, based on the way wives described their 'when sober' alcoholic husbands, was put forward by Kogan and Jackson (1961). They reported that, while there was relatively little variation in the way in which wives described their husbands 'when drinking', some gave very favourable descriptions of their husbands 'when sober' while others gave unfavourable descriptions. There were thus quite a number of wives who described their husbands in unfavourable terms whether drinking or sober. Kogan and Jackson considered this high frequency of 'atypical perceptions', regardless of drunkenness or sobriety, to be surprising, and they suggested that, 'These are uncomfortable and unrewarding marital situations which would be little changed by the cessation of drinking.' This is obviously a very important statement, the more so because it is made by two researchers, one of whom is still widely regarded as the major protagonist for the 'reaction to stress' model of the behaviour of the non-alcoholic spouse (Jackson, 1954). Data from the present study suggest that this feature of marital interaction, wives' perceptions of their husbands when sober, is fairly resistant to change over a period of twelve months despite radical changes in the alcoholic partner's drinking behaviour (p. 79).

Here again the specialist field has been structured in accordance with two extreme models neither of which accounts for all the facts, and which are not seriously expected to by writers in other fields.

MARITAL DISSOLUTION

Although the evidence suggests that wives are more likely to seek and obtain separation from their alcoholic husbands the more they have been exposed to hardship or deviance within their marriages (Haberman, 1965; Jackson and Kogan, 1963), none the less the cohesiveness of many alcoholism-complicated marriages has surprised a number of observers (e.g. Whalen, 1953). Endurance is quite likely to be attributed to fanciful intrapsychic mechanisms such as 'subconscious masochism' (Pixley and Stiefel, 1963).

Again the discussion in this area seems remarkably uninformed of theory and findings in the general marriage area. One useful framework is that put forward by Levinger (1965), who proposed a three-factor scheme as a basis for explaining findings on what makes a marriage stick or break. Viewing marital cohesiveness as a special case of group cohesiveness, Levinger listed factors relevant to dissolution or endurance under the following three headings: sources of attraction within marriage; sources of barrier strength; and sources of alternate attraction. Among the factors listed under 'sources of attraction' are a number with direct relevance to alcoholism-complicated marriage, such as 'esteem for spouse', 'husband's occupation and income', and 'sexual enjoyment'. As 'barriers' to breaking a marriage he lists such factors as 'feelings of obligation to dependent children', 'moral proscriptions' deriving from religion, for example; and 'external pressures' deriving from primary-group affiliations, community stigma, or legal or economic bars. Under the heading of 'sources of alternate attraction' are such factors as 'preferred alternate sex partner' and 'wife's opportunity for independent income'. None of these factors has been studied systematically in relation to alcoholism and marriage and their inclusion in Levinger's scheme provides a healthy corrective to the assumption that the endurance of unhappy marriages is to be accounted for solely in terms of the intricacies of interpersonal relationships or complex personality dynamics.

INFLUENCE OF MARITAL FACTORS ON TREATMENT OUTCOME

Relatively few investigations have been directed toward the question which Jackson (1954) asked some years ago: 'What are the factors within families which facilitate a return to sobriety or hamper it?' Smith (1967) reported a significant degree of association between favourable treatment outcome and the attendance of wives at weekly group meetings. Rae (1972) found that a wife's high Pd score on the MMPI was associated with a relatively poor prognosis for the alcoholic husband. A later chapter of this book will report some findings from the present study demonstrating an association between marital satisfaction or cohesion and the favourableness of outcome of treatment (p. 72).

Again these results are usefully seen in a more general light. Although concepts and methods of measuring family relationships have varied between studies, a number of investigations of the influence of family factors on the outcome of treatment for other types of psychological disorder can be seen as being roughly consistent with the above findings on alcoholism-complicated marriages (e.g. Brown et al., 1962, 1972; Freeman and Simmons, 1963; Morrow and Robins, 1964). If a general theme can be drawn, it seems to have to do with the importance of the continuing rewardingness, and mutual high expectations, of family relationships. Whether schizophrenia or alcoholism is the diagnostic category under consideration, breakdown in the mutual rewardingness of key family relationships appears to be predictive of a relatively unfavourable outcome following treatment or consultation for a psychological disorder (see CHAPTER V, p. 73 for a statement of a general hypothesis along these lines).

Weaknesses of Research Method

Most of the research on the subject of alcoholism and marriage which has been cited in this review has been methodologically unsophisticated. Without exception the studies have been descriptive rather than experimental and the descriptive methods have often been rudimentary. Interview or questionnaire items have frequently been indefinite (e.g. Haberman, 1965; Jackson and Kogan, 1963; James and Goldman, 1971; Lemert, 1960, 1962) or else analysis and interpretation have been subjective and inferential (e.g. Bailey, 1967). The reliability and validity of data have rarely been questioned. These faults are frequently compounded by the requirement that subjects recall past, often quite remote, periods of time (e.g. Bailey, 1967; Haberman, 1965; James and Goldman, 1971; Lemert, 1960; Macdonald, 1956), and in some instances it even appears that certain groups of subjects have been asked to recall more remote time periods than others (Bailey et al., 1962; Haberman, 1965). Such retrospective designs completely ignore the possibility of selective recruitment to groups. For example, the lower frequency of disturbance of wives in 'husband sober' groups may be the cause, not the result, of group membership (Bailey, 1967; Bailey et al., 1962; Haberman, 1964). Even when prospective designs have been employed, it is impossible to attribute causal significance to marital variables (Kogan and Jackson, 1961; Rae, 1972; and the present study).

In several instances the task set for research subjects has been too 'obvious', and 'demand characteristics' have been ignored. To ask wives whether they reacted more strongly when their husbands were drinking 'socially' or when their drinking was 'alcoholismic' (James and Goldman, 1971), or to ask them whether they experienced more personal disturbance when their husbands were actively drinking or when they were abstinent (Bailey, 1967; Bailey et al., 1962; Haberman, 1964), is to adopt a weak research procedure. Those who have investigated interperson perception (Drewery and Rae, 1969; Kogan and Jackson, 1963a and 1963b) appear to have ignored differences in 'set' between troubled subjects and ostensibly trouble-free controls.

A major deficiency throughout the literature on alcoholism and marriage is the failure to describe and define samples or to take account of differences between samples. Because the focus is on 'marriage', it appears to have been thought unnecessary to define 'alcoholism'. There is little recognition of the heterogeneity of persons who fall under this heading. The several papers by Jackson and Kogan are based on data provided by wives all of whom had had contact with Alcoholics Anonymous, and they may be untypical (e.g. Jackson, 1954; Kogan and Jackson, 1961, 1963a, b; 1964). There is also the question of 'norms' and control groups. In some cases the absence of a control group makes it impossible to know what is 'normal' in marriage (the present study, for example), and in other cases statements about the abnormality or atypicality of aspects of alcoholism-complicated marriages have been based on a comparison with data from control groups chosen in an unusual or unsatisfactory manner (e.g. Drewery and Rae, 1969; Kogan and Jackson, 1963a, b; Lemert, 1962).

TOWARD A MORE COMPLETE SOCIAL PSYCHOLOGY OF ALCOHOLISM AND MARRIAGE

The two major 'theories' in the field clearly have serious limitations. Neither does justice to marriage as an ongoing social system with a history of variable length measurable in years rather than weeks or hours. The current state of such a system must be influenced by the original inputs to that system, by processes of adaptation which have occurred within it during its history, and by external influences to which it has been exposed during that time (von Bertalanffy, 1966). Prevailing conceptions of alcoholism-complicated marriages involve a one-sided view of the marital relationship which artificially puts individuals into specialized roles, such as that of the 'stress victim', 'character disorder', and indeed the 'alcoholic' himself. This artificial 'punctuating of the sequence of interactional events' (Watzlawick et al., 1968) as often as not allows a one-sided evaluation and an apportionment of blame to one or the other party.

There is little recognition of the 'reciprocally contingent' nature of social interaction (Shannon and Guerney, 1973). In related fields, studies of the influence of family factors on treatment outcome have had to face the fact that causal significance cannot be attributed to the behaviour of one family member alone (the parent of a schizophrenic adolescent, for example), because the interpersonal behaviours of the interactants in a family system are intertwined and inseparable. For example, Brown et al. (1962) found that relatives were most likely to be hostile toward a family member returning from hospital when the latter was relatively hostile himself.

There have been a number of other demonstrations of the complex way in which variables inter-relate. A major demonstration of this was Kogan and Jackson's finding (1965) that a wife's self-reported current psychopathology, her perception of abnormality in her own childhood upbringing, and her report of recently experienced personal stress in marriage, were all positively inter-correlated. Although wives of alcoholics reported higher levels of all these variables than control wives, the relationships between these variables were similar in both groups.

Edwards, Harvey and Whitehead (1973) referred to a third 'psychosocial' view of wives of alcoholics. However, not only were they concerned with theories of spouses, rather than theories of marriage, but they set up a polarity between the 'stress' and the 'decompensation' views, and on the basis of their view of the evidence incorporated the former but not the latter in their psychosocial theory. Game theory (Berne, 1964; Steiner, 1969) represents one potentially sophisticated psychosocial model of alcoholism and marriage, but it is as yet not clearly formulated and little objective research has stemmed from it.

The wider social–psychological and sociological literature on marriage, as well as testifying to the non-uniqueness of the alcoholism–complicated marriage, provides the guidelines for the development of a more truly social–psychological theory of alcoholism and marriage. For a start, the initial process of bond formation leading to marriage may be best thought of as a complex, multi-stage, multi-factor process. Of the relatively simple views of the process, there is greatest support for mate similarity. Social habits, including heavy drinking, as well as 'personality' attributes which may be associated with future alcoholism, must be among the constellation of elements which influence person perception and mate choice at this early stage in the history of a marital dyad. Subsequently, during the dyad's existence the social influence process is undoubtedly highly complex and not easily understood, but probably involves a variety of processes some of which can be understood as 'social conditioning', 'contract formation,' 'modelling', and 'contagion'. In the history of some marriages a point may be reached where the behaviour of one partner is so deviant that the resulting state of affairs may be well construed as a source of stress, originating in one partner, and necessitating 'coping' by the other. Even then, it is arguable that the mutual influence process is still best analysed without the constraints imposed by assigning to the partners the roles of 'deviant' and 'coper'. Finally, the process of bond dissolution is likely to be subject to the influence of a wide variety of factors.

THE PROJECT

CHAPTER III

BASIC RESEARCH DESIGN

THE SAMPLE

The sample consisted of 100 marriages in which the husband received a diagnosis of alcoholism: to describe the sample as being of *marriages* rather than simply of *patients* is to emphasize a major perspective of the whole study. Nevertheless, the husbands were in the formal sense, 'the patients'. They were consecutive attenders at a Maudsley out-patient clinic (the Alcoholism Family Clinic). Referral was from a number of possible sources such as general practitioners, other hospitals, AA, and the probation service. Some patients were self-referred. Attendance was in strict terms voluntary, although there were obvious coercive pressures in many instances.

Criteria for inclusion in the series were that a referring agent considered the patient to have a drinking problem; the willingness of both partners to attend together an initial assessment session; the psychiatrist's confirmation that a drinking problem actually existed (a criterion which pilot work had rather surprisingly shown to be necessary); patients aged twenty-five to sixty years; and a reasonable travelling distance from the hospital so as to facilitate the family's subsequent attendance and home visiting. The only medical criteria for exclusion were progressive or painful physical disease, underlying psychotic illness, or clinically evident brain-damage.

INITIAL ASSESSMENT

Husband and wife came to the clinic at 9 a.m. and about three hours were spent in assessment. The husband was seen by a psychiatrist and a history recorded on a precoded schedule, physical examination was carried out and blood tests arranged for liver function and routine haematology, and radiographic investigations arranged when appropriate. The husband was then seen by a psychologist who made standard assessments relating to personality, self-esteem, marital relations, and perception of drinking problem. The wife was interviewed by a social worker who completed a pre-coded schedule, several sections of which paralleled the inquiry which the psychiatrist made of the patient. The wife in addition completed a number of questionnaires relating to her coping behaviour, marital interaction, and her appraisal of the severity of her husband's drinking. Details of these various assessments are given in CHAPTERS IV, V and VI.

RANDOMIZATION FOR PURPOSES OF THE CONTROLLED TRIAL

Only when the assessment procedures had been completed, was a randomization table kept by the project's secretary consulted, and patients allocated to either the Advice or Treatment group. The rules entailed separate randomization for sub-sets of patients defined by occupational status (three levels), and severity of drinking symptomatology (two levels), so as to maximize the likelihood of satisfactory group matching.

INITIAL COUNSELLING SESSION

With randomization determined, the morning then continued, and a joint session was held for husband and wife together with social worker, psychologist, and psychiatrist. As a further element in assessment, the psychiatrist asked a number of structured questions of the couple and marital interaction was observed. This joint interview is described more fully in CHAPTER V. The psychiatrist then stated that *the husband was suffering from alcoholism*, and advised that *the treatment goal should be total abstinence*, that *the husband should continue work or return to work*, and *that husband and wife should attempt to make the marriage viable*. A free discussion then followed, with a more individual and personal interpretation now given to the situation.

TIME-BASE FOR THE CONTROLLED TRIAL

The time-base for the controlled trial was the first twelve months after initial assessment and randomization: the research design was such as to maximize the contrast in treatment experience of the two groups over this period.

THERAPEUTIC APPROACH TO ADVICE GROUP DURING FIRST YEAR

The Advice Group couples were told at the initial counselling session that responsibility for attainment of the stated goals lay in their own hands and could not be taken over by others. This message was given in sympathetic and constructive terms. It was explained that the husband would not be offered a further appointment at the clinic, but that the social worker would call each month to see the wife and collect news of progress. It was stressed that this social worker would merely be collecting follow-up data which would be used for record keeping, and would be acting as someone simply holding 'a watching brief'. Advice was given that if the husband should be suffering from withdrawal symptoms, he should contact his general practitioner, but no medication was given by the clinic.

THERAPEUTIC APPROACH TO TREATMENT GROUP DURING FIRST YEAR

At the counselling session all husbands in the Treatment Group were offered an introduction to Alcoholics Anonymous, offered a prescription of citrated calcium carbimide, and prescribed drugs to cover withdrawal if this was indicated. A further appointment was then made for the husband to see the psychiatrist whose personal responsibility it was to evolve a continuing treatment programme with the husband, while the social worker took a similar responsibility for the wife. The husband's care subsequently continued on an out-patient basis with emphasis on strategies for abstinence, reality problems, and interpersonal and particularly marital interactions. Some other psychotherapeutic explorations were made when indicated, but with generally a rather cautious approach in this regard. If the husband failed to respond to out-patient care he was offered admission to a specialized in-patient alcoholism unit for detoxification, and subsequent involvement in in-patient group therapy, occupational therapy, and the ward milieu: the expected stay was about six weeks. The social worker was, if required, available to all husbands in the Treatment Group for advice on problems such as employment, housing, family finances, and court involvement. She largely, however, worked with the wife, on reality problems and the marital situation. The psychiatrist and social worker regularly discussed their cases together. Information was regularly passed to the G.P., and care was taken to establish effective liaison with any agencies which might already be involved with the case. The total treatment programme thus allowed wide latitude for varying intensities as determined by the needs and responses of individual couples, rather than the programme being conceived in terms of a stereotyped regime: the general strategy was to give more intensive care at the beginning of the twelve month treatment period and then, as indicated by individual response, to widen if possible the intervals between appointments. When a husband failed an appointment he was offered another, and the social worker might through the wife, or directly on a home visit, encourage the patient to re-attend.

This treatment model is seen as generally in accord with present-day thinking on help for the alcoholic, and in particular as largely congruent with the view of the special unit's functions outlined in the recent DHSS White Paper (DHSS, 1975).

FOLLOW-UP ASSESSMENTS DURING FIRST TWELVE MONTHS
     AND AT END OF YEAR

1. At the end of each successive four-week period within the twelve months between intake and one-year follow-up, the social worker gathered structured information from the wife. This applied to both Advice Group and Treatment Group wives: for the Advice Group the social worker was given the role of data collector, and was strictly instructed to confine the interview to data gathering on the basis of a structured schedule. Time spent with each family by the social worker was recorded.

2. On Treatment Group husbands the psychiatrist completed a monthly record of all therapeutic interventions: the social worker completed similar information on contacts with the wife (and sometimes husband).

3. All husbands (both groups) were to be seen by the psychiatrist as near as

possible to the twelve-month anniversary of study intake, and a reconstruction made using a structured schedule. A similar twelve-month reconstruction was made by the social worker interviewing the wife. Various standard assessments of both husband and wife, paralleling those made at intake, were undertaken by the psychologist.

Details of type of data gathered at intake and at follow-up will be made explicit in following chapters.

TREATMENT OF BOTH GROUPS DURING SECOND YEAR

It was realized that the possibility of observing two groups with contrasting treatment experience, would be progressively eroded by help-seeking engagement elsewhere, together with inevitable further losses to follow-up. During the second year, families from either group who actively wished treatment were therefore offered help (or further help), and there was purposely no effort to maintain the separateness of the two original groups. In fact this second year should be seen as a fairly free-wheeling period, with patients making their own choices, and relatively few families engaging in very active therapy.

FOLLOW-UP AT THE END OF TWENTY-FOUR MONTHS

At the end of the second year a member of the research team administered a follow-up questionnaire to husbands and to wives separately. These were relatively short inquiries, focusing particularly on the patient's drinking behaviour over the preceding twelve months, and on any evidence of his having drunk in a controlled fashion (see CHAPTER VII).

PILOT WORK

The study was extensively piloted. The initial work was on separate sections of the study and design of particular assessments, but before case intake was started a complete run-through of all procedures and assessments was carried out on a number of families.

THE TRIAL: ETHICAL CONSIDERATIONS

For the twelve-month trial it was considered absolutely necessary to operate stringent and continuous safeguards. Immediately after case intake, a full letter was written to every husband's general practitioner which explained the course of action which was being taken, and in particular alerted the doctor to any physical complications which might require treatment or specialized referral: results were forwarded of any positive laboratory investigations. The social worker's monthly contact with wives in the Advice Group provided a form of safety monitoring; it was understood that any worrying situation would be discussed in the staff group, and that the husband might if necessary then be taken out of the study. Patients in the Advice Group were of course free to seek the help of any other treatment agency if they so wished.

CHAPTER IV

RESULTS OF THE TRIAL
AT TWELVE MONTHS

THIS chapter reports the treatment trial aspect of the study. The basic methodology is described in CHAPTER III, but it may be useful here briefly to summarize the essential features of the trial design.

1. One hundred consecutive families in which the husband sought treatment for alcoholism were, at an initial session, assessed on multiple criteria, with independent information from both marriage partners.

2. Families were randomized between two sharply contrasting therapeutic approaches:

(a) The Treatment Group, modelled on present British ideas of what would constitute an energetic offer of help to husband and wife.

(b) The Advice Group, which was tantamount to giving families carefully considered and personal instruction on how to get on with things by themselves, and without further help from the clinic.

3. Exactly parallel monthly follow-up information was collected from wives of patients in both groups (and additional information from patients in the Treatment Group).

4. Comprehensive twelve-month follow-up assessments on multiple criteria were separately obtained from husbands and from wives in both groups.

RESULTS

Statistical note. Throughout this chapter a statement that 'no significant difference' has been demonstrated implies relevant differences between means (by t test), or departures from expected distributions (χ^2 on raw scores), with a chance probability greater than 5 per cent. The notation $\pm$ attached to a mean indicates the standard error of the mean.

1 MATCHING OF INTAKE SAMPLES

The process of randomization resulted in satisfactory matching of the Advice and Treatment Groups, and on no parameter measured did the two groups differ significantly.

(a) *Demographic and Social Characteristics.* TABLE 5 shows satisfactory matching for age and 'highest ever' occupational status and for variables which might be seen as reflecting degree of social stability. Occupational status was rated on the Hall-Jones scale of occupational prestige for males (Hall and Jones, 1950; Oppenheim, 1966), with categories collapsed to I–IV (professionally qualified and higher administrative to inspectional, supervisory and some non-manual) and V–VII (routine grades of non-manual to routine manual). 'Time off work' was a summation of reported sickness absence, unemployment, etc.

(b) *Matching on Drink-Related Variables.* On this set of variables the two groups of fifty patients again showed no significant difference (TABLE 6)— 'Age first experienced damage' was the husband's retrospective estimate of the age at which he first experienced any deleterious effect of drinking on mental or physical health, or social functioning. 'Age first realized problem' was the age at which he had actually first admitted to himself that he had a drinking problem, a point which in each group followed 'first damage' by a mean of 2·6 years. 'Weeks heavy drinking' in previous twelve months was based on (a) establishment of what for the *individual* patient (H or W's estimate respectively) constituted 'heavy drinking', (b) careful reconstruction of drinking behaviour over the twelve months and summation (H and W respectively), of all 'heavy drinking' days, to the sum of the nearest week. Such reconstruction is of uncertain accuracy but the aim was to establish between-group comparisons rather than absolute measures. 'Longest abstinence' is longest continuous period of total abstinence in the preceding twelve months. 'Trouble score'[1] is an index of the patient's self-report of drinking symptomatology during the preceding twelve months: this scale gives a possible range of 0–10, 'Hardship score'[2] is a similar index of the wife's report of hardship she had experienced over the previous twelve months in association with her husband's drinking: the possible range was again 0–10.

2 OUTCOME OVER TWELVE-MONTH FOLLOW-UP

(a) *Number of Couples Available for Analysis.* The core of couples for whom twelve-month follow-up data was available for analysis was forty-six for the Advice and forty-eight for the Treatment Group. The loss to follow-up of four couples from the Advice Group was accounted for by one couple being withdrawn from the study because of the dangerous impact of the husband's drinking on his family, by one patient being withdrawn because of the development of florid schizophrenia, and finally by two couples being untraceable at twelve months. The loss of two couples from the Treatment Group was accounted for by one husband having died and by loss of contact with a further couple. On some individual items there were missing data; this will be duly noted in subsequent tables.

[1] The internally homogeneous tens-item Trouble scale was derived by item analysis from a set of twenty-eight questions put to husbands. The ten items related to morning tremor, morning nausea, morning drinking, inability to stop drinking, hallucinatory experience, 'passing out', secret drinking, debts, pawning possessions, losing time from work (Orford, 1974).

[2] By a similar process to that used in construction of the Trouble scale questions relating to ten aspects of the husband's behaviour were selected for inclusion in the Hardship scale (Orford, 1974; Orford *et al.*, 1976a). This scale is discussed in more detail on pp. 75–6 and in TABLE 22, CHAPTER V.

(b) *Patient's Drinking Behaviour During Twelve Months from Intake to Intake Anniversary*. The intake date was for each patient the date of initial assessment, and the day on which he was allocated either to the Advice or Treatment Group. The anniversary date was for each patient exactly fifty-two weeks later. The follow-up information was obtained either on that anniversary date or as soon thereafter as possible, with independent information from the husband (obtained for different items separately by the psychiatrist and by the psychologist), and from the wife (obtained for different items separately by the research social worker and the psychologist). The outcome data deriving from these fifty-two week reconstructions were in certain instances supplemented by the thirteen four-weekly tallies of information from wives obtained throughout the study period by the research social worker. Relevant data are set out firstly in TABLE 7, which gives assessments both by husband and wife. The method of categorizing patient's report of his drinking behaviour used at twelve-months' anniversary was different from that employed at the study intake. Instead of totting up actual number of days at different drinking levels during the previous year, each of the fifty-two weeks was characterized by the highest drinking level during that particular week. The four different drinking levels shown in TABLE 7 were defined.[1] The drinking categorization used by the wife was also revised for the outcome measures. It was more in accord with the wife's own intuitive assessment of the husband's drinking to ask her to describe his drinking in terms of its being 'acceptable' or 'unacceptable' rather than asking her to make any assessment of actual levels. As with the husband's outcome ratings, description of the week in terms of highest category on any day in the given week (rather than totting up days), was found to be more satisfactory. On none of the measures reported in this table was there a significant between-group difference in outcome.

TABLE 8 presents data calculated so as to correct for the fact that some patients spent part of the study year in hospital (and hence in a situation of enforced abstinence). The table makes between-group comparison only as regards drinking behaviour during that part of the year spent outside hospital (the periods when drinking was an option), with time in each instance proportionately corrected up to a notional total of fifty-two weeks. From the results given in TABLES 7 and 8 together, it may therefore be concluded that the drinking behaviour of the two groups over the period of the study year was closely similar, with the impact of hospital-related abstinence not significantly altering this situation.

(c) *Subjective Ratings of Drinking Problem*. Husband and wife were each asked to give an overall rating of the severity of the patient's drinking problem as it was on the anniversary date, and of the degree of improvement over the

---

[1] One pint of beer contains 16–20 g of absolute alcohol. A pint of beer was for purposes of this categorization taken as equivalent to two single measures of spirits, or two glasses of wine.

preceding fifty-two week period (TABLE 9). Again no significant between-group differences are revealed. Husbands tended to give a rather more optimistic picture than wives. On the conservative estimate given by the wives, the results would indicate that at the anniversary about one-third of patients in either group had a 'slight or no' drinking problem.

(*d*) *Social Adjustment*. On indices of social adjustment there were no significant between-group difference in outcome (TABLE 10).

(i) The Treatment Group showed an average of three to four weeks greater time off work than the Advice Group (the difference just failing to reach significance).

(ii) Husbands gave a very slightly more optimistic estimate than wives regarding overall improvement in 'marital problem', with the picture (both for husband's and wife's accounts), very alike for the two groups.

(*e*) *Trouble Scores: Comparison between Pre-treatment and Study Year.* Trouble scores were determined by identical inquiry at two points in time—at intake for the preceding twelve months, and at twelve-month intake anniversary for the twelve months of the study period. Husband's report for *Advice Group* gave a mean score of 5·2 ± 0·4 at intake, and 3·2 ± 0·4 at anniversary, with a change of −2·0 scale points (38 per cent): for *Treatment Group* there was a mean score of 5·1 ± 0·4 at intake, 3·1 ± 0·4 at anniversary, with a change of −2·0 scale points (39 per cent).

3 TREATMENT EXPERIENCE OF THE TWO GROUPS OVER TWELVE-MONTH FOLLOW-UP

A crucial matter to determine was whether over the twelve-month period a considerable distinction between the treatment experience of the two groups had been maintained. Advice Group patients were at liberty to seek psychiatric treatment elsewhere or to seek help from many other available agencies. Furthermore, for the Treatment Group, treatment was not in any sense compulsory, and it was open to patients and wives to reject any or all of the help offered.

The study design therefore left open the possibility of patient behaviour, which would over twelve months erode the difference in treatment experience between the two groups. The Advice Group might have sought help elsewhere and the Treatment Group have rejected the help offered by the Clinic, and all this to such an extent that any notion of the study constituting a trial of two markedly different intensities of therapeutic interventions would be vitiated. To check on this possibility, detailed information was collected about contacts which couples in either group made during the study period with a wide variety of helping agencies. These data came variously from the monthly contacts made by the social worker with each wife in each group, 'anniversary' information separately from husband and wife, and a check on hospital records. The essential conclusion is that a large distinction between the quantity and type of help received by the two groups was indeed maintained. Although some Advice Group patients sought help from other sources, and some Treatment Group patients engaged in only a rather minimal degree of contact with the Clinic, the overall between-group differences remained at a level which can leave no doubt that two very different types of therapeutic engagements are being compared.

(a) *Both Groups: Time spent in psychiatric hospitals* (TABLE 11). The percentage of patients in Advice and Treatment Groups who were psychiatric in-patients during the twelve-month follow-up did not differ significantly. However, the mean duration of admission was considerably different for the two groups (P <0·01), with the overall group mean for the Advice Group being less than one week, and for the Treatment Group over three weeks. The great majority of the Advice Group who were admitted, had admissions of less than four weeks, while for the Treatment Group the majority of admissions were for over eight weeks.

Behind the data presented in this table lies the fact that all the recorded admissions for the Treatment Group were to the one specialized alcoholism in-patient unit (Bethlem Royal Hospital), where in the majority of instances a planned programme of specialized treatment was completed. On the other hand, the patients in the Advice Group who during the twelve months found their way to in-patient psychiatric care were admitted to a variety of hospitals, usually in response to crisis, and largely for relatively short periods of 'drying out'.

(b) *Both Groups: Help-seeking outside the Family Clinic's Services.* TABLE 12 records the contact of both groups with a variety of helping agencies during the follow-up twelve months. Other than the entry in the bottom line of the table, the data are derived from summation of the monthly reports given by wives. The results show that the Advice Group did not compensate for lack of proffered Family Clinic help by seeking help from agencies other than the Clinic: the extra-Clinic contacts of the Advice Group over the twelve-month period were not significantly in excess of such extra-Clinic contacts by the Treatment Group. For instance, not only was there no significant between-group difference in number of visits to Alcoholics Anonymous, but the non-significant tendency was for the Treatment Group to have the greater AA contact—an active effort had of course been made by the Family Clinic to persuade all patients in the Treatment Group to attend these meetings. Visits to general practitioners, out-patient psychiatric attendances, and out-patient general hospital visits were all recorded, and there were no significant between-group differences.

(c) *Both Groups: Contact with the research social worker.* For the Advice Group the social worker (acting simply in data-collecting capacity), recorded monthly the time spent in contacts with each family, and for the Treatment Group time spent in social work contact was similarly recorded. The mean total time for the twelve months for the Advice Group was 4·7 ± 0·5 hours and for the Treatment Group 18·3 ± 1·5 hours (P < 0·01). The data thus confirm that the social workers were in this regard successful in maintaining a considerable difference in the quantity of contact offered to the two groups.

(d) *Treatment Group: Analysis of Alcoholism Family Clinic Out-patient care.* For each patient the psychiatrist concerned with that patient's treatment completed a four-weekly tally of out-patient contacts and of all therapeutic effort (TABLE 13). There was wide variation in the count of out-patient psychiatric consultations. It should be remembered that on average the Treatment Group spent rather more than three of the fifty-two study weeks as in-patients, which decreased the group's overall 'availability' for out-patient appointments—the 'corrected' degree of co-operation in clinic attendance would therefore be slightly greater than a reading of TABLE 13 would suggest. About one-third of patients had rather minimal contact (0–6 visits), about one-third medium intensity contact (7–12 visits), while the remaining third had more intensive contact (13+ visits). The fact that on average each patient failed about six offered appointments is an indication of the degree to which the Clinic attempted to maintain treatment contact, and the average duration of interview with the psychiatrist (about half an hour), provides a further quantitative measure of the type of care which the Clinic was offering. Psycho-active drugs were prescribed by the Clinic only sparingly and in terms of a purposely rather conservative policy which sought to avoid the hazards of concurrent drug taking and heavy drinking, or the dangers of iatrogenic cross-dependence: such drugs were given to out-patients only as part of a carefully and individually planned aid to alcohol withdrawal, or where there were other unequivocal indications. About two-thirds of the patients at some time accepted prescription of a drink-deterrent drug (citrated calcium carbimide): this drug was prescribed only with full warning of the dangers which would result from drinking, and no serious untoward incident was recorded.

4 DIFFERENCES IN HELP-SEEKING ENGAGEMENT BETWEEN THOSE
   PATIENTS WITH RELATIVELY POOR AND RELATIVELY
   GOOD OUTCOME

It could still be argued that a failure to demonstrate broad between-group differences in outcome did not logically preclude an interpretation that 'Treatment' was a more effective intervention than 'Advice', provided that further analysis could show the following to be the facts:

(i) In the *Treatment* Group, within-group analysis showed that those with better outcome had received more treatment.

(ii) In the *Advice* Group, those with better outcome were found to be a sub-group which had compensated for the absence of a treatment offer from the Family Clinic by finding similar help elsewhere.

In essence, the facts would then propose that for both groups a gradient of less → more therapeutic engagement paralleled a gradient of less → more improvement, with the inference that a causal connection between therapeutic engagement and outcome was not an unreasonable hypothesis. TABLE 14 examines these questions in terms of two different outcome variables—the husband's subjective assessment of improvement in drinking problem at twelve months,[1] and composite Outcome Categories.[2] The latter three-part categorization gives only rather small numbers in cells, but is probably more valid and closer to clinical meaning than a rating based simply on answers to the one subjective question.

The evidence bearing on the preceding hypothesis is then as follows (TABLE 14):

(i) Of the comparisons involving the *Treatment Group*, only three produced differences which were statistically significant. Patients reporting 'some' improvement at follow-up had more contact with G.P.s and general hospital out-patient departments. The three-category outcome classification showed patients in the best outcome group as having fewer social work contacts than patients in either of the other two groups.

(ii) Of comparisons involving the *Advice Group*, none produced significant differences. A non-significant difference in distributions between different frequency categories of A A attendance should however be noted: whatever their outcome, most patients in the Advice Group did not attend A A at all, but among those with better outcome there was a small segment of specially keen attenders. As with the Treatment Group, psychiatric hospital admission tended to be related to poorer outcome. The relationship between number of G.P. attendances and better outcome was non-significant but in the same direction as for the Treatment Group.

Because of the large number of comparisons made in TABLE 14 some chance associations might be expected. The data are best therefore interpreted rather guardedly and the picture which emerges taken in the round. With this approach, it might be concluded that in terms of the original hypotheses (i) for the Treatment Group better outcome was not associated with more in-

---

[1] Subjective assessment of drinking problem was coded on a seven-point scale from 'distinctly worse' (o) to 'distinctly improved' (6), and the distribution was then dichotomized between a rating of '4' ('slightly improved') and '5' ('moderately improved').

[2] The details of this categorization of drinking outcome are recorded elsewhere (Orford *et al.*, 1976a), but, in summary, the following may be said: To qualify for the good outcome group husband and wife had to agree independently that relatively little of the intervening year had been spent in excessive drinking (less than ten weeks at 5+ pints or approximately 100+ gms, or at an 'unacceptable' level), and that the husband's problem was now slight at most, or that considerable improvement had occurred since intake. To qualify for the bad outcome group husbands and wives had to agree independently that more than half the year had been spent in excessive drinking, and that the problem was still considerable or had shown negligible improvement since intake. Information was not sufficiently complete to make a classification in eleven cases, and in thirty-three other cases ('equivocal' outcome) the criteria for inclusion in one or the other of the extreme outcome groups were not satisfied.

tensive specialized treatment (use of psychiatric out-patient and in-patient facilities), but was possibly associated with marginally greater use of the G.P. and general hospital out-patient facilities, while (ii) for the Advice Group better outcome was probably not to any important degree associated with more frequent involvement with medical or psychiatric agencies, although there is a hint that a small group of specially keen AA attenders may have attained better outcome.

5 PATIENT'S VIEW ON WHAT HAD HELPED THEM

At the end of the twelve-month study period, each husband was seen by the research psychologist and asked to mark a check list relating to factors which might have aided in whatever improvement the patient saw himself as having achieved over the year. What is being obtained is of course a crude, and entirely subjective measure, but it is the husband's view of causality rather than anything more objective which is here the focus of interest. TABLE 15 suggests the following broad conclusions:

(i) In rank order, and both for Treatment and Advice Groups, the four items which are accorded the highest rating do not include in-patient care, out-patient care, AA, or other helping agency contact. What might be deemed the elements of the overt package of help, are being seen as less helpful than the three items relating respectively to changes in external reality, intra-psychic change, and change in the marital relationship. It might of course be argued that these three items could in some degree reflect change due to therapeutic intervention rather than being in any sense spontaneous, but that is conjecture. The second point to be noted here is that among the four top-rank items is the Family Clinic 'intake' advice—the single session of directive counselling which was given to patients and wives in both groups on the day of intake to the study. Changes in physical health, and social pressures to stop drinking, are not seen as important.

(ii) When comparison is then made between ratings given by the Advice and by the Treatment Group, the only between-group difference which reaches a level of significance ($P < 0.01$), is patients' assessment of the helpful influence of change in external reality. That this category of happening is seen as related to improvement by 54 per cent of the Advice Group as opposed to 27 per cent of the Treatment Group contradicts the inference that change in external reality is usually only a consequence of change brought about by therapeutic intervention. On other items it is the absence of significant between-group differences which calls for comment. For instance, both groups place equal emphasis on the value of in-patient treatment although the mean time spent in in-patient care was significantly greater for the Treatment Group: evaluations of importance of change in marital relationships are almost identical for the two groups despite only the

Treatment Group wives having been specially offered social work help: the influence of A A is assessed at an almost identical and low level of helpfulness by the two groups, despite all the patients in the Treatment Group having been advised to attend A A.

The conclusions must be that patients in both groups were generally rather unimpressed by any helping intervention other than the initial counselling, and the subsequent efforts of the Family Clinic certainly were not rated specially highly.

6 Correlations Between Initial Trouble Score and Outcome

The facts so far reported establish that there was no significant between-group difference in outcome. Such a finding might of course conceal within it a possibility that patients with particular characteristics might respond differentially to one or other therapeutic approach. To examine this question, correlations were calculated for both groups between Trouble Score at intake, and twelve-month outcome, in terms both of the three category outcome criterion and the 0–6 improvement scale (TABLE 16). With neither outcome measure are the correlations achieved other than small. On both outcome measures the difference between corresponding correlations for Advice and Treatment Group fails to reach a 5 per cent level of significance. There is thus no evidence here of a significant treatment/patient-characteristic interaction effect: the argument cannot be sustained that it is the 'more ill' patients who did better with Treatment and worse with Advice.

DISCUSSION

The discussion section of this chapter will be presented under two major sub-headings. Firstly, examination will be made of problems in the study's design and methodology which might affect the validity of the results obtained. The second section will discuss a series of factual conclusions which may be drawn from those results. The implications of these conclusions for the future organization of treatment services, and their bearing on related research needs, will be considered in CHAPTER VIII.

A Methodological Considerations

1. *Absence of double-blind procedures.* The bias which might have been introduced is of two varieties. Firstly, the couples in the Advice Group might have perceived the treatment which they were offered as inferior or second-best, and such a perception might be expected to affect outcome adversely (Emrick (1975) and see p. 19). However, as regards the present study, this would have acted to increase rather than decrease group differences.

The possible influence of observer bias is more difficult to discount. The bulk of the data was however obtained by structured inquiry, with different team members separately obtaining information from husband and wife. There was no obvious consensus of expectation among team members as to the likely outcome of the trial.

2. *Matching of groups.* The procedure for randomization resulted in satisfactory matching of groups. (TABLE 5 and TABLE 6).

3. *Loss of cases to follow-up.* The loss to follow-up of four cases from the Advice Group and two from the Treatment Group (p. 44), and further missing data on individual items, must be noted. Other than the loss to the Advice Group of the one patient who had to be taken out of the study because of the threat which his behaviour constituted to his family, there is no obvious reason for supposing that these missing data have produced between-group bias. This particular patient was given intensive help and admitted to hospital, but in hospital he immediately fell and fractured his femur: paradoxically therefore treatment was immediately associated with the patient's sustaining a serious injury.

4. *Influence of social worker assessments.* The social workers who obtained monthly follow-up information from wives in the Advice Group were specially instructed to avoid being drawn into therapeutic contact, and monitored their contacts by keeping an exact timing of the length of each interview. The difference in mean social worker time between the two groups (pp. 47–8), suggests that a considerable distinction was, however, successfully maintained. It is possible that they accidentally exerted a degree of therapeutic influence by the mere fact of collecting information, but if so this would certainly challenge conventional assumptions as to what constitutes social work.

5. *Duration of follow-up.* The study period was twelve months from initiation of treatment, rather than twelve months from completion of treatment. The latter approach is the more conventional, but it enshrines an unrealistic concept of the treatment process—for many patients it would be artificial and against normal clinical practice to suppose that the treatment process is abruptly terminated after a certain number of months, or at the moment of in-patient discharge. The choice of time-base taken for the present research would more probably pick up difference in outcome than would a rather longer follow-up period which would give more opportunity for fall-off in any response to the more intensive regime. Whether the prolongation of the Treatment regime at a high level of intensity for, say, two years rather than one, would have produced between-group differences, is another question. It seems unlikely that a Treatment regime which fails to establish any significant edge over Advice at twelve months, would produce a differential impact of any very great importance if more prolonged. In a review which dealt specifically with duration of follow-up as a factor influencing outcome, Gerard and Saenger (1959) concluded that a twelve-month period generally gave a good pointer.

6. *Outcome variables.* There has been much discussion about the variables which are appropriate and sufficient for delineation of alcoholism treatment outcome (Gerard *et al.*, 1962; Pattison *et al.*, 1968; Belasco, 1971; Emrick, 1974). The range of variables employed in the present study was not exhaus-

tive, but included both drink-related variables (consumption levels, troubles related to drinking, wife's hardship, self-rating and wife's rating of drinking problem), as well as other variables (time off work, marital status, improvement in marital problem). A conclusion based on these key parameters might be considered reasonably robust. Other aspects of marital adjustment were in fact also measured but are reported elsewhere (Orford et al., 1976b) and in CHAPTER V (pp. 73–9).

7. *The patient population.* No one study sample drawn only from couples presenting for treatment at a single hospital, can be claimed as representative of the possible universe of alcoholic patients which is the basis on which representativeness should be judged (and a base population the characteristics of which remain in many ways unknown). Close inquiry should though be made concerning the possible major sources of sampling bias which might vitiate the legitimacy of extrapolation. The only obvious manner in which the present subjects may have differed from those on whom a number of previous studies have reported, is that alcoholism treatment research has frequently focused largely or exclusively on patients who have been willing to accept in-patient care. This has been particularly the case in the British literature (e.g. Davies et al., 1956; Glatt, 1961b; Vallance, 1965; Rathod et al., 1966; Walton et al., 1966; Ritson, 1968; McCance and McCance, 1969; Willems et al., 1973a, b)—those who have been unwilling to accept these terms of treatment are not then reported on. The experience of some specialized in-patient centres has indeed led to prospective patients being asked, as a precondition, to accept an in-patient stay of two or three months, with this seen as a necessary test of motivation.

There is a likelihood therefore that our 100 subjects will have included a number who were less hopeful candidates than those typically making up some of the more important recent published series. If our bias was overwhelmingly toward selection of patients who were from the start quite hopeless treatment prospects, the failure to find a difference in efficacy between the Advice and Treatment regimes might speak only to the fact that patients of poor prognosis fare badly whatever the offered help. That this is not a potent criticism is suggested by the fact that overall treatment outcome of the two groups reveals that a fair segment of patients did well—the study population was by no means composed exclusively of alcoholics with no potential for recovery. Comparison of the results of our study with those of other researches can only be of limited meaning because of different operational definitions. However, between 1952 and 1971, Emrick (1974) reported a mean rate of patients 'improved' of 67·2 per cent (SD 18·2 per cent). TABLE 9 of the present study shows, on self-assessment, a 59 per cent rating of 'improved' by the Advice Group and 63 per cent rating by the Treatment Group, which in crude terms might suggest that outcome for our patients fell well within generally expected limits.

However, by definition and intent the design was such as to lead to atypical sampling in two respects, and here the possible implications have to be examined. Firstly, the population was drawn entirely from patients who had an intact marriage (or steady cohabitation), at the time of entering treatment, so that independent information would be available in every instance. This factor must have led to a sample which was biased toward a rather greater degree of social stability than would be found in a random sample of alcoholics presenting for treatment. This point certainly deserves note and is perhaps the most obvious limit on extrapolation: patients with a lesser degree of social support might for instance be less able to respond to the Advice regime— extrapolation to a population of homeless men would be risky (Pittman and Tate, 1972). The second intentional sampling bias was the decision to limit the series to men, for the sake of homogeneity: it must remain an open question whether similar results would be found with a series of women alcoholics.

8. *Limited sampling of treatment methods.* The study compared the efficacy only of two stated treatment approaches, as applied by the staff of one treatment centre. The possible influence on treatment outcome of variations in the skills and training of therapeutic staff is not assessed.

B FACTUAL CONCLUSIONS

The aim of this section is to determine what might with reasonable confidence be seen as factually established by this study—the question of what policy implications might stem from these facts is reserved till later (CHAPTER VIII).

1. *Within the defined alcoholic population, if after assessment and one session of counselling, treatment of the type described is then offered to half the couples, then on average the twelve-month outcome (on the variables delineated), is not improved as compared to outcome for the half to whom no such offer is made.* To say that the Advice regime gave as good results as the Treatment regime would be a less cumbersome phrasing, but less properly conservative. Such an assertion has to be modified by a number of qualifying clauses, hence the rather lengthy sentence which heads this sub-section. These qualifications require individual consideration:

(a) *The defined alcoholic population.* The limits which should be placed on extrapolation to other clinic populations have already been noted.

(b) *Assessment.* The assessment process in all cases involved the participation of both husband and wife for the best part of a morning. The possible impact of a process involving the family's sharing in a major review of drinking history, the marriage, and the general life situation, should not be overlooked as a potentially therapeutic experience.

(c) *Counselling.* The content of this counselling session has already been described. It is important to note that such an approach would not be replicated by a mere few minutes of cursory and impersonal advice—the session was carefully structured, carried a number of specific pieces of advice addressed to explicit behaviour choices, and was made personal. Seen as a 'persuasive communication', the probable degree of credibility attaching to the psychiatrist as informant should also be taken into account, with the prior assessment experience perhaps enhancing the relationship.

(d) *Treatment*. The treatment regime in this clinical trial was intended to resemble the sort of care which might today be provided by most specialized alcoholism treatment clinics in the Western world. The intensity of care which was offered (a psychiatrist available to every patient, social worker available to every wife), would place this regime toward the more privileged end of the spectrum of North American clinics. For instance, in a detailed study of help given to 786 patients attending eight American state-supported alcoholism clinics, Gerard and Saenger (1966) found that over a twelve-month period only about 20 per cent of patients attended a clinic for ten or more visits (compared with 30 per cent of the present Treatment Group attending thirteen or more times): 63 per cent attended six or fewer times (Treatment Group 35 per cent): in 30 per cent of cases a family member was seen (Treatment Group 100 per cent): disulfiram was prescribed for 7 per cent (63 per cent Treatment Group prescribed citrated calcium carbimide). The only aspect of the regime which would suggest a less intensive approach than that of some other centres, was that in-patient care was offered only if there was failure of response to out-patient care, and not as a routine. Previous work had however shown that in-patient care on average gave no advantage over out-patient care (Edwards and Guthrie, 1966, 1967).

(e) *Offered*. The trial was of what happened subsequent to the moment when a clinic *offered* one of two contrasting helping responses. This aspect of the study's design requires particular emphasis: it compared efficacy of two treatment regimes, but with the *acceptability* of the regime an aspect which was being tested at the same time. In many published reports of series limited to in-patients, there is no indication of the percentage of patients who refused the in-patient offer. In the Treatment Group, greater acceptance of the treatment on offer does not appear to have been followed by greater improvement.

(f) *On average*. The present study is concerned with broad differences between group behaviours.

(g) *Twelve months outcome*. Reasons for believing that the choice of twelve months from intake date provided a satisfactory time-base for group comparisons have already been given (p. 52).

(h) *On the variables delineated*. Speculatively, wider choice of variables might have shown between-group differences of a sort that have not been detected. However, it cannot be gainsaid that no outcome differences between groups were found in terms of the present crucial variables.

(i) *No such offer*. The Advice Group was not offered treatment, but the wives were seen over the course of the subsequent year by a research social worker.

So much for the necessary qualifying phrases. None the less, it is important not to lose sight of the basic simplicity of the assertion which is being made. These results point to the conclusion that the offer of a reasonably intensive and conventional treatment regime confers no additional benefit over an extremely simple approach. It is then important to examine some interpretations which are linked to the core conclusion and which modify or fill out its meaning.

2. *Failure to demonstrate difference in outcome between Advice and Treatment Groups is not due to compensatory help seeking by the Advice Group.* This assertion is supported by the data given in TABLES 11 and 12 and which have already been discussed (p. 47). On average Advice Group patients certainly did not obtain significant psychiatric help elsewhere, and in fact went to AA with lesser (but not significantly lesser) frequency than did the Treatment Group. By and large those Advice subjects who had better outcome were not those who had engaged in more energetic help-seeking (TABLE 14).

These findings can perhaps be given a further interpretation beyond the obvious one that the present trial offered a comparison between two treatment regimes with a large degree of contrast maintained. It may be that the appetite of many Advice Group patients for help-seeking was to a large degree 'satisfied' by the offer of one counselling session, whereas for many of the Treatment Group for whom more intensive help was offered, an appetite for further engagement in treatment was created. Intensity of offered treatment may not influence behaviour in terms of treatment outcome, but it certainly has the ability to influence behaviour in terms of subsequent help-seeking engagement—the results suggest that these two aspects of behaviour should be kept distinct.

3. *When patients are offered a conventional treatment regime, the degree to which they utilize the offered help is not related to subsequent outcome.* The lack of close association between degree of help received and quality of outcome in the Treatment Group mirrors what has been said above, regarding the help-seeking of the Advice Group (TABLE 14). As regards periods spent in in-patient care during the study year, it should of course be noted that a particular policy of the Treatment regime was that of admitting subjects to hospital only if they failed to respond to out-patient care: the effect would be to bias the admission sub-group toward poorer twelve-month outcome.

4. *Patient statements on reasons for improvement generally do not favour formal therapeutic intervention. However, a single counselling session is reported on quite favourably.* The data which support this interpretation are given in TABLE 15 and have been discussed (pp. 50–1). This table is based on subjective accounts, but it at least serves as a useful reminder that the patient's view of things may be different from the conventional assumptions of the treatment agency. The interpretation of what is effective seems to an extent to be overlaid by the influence of help subsequently given—more intensive help demotes the importance given to change in external realities and internal psychic change, and

the significance given the counselling session. The inner meaning of this data is probably highly complex, but it would seem fair to conclude that the results must at the least be taken as indicating lack of support for any claim that patients themselves look upon conventional treatment as exceptionally helpful.

5. *Directing clinic patients towards Alcoholics Anonymous can enhance the likelihood of A A involvement, but evidence for the contribution of A A as an adjunct to clinic treatment is not easily found. Among patients who are not receiving clinic treatment but who find their way to A A by various routes, there is some suggestive evidence that for a few of them more frequent A A attendance is associated with better outcome.* This statement rests on data which is to be found in TABLES 12, 14, and 15. A psychiatrist's advice to patients that they should attend A A increases the likelihood of their so doing. All the Treatment Group patients received such advice, and during the course of the year almost 60 per cent went to a meeting, with 24 per cent attending on average more than once a month. The Advice Group were not told about A A by the clinic, and 33 per cent found their way to a meeting, with 13 per cent in the highest frequency category. The route by which the Advice Group patients found their way to A A is not known, but as with the Treatment Group some may have already been in contact with A A at the beginning of the year.

The interpretation that there is no evidence for A A having helped the Treatment Group patients comes from TABLE 14: better outcome is associated neither with a greater likelihood of having attended A A at all, nor with greater frequency of such attendances. Turning to subjective report (TABLE 15), only 8 per cent of these patients see A A as having helped their recovery. In the Advice Group there were the four or five patients with good outcome who stand out as frequent A A attenders, and this is neither a finding to be dismissed, nor one on which firm conclusions can be reached: attendance may actually cause improvement for a small sub-group, or A A attendance may be an epiphenomenon.

Far from being seen as revolutionary, the central conclusions to be drawn from the present trial might be viewed as simply adding some further support to buttress what was already a largely apparent truth—the results are entirely congruent with the conclusions to be drawn from previous treatment research (pp. 18–21).

THE PROVISIONAL IMPLICATION

Discussion of the implication of these results for individual treatment, planning of services, and for further research, will be held over to the last chapter. What may here provisionally be said is that the results add to evidence which must radically challenge the assumptions on which treatment has generally been based. But as will be insisted in the later discussion, the results of this trial must be taken as challenge to better design of help, rather than accidentally being seen as excuse for nihilism.

CHAPTER V

MARITAL AND OTHER SOCIAL–ENVIRONMENTAL FACTORS AND TREATMENT OUTCOME

INTRODUCTION

ONE approach to the study of alcoholism is to see drinking as the central problem and all else as peripheral—the individual's social environment is acknowledged as important in so far as it may influence drinking, but that person's marriage, for instance, is conceived as essentially of secondary importance to the core concern. The problem resides in the individual, and it is his drinking which is the focus of study and the target for modification. This represents a relatively simple individual behaviour model. In contrast, a comparatively complex social–psychological view of behaviour disorder proposes that drinking behaviour is only completely understood within its social and interpersonal context. The emphasis shifts from the study of a lone individual to the study of the relationships between individuals. It is this latter approach which guided the design of that part of the research to be reported now.

This chapter will examine the role of one aspect of family life, namely the marriage partnership, in the process of modification of excessive drinking habits. Some mention will be made of other social and environmental influences, notably current occupational status, but the emphasis will be upon marital matters. Indeed the present sample was deliberately chosen with this principal concern in mind.

The chapter will begin with a *description* of the methods used to assess aspects of marriage relationships at the time of intake to the study. It will proceed to an analysis of the *predictive relationship* between these, and other intake variables, and subsequent drinking outcome for husbands. There will then follow an analysis of *change* in marriage variables between intake and twelve-months follow-up. Finally there will be a closer look at one particular aspect of these marriages, namely wives' *coping behaviour*.

THE MEASUREMENT OF MARRIAGE RELATIONSHIPS

THE CHOICE OF VARIABLES

Marriage relationships vary widely in terms of numerous dimensions which are interrelated in complex fashion. Much of the literature reviewed in CHAPTER II demonstrates the truth of this assertion when the subjects of study are marriage partners one of whom has been identified as suffering from alcoholism. Variables that have been examined by different investigators include atypical wife perceptions of sober husbands, wife's stereotype accuracy in perceiving husband, role dependency, hardship or exposure to deviance, marriage/drinking ratio or length of problem-free marriage, and wife's psychopathology. Evidence for the complex inter-relatedness of many subsets of these variables (see particularly Lemert, 1962; Kogan and Jackson, 1965; and Rae, 1972) suggests that more economical description might be gained by identifying higher-order variables. The latter might prove to be the more heuristic, both in the specific study of alcoholism and marriage, and in the general study of marriage and psychological disorder. The first task in this part of the present investigation was to make a choice of individual marriage variables amongst which such higher-order dimensions might be identified.

A number of principles guided this choice. The most important constraint was that the variables to be measured should be essentially *social* in nature. They should therefore involve assessment of some aspect of a husband's (H's) and wife's (W's) joint performance or behaviour, or H's behaviour towards, or perception of, W (or vice versa).

Otherwise, variables were chosen to cover some of the major areas, (*a*) which the review of the literature on alcoholism and marriage suggested as important sources of variation within such marriages, (*b*) which the more general marriage literature suggested to be important sources of variation in marriages generally, but which appeared to have been ignored in the specific alcoholism literature (e.g. marital satisfaction or mutual affection), and (*c*) which appeared to have been of predictive utility in studies on outcome following treatment for some other form of psychological disorder (e.g. hostility displayed in a joint interview—Brown *et al.*, 1962).

It was necessary that the measurement of marriage variables be feasible within the limits set by a single out-patient assessment session. What is more, couples were in varying states of distress at the time of entry to the study, and had varying expectations about the treatment which they would receive. These circumstances imposed fairly severe limitations; the set of procedures had to be neither too time consuming, nor stressful, not had they to involve instructions or operations of any great complication.

Bearing these criteria in mind, an existing scale of marital affection and an existing person perception technique were modified for this study, a new questionnaire measure of task involvement and decision-making was designed, as well as a new standard joint interview procedure, and a number of questions relating to marriage were included in the standard intake interviews. These procedures will now be described in greater detail.

1. *The marital patterns test*

As a brief self-report measure of marital affection, a modified version of the marital patterns test (Ryle, 1966) was administered to each husband and each wife. The version employed consisted of ten items (the items, as well as details of how the modification of the original, longer, version was effected, are given in APPENDIX I), each item containing a pair of statements of the following form each requiring a response of 'true', 'uncertain', or 'not true':

(a) I am usually very patient with her (him).
(b) She (he) is usually very patient with me.

Items were scored I or o ('uncertain' replies mostly taken to imply lack of affection) and the ten items summed to form an 'affection given' score (the first statement of each pair) and an 'affection received' score (the second statement of each pair). In each case scores ranged from o to 10. Ryle (1966) presented evidence that these were internally reliable, that scores were significantly associated with interviewer ratings of the 'satisfactoriness' of marriage, and that there was a significant, although modest, degree of positive husband–wife agreement. In the present data internal reliabilities of the ten-item scores (Kuder and Richardson, 1937) were 0·77 for affection given scores (combining husband and wives), and 0·78 for affection received scores. The two scores from the same respondent can also be summed to form a 'total affection' score (possible range o to 20).

TABLE 17 shows the actual ranges, means, and standard deviations of affection given, affection received, and total affection scores obtained from husbands and wives in the present sample. Three points about these data are worthy of note.

Firstly there is the wide range of scores represented. The sample includes informants who have totally good things to say about the degree of affection being shown within their marriages, informants who have nothing good to say on this score, and all shades in between.

Secondly is the higher degree of affection which both sets of informants, as groups, attribute to wives, rather than husbands. This is shown by two kinds of statistic. TABLE 17 shows significant differences between AG and AR scores for both husbands and wives, with husbands reporting more affection received than given, and wives reporting the reverse. Of the husbands, sixty-seven attributed more affection to their wives than to themselves and only eighteen attributed more affection to themselves than to their wives (Sign test, $z = 5·20$, $P < 0·001$). Similarly, sixty-four wives attributed more affection to themselves than to their husbands whilst twenty-two attributed more affection to their husbands than to themselves ($z = 4·42$, $P < 0·001$).

Thirdly there is the question of overall husband–wife agreement. There was in fact a modest, but statistically significant, level of agreement about the amount of affection which husbands gave (H's AG versus W's AR, $r = 0·36$), about the amount of affection given by wives (H's AR versus W's AG, $r = 0·41$), and about the total amount of affection (H's versus W's AG + AR $r = 0·46$) (each correlation significant at $P < 0·001$).

2. Adjective check-lists

Each husband and each wife was asked to provide a self-description, a description of his or her spouse, and a meta-description (i.e. how he thought she would describe him, and how she thought he would describe her). It was also thought advisable to obtain ideal-spouse descriptions, in case of marked individual differences in ideals. In addition, two considerations suggested that descriptions with husbands as objects should be split into descriptions of 'sober husbands' and perceptions of husbands 'when drinking'. The first consideration was a knowledge of Kogan and Jackson's (1961, 1964) work specifically focusing upon atypical wife perceptions of 'sober husbands'. The second consideration derived from our experience that wives, when asked informally to describe their husbands, frequently wished to distinguish between their husbands sober and drinking. The full set of descriptions required (five from each husband, five from each wife) is, therefore, as shown in the first column of TABLE 18.

The vehicle for these descriptions was a shortened version of the 128-item adjective check-list (Leary, 1957; LaForge and Suczek, 1955) which had been used in much of the general marital, as well as specific alcoholism and marriage research (e.g. Kogan and Jackson, 1963b), on the topic of interperson perception. The 128 adjectives, or adjectival phrases, of the full version represent the following eight octants of the interpersonal behaviour circle, or circumplex:

AP	Managerial–Autocratic	HI	Self-Effacing–Masochistic
BC	Competitive–Narcissistic	JK	Docile–Dependent
DE	Aggressive–Sadistic	LM	Co-operative–Overconventional
FG	Rebellious–Distrustful	NO	Responsible–Hypernormal

Within each octant, four levels of social desirability are represented. Two adjectives, or adjectival phrases, represent socially desirable aspects of the type of behaviour represented by that octant (Level 1), six represent each of the two intermediate levels, and two represent socially undesirable aspects of the type of behaviour represented (Level 4).

For the present study the check-list was shortened to forty items. This was carried out in two ways. Firstly items were only included that represented the poles of two major axes within the interpersonal behaviour circle (Affection or LM versus Hostility or DE; Dominance or AP versus Submissiveness or HI). Secondly, within the four chosen octants of the circle, both adjectives or phrases representing social desirability Level 1 were omitted, and two of the six adjectives or phrases at each of Levels 2 and 3 were also omitted. The full set of items chosen for the shortened version, along with an indication of the octants from which they were taken, are shown in APPENDIX 2.

In an attempt to confirm the two-dimensional structure assumed to underlie this shortened version of the check-list (Affection versus Hostility and

Dominance versus Submissiveness), separate factor analyses were carried out for husbands, and for wives, for self-descriptions, and spouse-descriptions (making four analyses in all). The assumed structure was not confirmed and it was decided to base the scoring of the check-lists upon three factors which were interpretable and emerged consistently from the different analyses. The item weights used to obtain these three scores, along with details of the factor analyses and the method of assigning weights to items, are also shown in APPENDIX 2.

An inspection of these item weights suggested that these three factors are appropriately called *desirability* (affection items combined with the more desirable dominance items), *hostile-dominance* (hostile items combined with less desirable dominance items), and *submissiveness* (high weights given to submissiveness items, low or negative weights given to dominance items).

One way of presenting data of this sort (a way which is relatively unaffected by the acquiescence response-set bias which can be shown to influence data of this kind), is to rank the three factor scores for each description and then to report the frequency with which each of the three factor scores achieves 'rank one'. TABLE 18 presents the data in this form for each of the five descriptions provided by husbands and each of the five descriptions provided by wives.

A number of points are immediately apparent from an inspection of TABLE 18. Firstly and not unexpectedly, Factor 1 (desirability) almost invariably achieves the position of rank one when either husbands or wives are describing their ideal spouses. In fact the general concept of 'ideal husband' held by wives corresponds very closely to the general concept of 'ideal wife' held by husbands. Quite different results are obtained when wives describe their husbands 'when drinking'. In no less than 88 per cent of these descriptions it is Factor 2 (hostile-dominance) which achieves the position of rank one, and in only 6 per cent of such descriptions is it Factor 1 which achieves this rank. When husbands describe themselves 'when drinking' the position is similar but not so extreme. In this case as many as 23 per cent of husbands put Factor 1 (desirability) first.

Self-descriptions (wives describing themselves, and husbands describing themselves 'sober') and husbands' perceptions of wives, are more mixed, but Factor 1 is the most popular factor of rank one. However, wives' perceptions of 'sober' husbands very frequently depart from the ideal, or desirable, stereotype. As many as 58 per cent of wives give greater prominence to hostile-dominance (38 per cent) or to submissiveness (20 per cent) than to desirability in their descriptions of their husbands when sober. Meta-perceptions also depart considerably from the ideal. Only 22 per cent of husbands think that their wives will give prominence to the desirability factor in their descriptions of them, and only 37 per cent of wives think that their husbands will give prominence to this factor when describing them. Meta-perceptions are also more negative than the corresponding spouse perceptions for both husbands and wives. Thus wives think their husbands describe them in less desirable terms than they actually do, and the same is true for husbands.

3. Marital role inventories

Traditional self-report, forced-choice, methodology (e.g. Blood and Wolfe, 1960) was followed in asking subjects to report on the balance of husband–wife participation in ten family decision-making and task-performance areas 'in the last month'. The choice of items (see TABLE 19) was dictated by preliminary discussions with individual alcoholic husbands and their wives, and items ranged from the relatively concrete-specific (e.g. 'who does repairs?') to the abstract-general (e.g. 'who is at hand when needed by the family?'). Respondents were required to state their answers in terms of the husband–wife balance of involvement. There were five alternatives (husband does all; husband does most; husband and wife equally; wife does most; wife does all). As well as requiring subjects to report on participation during the previous month, the inventory was administered under two further conditions, namely *ideal* husband–wife participation and recalled participation in the *first year of marriage*.

TABLE 19 shows the ten items, the method of scoring, and means and standard deviations under 'last month' and 'ideal' conditions. For no fewer than nine out of the ten items, differences between 'last month' and 'ideal' means indicate that husbands were seen by both sets of informants as less involved in nearly all aspects of marital role performance asked about than was considered to be ideal. In most cases the differences between ideal and last month were significant. The single exception is 'deciding frequency of sexual relations', and in this case it appears that both sets of informants considered husbands to have been relatively *highly* involved in recent decision-making in this area, in comparison with the ideal.

In eight cases out of ten (the exceptions being deciding about frequency of sex and deciding which friends and relatives to see), husbands as a group reported more husband participation than did wives (in five cases the difference was significant).

When role inventory items were inter-correlated for each set of informants separately, and for each of the three conditions of administration separately, it was found that not all items were consistently positively inter-correlated, although a sub-set of six items (items 1, 2, 3, 7, 8, and 10) were. This sub-set of items appears to concern the balance of husband and wife *task participation* as distinct from decision-making. It is these six items which show the greatest degree of recent husband under-involvement in comparison with stated ideals. Two twelve-point scales (one based upon husband replies, the other upon wife replies) were computed from these six items. A score of twelve represented extreme wife over-involvement and husband under-involvement in comparison with the state of affairs most frequently considered to be ideal by members of this sample, whilst a score of 0 represented the reverse.

A classification of each couple, for 'last month', 'when first married' and 'ideal' (which could of course be different from the state of affairs most frequently considered ideal in the sample as a whole), was then made on the basis of husband's and wife's scores combined. Couples were classified as 'wife dominated', 'egalitarian', or 'husband dominated', with additional intermediate categories of 'wife dominated–egalitarian' and 'husband dominated–egalitarian' if one informant reported an egalitarian balance and the other reported a mildly dominated balance. In addition some couples had to be categorized as 'disputed' (one reported husband domination the other wife domination), or 'disputed–egalitarian' (one reported an egalitarian balance, the other reported fairly extreme domination by one or other partner).

The results of this classification are shown in TABLE 20. No less than fifty-two families are classified as 'wife dominated' on the basis of both husbands' and wives' reports of task participation in the last month. There is only one family, out of all the hundred families, that considered this pattern to be ideal. Only a minority of families (18 per cent) were agreed that the recent pattern had been 'egalitarian' or 'husband dominated–egalitarian', which were the patterns considered to be ideal by the majority.

The results for 'when first married' lay somewhere between those for 'ideals' and 'last month'. There were no fewer than 23 per cent of families who reported a 'wife dominated' pattern of task participation even when the couple was first married, and a further 14 per cent who reported the pattern as having been a 'wife dominated–egalitarian' one. On the other hand, there were clearly many families who felt that the pattern of task participation had moved towards a more 'wife dominated' pattern since the couple was first married.

Of the remaining four items of the role inventories, three of them (items 4, 6, and 9) also showed a uniform pattern of positive inter-correlation. These items seem to reflect *decision-making about social or sexual matters*, and appear to be areas where husbands, as a group, have retained involvement or may even be (as for item 9 about sexual behaviour) over-involved in comparison with the ideal.

There is evidence, then, for the importance of the distinction which is traditionally drawn (e.g. Blood and Wolfe, 1960) between *task performance* and *decision-making* elements of marital role functioning. The role inventory items which were fairly consistently positively correlated, and which showed the clearest discrepancy between reported recent and ideal performance, were those which could most easily be subsumed under the former heading. Items which appeared to reflect decision-making in social or sexual spheres were much less likely to produce reports of husband under-involvement. Although 'norms' are lacking, it seems probable that alcohol dependence in husbands is more likely to be associated with a reduced involvement in the performance of tasks necessary for the family's functioning, than with reduced assertion in influencing the family over important social and sexual matters. However, it is *described   described*

unlikely that this is specific to marriages in which husbands are diagnosed as suffering from alcoholism (Collins *et al.*, 1971; Herbst, 1954).

4. *Joint interview ratings*

The three techniques so far described differ slightly in format, but are all of the basic self-completion inventory type. They require husbands and wives, separately, to record their opinions about some aspects of the 'state of their marriage'. No attempt is made, in the course of applying these techniques, to study such aspects of marriage as 'communication' or 'interaction' directly. The first part of the last phase of the intake assessment session (when husband and wife came together in the presence of all three members of the assessment team) was therefore scheduled for a 'standardized joint interview'. The problem of design was that of standardizing the situation presented to the couples to a sufficient degree to make comparisons between couples possible, whilst at the same time preserving a degree of naturalness and relevance compatible with an out-patient assessment session. To keep the situation as standard as possible, it was decided that two members of the assessment team should remain silent during this period, and that the third member (the psychiatrist) should ask four standard questions at four-minute intervals. In the four-minute period between questions the instructions allowed the psychiatrist only to repeat the question or to make some non-informative remark or grunt. The instructions also encouraged the interviewing psychiatrist to take care that he did not 'lead' the interview by differential eye-contact, or by the use of re-marks or noises which might imply disapproval or disagreement. The first question asked ('How do you see things now?') was a deliberately vague question, and the following three questions ('Is drinking the real problem do you think?', 'How can a wife help her husband in this situation do you think?', and 'How much do you blame one another?') were those which discussions with husbands and wives prior to the study suggested were contentious areas of high relevance to marriage complicated by alcoholism in the husband. Although this procedure was sometimes stressful, particularly when both husband and wife were reticent and seemed to invite interviewer directiveness, it gave rise to discussions and husband–wife exchanges which frequently impressed members of the assessment team as being both spontaneous and 'natural'.

One of the two silent members of the assessment team (the psychologist) recorded whether it was husband or wife who initiated discussion after each of the interviewer questions, and each member of the assessment team made a number of independent ratings when the couple finally departed at the end of the assessment session. Six ratings were made: husband to wife warmth, dominance, and hostility; and wife to husband warmth, dominance, and hostility. Each rating was made on a 4-point scale (0 = 'none'; 1 = 'a slight amount'; 2 = 'a moderate amount'; 3 = 'a distinct amount').

Inter-rater reliabilities (psychiatrist *v.* psychologist; psychiatrist *v.* social worker; psychologist *v.* social worker, for each of six ratings, making eighteen coefficients of reliability in all) were all positive and statistically significant but of only modest magnitude (varying between +0·22 and +0·51). It should however be noted that two different psychiatrists and no less than four different social workers were involved. Furthermore, it can now be seen with hindsight that more training in the use of these ratings would have been an advantage.

Each of the fifteen correlations within the complete set of inter-correlations of the six joint-interview ratings was statistically significant. Ratings of warmth and hostility were, as expected, negatively correlated (H to W, r = −0·54; W to H, r = −0·45). Dominance ratings were positively associated with hostility ratings (H to W, +0·66; W to H, +0·60), and negatively associated with warmth ratings (H to W, −0·31; W to H, −0·24).

H to W and W to H ratings were also significantly inter-correlated. Raters tended to ascribe the same level of warmth to both members of a marital pair (r = +0·50) and the same was true of hostility (r = +0·68). The same tendency, but much diminished, was true of dominance also (r = +0·23).

The number of times W spoke first after a new interviewer question correlated substantially with W to H dominance (r = +0.50) but insignificantly with H to W dominance (r = −0·16).

5. *Intake interview questions*

Husbands and wives were also asked a number of direct questions relevant to their marriages in the course of the standard intake interviews administered by the psychiatrist and research social worker. Questions were asked about periods of separation and about the initiation of divorce or legal separation proceedings. Such proceedings had been started or inquired about, within the previous three years, in 23 out of the 100 marriages (by the wife in all cases except one), and in a further twenty-nine cases the wife had 'left home' for a period of twenty-four hours or longer on at least one occasion within the previous three years.

Both partners were also asked about the frequency of recent marital sexual intercourse. Husband–wife agreement was high (six categories from 'not at all in the last twelve months' to 'two or three times a week', r = +0·82). When a rough comparison was made with Kinsey *et al.*'s (1948, 1953) data collected in the U.S. over twenty years ago, it was apparent that median frequencies for all age groups (except the youngest, twenty-six to thirty-year-olds) were low in comparison with Kinsey's data. Reported frequencies showed the same marked negative correlation with age in the present data as in the comparison data. Low levels of marital sexual behaviour were thus particularly likely to be reported by husbands and wives in the present sample who were aged forty-one or over.

Husbands and wives were also asked about the likelihood of future marital breakdown. A small minority of both husbands and wives (six husbands, four wives) admitted that their marriage might break up even 'if things did get better'. The majority (57, 55) thought their marriages would break up 'if things got no better'; some (16, 20) 'if things got worse or much worse'; and about one fifth (21, 21) considered that their marriages would remain intact even if things did get much worse. Husband–wife agreement on this matter was statistically significant but modest (five categories, $r = +0.37$).

Three additional variables were included in these interviews as possible indications of a dominance discrepancy within the marriage (husband–wife age discrepancy, social class background discrepancy based upon the Hall-Jones classification of the occupational status of husband's father and mother's father, and discrepancy in age of completion of full-time education). Wife's work status was also recorded (no employment outside the home; part-time; full-time).

HIGHER-ORDER DIMENSIONS

The 100 couples therefore varied widely in terms of a number of variables, such as levels of affection reported, the way they described themselves and each other, the amount of involvement of each partner in family tasks and decisions, amounts of warm, hostile, and assertive behaviour during joint discussion, and optimism about the future of their marriage. Certainly these variables overlap and a description of a marriage in terms of so many variables is both redundant and uneconomic. Hence the attempt, reported in this section, to identify higher-order factors or dimensions that might allow a simpler method of description.

Forty-six relevant variables were inter-correlated and subjected to a factor analysis. The variables are those shown in APPENDIX 3. Four of these variables derived from the marital patterns test, four from the role inventories, seven from the joint interview, seven from the intake interviews and twenty-four from the adjective check-lists. (Three factor scores from each of three check-lists provided by husbands and each of three provided by wives—descriptions of ideal spouses and of husbands when drinking were omitted. Also included in order to control for acquiescence response bias were the 'check frequencies', i.e. the number of adjectives checked for each of these six descriptions.)

The total 46×46 correlation matrix contained many more significant correlations than would have been expected by chance (e.g. 122 > + or − 0.31, P < 0.001). This was still the case when check frequency variables were omitted from the matrix. Eigen values dropped after the sixth factor, and accordingly the first six factors (accounting for 52 per cent of the variance) were rotated using the Varimax method.

Rotated factors 1 and 3 were almost entirely specific to adjective check list variables (husband variables in the case of factor 1, wife variables for factor 3) and in each case check frequency variables had the highest loadings of all. These two factors therefore appear to be 'method factors' mainly measuring response bias on the adjective check-lists. The remaining four substantive variables will be discussed in greater detail.

'OPEN HOSTILITY'

Loadings on factor 2 are shown in the second column of figures in APPENDIX 3. Each of the joint interview ratings has substantial loadings on this factor, with both hostility ratings having the highest positive loadings, dominance ratings having positive loadings, and warmth ratings loading negatively. This factor therefore appears to reflect hostile-dominance versus affection displayed openly in the joint interview. The degree of affection which husbands ascribed to their wives on the marital patterns test also has a substantial negative loading, and hostile-dominance descriptions of wives provided by husbands on the adjective check-list have a moderately high positive loading. Again these two variables probably reflect the openness of hostility in a marriage, as it was relatively unusual in this sample for husbands to ascribe low affection to their wives or to describe them in hostile-dominant terms (in comparison with things that wives said about their husbands).

'WIFE'S SUBMISSIVENESS'

Loadings on factor 4 are shown in the fourth column of APPENDIX 3. In terms of the adjective check-lists this dimension is reflected in wives' views of their own submissiveness, and in husbands' opinions about their wives' submissiveness. In terms of the joint interview this dimension is reflected in lack of initiative by wives in being the first to answer interviewer questions, and in low staff ratings of wife to husband dominance. It is also reflected in the role inventory in terms of wives' opinions about the greater relative involvement of their husbands in decision-making on social and sexual matters. There is also a suggestion that husbands of the more submissive wives use relatively few hostile-dominance adjectives or phrases to describe their wives, but also use relatively few 'desirability' adjectives or phrases about them also. Also that submissive wives attribute greater hostile-dominance to their husbands when the latter are sober.

'HOSTILE-DOMINANCE BALANCE'

The next column of APPENDIX 3 shows loadings on the fifth factor. In terms of the adjective check-lists, the positive pole of this factor is reflected in high husband hostile-dominance (wife-, meta-, but especially self-perceptions), and low wife hostile-dominance. The positive pole is also reflected in wives' working status (an incongruent finding, with working wives having the relatively more hostile-dominant husbands), husbands' views of their own relatively great participation in socio-sexual decision-making, and in relatively high joint interview ratings of husband to wife dominance.

'LACK OF COHESION'

Variables derived from a number of different techniques have moderate to high loadings on this factor (shown in the last column of APPENDIX 3). Contributions to the positive pole came from low scores on several of the affection scales in the marital patterns test (particularly wife scales), from both sets of informants' views on low husband participation in family tasks, and in adjective check-list scores which seem to indicate a departure from mutual positive regard (wives describe their husbands when sober in undesirable terms, husbands expect their wives to see them that way, and wives think their husbands see them as hostile-dominant). Furthermore the felt likelihood of future marital breakdown has a moderate positive loading on this factor.

DISCUSSION

Although the present findings confirm the wide-ranging variability to be found within a sample of marriages complicated by alcoholism in husbands, and hence it is impossible to generalize about such marriages, some order has been brought to this field by the identification of four dimensions. Two of these ('open hostility' and 'lack of cohesion') principally concern themes of affection, hostility, and cohesiveness. They reflect sources of variation which were separate (even though as *scored* they were correlated, see p. 70) and should not be confused. One ('open hostility') reflected the degree of overt hostility and mutual attempts to dominate one another, and was particularly apparent in the standard joint interview when husband and wife were interviewed together and asked questions extremely pertinent to the husband's drinking problem. The second ('lack of cohesion') may have had more to do with variation in basic regard for one another, affection displayed in everyday life, and joint involvement in family tasks.

The remaining two factors ('wife's submissiveness' and 'hostile-dominance balance') contained different themes, namely those of submissiveness and dominance in marriage. Again they represent independent dimensions, not to be confused with 'open hostility' or with 'lack of cohesion' or with one another. Wife's submissiveness is apparently not the same thing as a balance of hostile-dominance in favour of the husband. However, the meaning and implications of this distinction are not clear from the present findings. It may be that the 'wife's submissiveness' factor has more to do with public behaviour, and that 'hostile-dominance balance' has more to do with the exercise of power 'indoors'.

Incidentally, the distinction between task and decision-making aspects of marital role performance is supported by the different pattern of loadings on marital factors. Whereas task performance variables loaded quite strongly on 'lack of cohesion', decision-making variables loaded on the two factors with themes of submissiveness and dominance. The former therefore appears to have much more to do with a breakdown of involvement and mutual regard, whilst the latter has more to do with variation in husband–wife 'power'.

PREDICTING DRINKING OUTCOME AT TWELVE MONTHS

Predicting from Marital Factors

We turn now to the heart of the matter. Having identified interpretable dimensions relating to the state of a marriage complicated by alcoholism in the husband, is it possible to show that a couple's standing on any of these factors is predictive of the response of the husband's drinking problem to the treatment or advice which the couple received?

Each couple was given a score for each of the four factors described above. The method of computing scores was as follows: The distribution of scores on each variable was dichotomized at the median, and scores above the median given a weight of 1. Each factor score was then based upon those ten variables having the highest loadings on that factor. Scores above the median on a variable with a positive loading contributed $+1$ to the derived factor score, and scores above the median on variables with negative loadings contributed -1. In the case of factor 6, for example, derived scores ranged from $+4$ to -6.

Despite its disadvantages, this approximate method was preferred to more mathematically exact solutions. For one thing the large size of the variable pool in relation to the number of cases made it unlikely that factor loadings would be very reliable. It was felt that the purpose of factor analysis in this instance was to provide a rough guide to the location of the more important higher order dimension(s) of predictive utility. This method of deriving scores resulted in a sizable correlation between factors 2 and 6 ($r = +0.56$). Tests were carried out on the relationship between scores on each of these four marital factors and the three-category twelve months drinking outcome classification described in CHAPTER IV (p. 49). In each case two statistical tests were employed. Firstly, factor scores were dichotomized as close to the median as possible, and a comparison of the frequencies of high and low factor scores in each of the three outcome groups was made, using chi squared tests. Secondly, mean factor scores were computed for cases in each of the outcome groups, and differences between means examined using independent t-tests. Results of applying these tests are shown in TABLE 21.

Dominance and submissiveness

There was a notable absence of any detectable predictive relationship between outcome and scores on either of the two marital factors which appeared to have aspects of submissiveness and dominance as their themes (factors 4 and 5). On the contrary, it was quite clear that it was the factors whose content appeared to revolve around themes of affection and cohesiveness which were predictive. This in itself may be of some importance. The 'controlling' nature of some women married to alcoholic husbands is a theme which often recurs in the literature on alcoholism in marriage (Bullock and Mudd, 1959; Whalen, 1953; Rae and Forbes, 1966). Dominance–submission themes are also prominent in more general writings and research on the subject of mate-selection (e.g. Winch, 1958; Dicks, 1967) and there is often the suggestion that the 'well' spouse is in some way attracted to, and therefore contributes to the continuation of, the deviant spouse's deviance (e.g. Taylor et al., 1966; Kreitman, 1968; Agulnik, 1970). Although most of these ideas are speculative they do provide some grounds for expecting that variables to do with wife dominance might have been predictive of the outcome of a husband's drinking problem.

There are, however, a number of rather general reasons why, in retrospect, the lack of predictive significance of the two dominance factors is not so surprising. For one thing, a closer examination of some of the statements which have been made about the 'controlling' nature of some alcoholics' wives shows that as much emphasis, if not more, is placed upon hostility and criticality towards the husband, resentment towards men in general, provocative behaviour towards their husbands, and hard and unforgiving attitudes (Bullock and Mudd, 1959; Whalen, 1953). The ambiguity of constructs such as 'dominating', 'controlling', and 'power' was equally apparent in the notes made by research social workers in the course of the present investigation. The term 'controlling' was frequently applied to wives in both low cohesion and high cohesion marriages. However, in the former cases the controlling behaviour described appeared to have a hostile, bitter, element which was frequently lacking in other cases.

Furthermore, recent research and writing on the subject testifies to the conceptual and methodological difficulty of assessing dominance, or power, balance in marital relationships (e.g. Olson, 1969; Turk and Bell, 1972). There seems to be agreement in the recent literature that an assessment of 'who wears the trousers' in a marital relationship is very much more complex than might be supposed, and that indeed the question itself is over-simple. It is of some methodological interest in this context that 'pure' measures of dominance, independent of hostility or affection, were not obtained from adjective check-list or joint interview rating data in this study.

HOSTILITY AND LACK OF COHESION

TABLE 21 shows a slight degree of association between outcome and scores on factor 2, indicating that relatively high levels of 'open hostility' were predictive of subsequent placement in 'equivocal' or 'bad' outcome groups.

However, the strongest predictive relationship involved scores on factor 6 ('lack of cohesion'). There was a regular increase in the frequency of high scores on this factor, and a regular increase in mean factor scores, from 'good' to 'equivocal' to 'bad' outcome groups. The difference between means for the two extreme outcome groups was significant (P < 0·002), as was the overall chi squared value (P < 0·001).

This is a major finding of the present study: relatively cohesive couples were more than twice as likely to find themselves in the 'good' than in the 'bad' outcome group at follow-up, whilst relatively non-cohesive couples were more than three times as likely to find themselves in the 'bad' group. However, the number of couples involved was relatively small and the finding requires replication.

The predictive significance of 'lack of cohesion' suggests that it would be valuable to know more about the meaning of this dimension. An inspection of the individual variables contributing to these scores shows that couples had a relatively poor prognosis if relatively many of the following conditions were satisfied at the time of intake: If wives reported that they both gave and received relatively little affection; wives used relatively few socially desirable adjectives or phrases in describing their 'sober' husbands; husbands expected their wives to use relatively few such adjectives or phrases in describing them 'sober'; husbands reported that they had been participating less in family tasks than was ideal; wives thought the same; wives thought their husbands would use relatively many 'hostile-dominance' adjectives or phrases in describing them; and pooled opinions of husbands and wives about the future of their marriage were relatively pessimistic.

Clinical material may throw further light on the meaning of these elements. In the case of many couples assigned to the treatment group, a research social worker had continued intensive contact with each family (particularly with wives). A close examination of the detailed notes which were made by research social workers in these cases throws further light upon the nature of the common thread predominating in families which we have construed as 'lacking cohesion'.

From reading these notes the impression was formed that low cohesion families contrasted with others in the following principal respects. The most generally shared feature in the former cases was the *dislike* which the wife expressed towards her husband. Expressions which wives used included: '. . . hate him . . .', '. . . unable to forgive him . . .', '. . . never loved him . . .', '. . . my feelings are dead . . .', '. . . no longer concerned with my husband . . .', and '. . . feelings of deep revulsion . . .'. The dislike expressed by wives was often explicitly *general*. For example, '. . . drinking is not the main problem . . .' and '. . . it's his person I don't like . . .'. It was often associated with *pessimism* about, and *lack of understanding* of, the husband's behaviour, combined with *resignation* about the future. Reference was frequently made to previous unhappiness. It was as if dislike of the husband was spreading both forwards, in terms of pessimism about the future, and backwards in terms of an unfavourable construing of the past. In two cases the wife recalled that she had left her husband during a period of cohabitation *before* their marriage, and in other cases the wife recalled unhappiness virtually throughout marriage. A number recalled problems other than alcoholism, such as the husband's gambling or excessive jealousy. In a number of cases the wife referred to a previous husband whom she now saw as better than her present husband.

These descriptions make much sense of the loading on 'lack of cohesion' of the 'desirability' of wives' adjective check-list descriptions of their *sober* husbands. It now appears that this method was tapping an aspect of marital attitude which impressed itself upon the social work observer who got to know wives relatively well. These findings also confirm and extend Kogan and Jackson's (1961, 1963b, 1964) findings concerning variation in wives' descriptions of their alcoholic husbands 'when sober'. Of their sample of forty-six wives, 61 per cent provided descriptions which departed from the generally favourable descriptions provided by most control wives. This figure is remarkably close to the 58 per cent of wives in the present sample who gave prominence to hostile-dominance or submissiveness, rather than 'desirability', terms in describing their husbands when 'not drinking'. This suggests that only a minority of wives may subscribe to the Jekyll and Hyde view of the excessively drinking husband as someone whose behaviour is deviant only when he is drinking. The present study has extended these findings by showing that this element of marital person perception is part of a general absence of marital cohesion which is itself predictive of the immediate future course of the husband's drinking behaviour.

Other major themes which emerged from the notes on low cohesion marriages were the presence of overt *mutual hostility*, and/or a *breakdown in communication*. Hostilities were often of dramatic proportions, involving physical violence, police involvement, and disputes over entry to the family home. Hostility and breakdown were reflected in expressions such as: 'It's not a married life. . . .', 'It's never been a family life. . . .', 'The marriage is finished. . . .', 'I'd like to get rid of him. . . .', and 'He gives nothing, neither do I. . . .'. In other, often less dramatic, cases it was withdrawal and breakdown in communication which were most apparent. References to sleeping separately, a bad family 'atmosphere', and long periods of silence (one husband reported that there had been no words for a whole year) were frequent.

THE INFLUENCE OF FAMILY FACTORS ON THE COURSE OF PSYCHOLOGICAL DISORDER: A GENERAL HYPOTHESIS

Despite conceptual and methodological differences, the major finding of this part of the study is broadly similar to the findings of several studies of the family correlates of outcome following treatment for mental disorder, as well as the findings of the single previous study of marriage and outcome following treatment for alcoholism (Rae, 1972). Husbands' and wives' scores on the psychopathic deviate scale of the MMPI, but particularly wives' scores, were predictive of outcome in the latter study, and Rae devoted some discussion to the question of exactly what this scale was measuring. He quotes from Welsh and Dahlstrom (1956) who state that high scores on the scale indicate a 'shallow emotional life and a capacity for only transitory or superficial loyalty . . . an egocentric personality who finds difficulty in accepting groups standards . . .'.

In related fields others have found that factors such as relatively high emotional involvement, particularly criticality, (Brown *et al.*, 1962, 1972; Vaughn and Leff, 1976), relatively high family activity and tension (Cheek, 1965), low levels of 'mutual love' and 'husband–wife consensus', and relatively high levels of 'subordination of the patient' by the spouse (Morrow and Robins, 1964), and atypicality of relative's personality (Freeman and Simmons, 1963), are predictive of relatively high rates of relapse in the months following treatment for a psychiatric disorder. The diagnosis was usually schizophrenia in these studies although Vaughn and Leff's study (1976) involved 'neurotic depressives' also.

Although the terminology, and methodology, differs between these studies, and between these studies and the present one, it is at least arguable that the theme of cohesiveness or satisfaction unites them. The general hypothesis may be proposed that: *A breakdown in the mutual rewardingness of marital or other family relationships is predictive of a relatively unfavourable outcome following treatment or consultation for any psychological disorder.*

THE ATTRIBUTION OF CAUSE AND EFFECT

In each of these studies a family relationship variable (X) has been assessed at one point in time and found to be predictive of an outcome variable (Y) measured at a later point in time. In all such predictive correlational studies, in which the manipulation of variables is not under deliberate experimental control, there is the ever-present danger of neglecting the importance of a 'third factor' (Z) with which X is correlated and which is equally, if not more strongly, predictive of Y. Any simple causal hypothesis of the type $X \rightarrow Y$ or $Z \rightarrow Y$ is then inadequate alone.

In fact in each of the studies relevant to the general hypothesis which we have put forward concerning the influence of family factors upon the outcome following treatment for psychological disorder, and these include the present study, some account was taken of Z-type variables. In almost every instance Z-type variables were themselves predictive of outcome, and furthermore X-type variables (family variables) were not independent of them. For example, Brown *et al.* (1962) found that the more hostile relatives tended to be those living with patients who expressed hostility in a joint interview. Relatives were more likely to demonstrate high emotional involvement if the patient in their family was still relatively ill at the time of discharge from hospital, and both factors (illness at discharge and relative's emotional involvement) were predictive of outcome. Similarly, Morrow and Robins (1964) found that their patient-wives were more likely to report that their husbands subordinated them if their own illness had been of relatively gradual, rather than sudden, onset, and again both factors (subordination of wife by husband and gradual versus sudden onset of illness) were predictive of outcome.

What it amounts to is that research on families and outcome has to face up to the complex inter-reacting nature of social groups particularly groups which, like families, have a previous history. Vast literatures attest both to the non-random assortative nature of mate-selection, and to the reciprocally contingent nature of social interaction. It should therefore come as no surprise to find that it is difficult to isolate the influence of one particular member of a family dyad or group.

PREDICTING FROM OCCUPATIONAL STATUS, HARDSHIP, AND SELF-ESTEEM

The difficulties of interpretation which arise in correlational, albeit pro-spective, studies of this kind, arose in the context of the present study. Marital variables were not the only ones predictive of one-year outcome. Three other variables in particular emerged as important social–environmental correlates of treatment outcome. Each of these variables was at least as strongly predic-tive of outcome as was marital cohesion itself. Furthermore, when each was partially controlled statistically, the association between marital cohesion and subsequent outcome remained statistically significant only for certain sub-groups.

Firstly, *intake occupational status* (rated on the Hall-Jones 7-point scale, 1950) showed quite a marked association with outcome. Of twenty-seven husbands with a 'good' one-year outcome,[1] thirteen had been working in a job at intake which could be categorized in one of the top four status categories (professional, administrative, supervisory, and other non-routine, non-manual, occupations). In contrast, only two of twenty-seven husbands with a sub-sequent 'bad' outcome[1] had jobs of this status (chi squared $= 9 \cdot 23$, 1 d.f., P $< 0 \cdot 002$). An intermediate proportion of 'equivocal' outcome husbands had jobs of this status at intake (twelve out of thirty-two[1]). (Overall chi squared $= 12 \cdot 65$, 2 d.f., P $< 0 \cdot 005$.) When occupational status ratings were made on the basis of the *highest status occupation ever held*, the relationship was found to be in the same direction but statistically insignificant ($15/28$ 'good' as opposed to $9/28$ 'bad' in categories I–IV).

In view of the general downward mobility of men in this sample, in terms of occupational prestige, current 'occupational status' should probably be inter-preted as compounded of 'social class' and occupational decline associated with alcoholism. Whatever its meaning, it is clearly a variable which in this investigation was strongly predictive of outcome and which also altered the relationship between marital cohesion and outcome (see below).

A second predictive variable (correlated with intake job status, r $= -0 \cdot 43$) concerned the degree of *hardship* reported by wives. Each wife was asked

[1] One husband in each outcome group had been unemployed for over three months at intake.

twenty-two questions relating to aspects of hardship which she might have experienced in her marriage as a result of, or in association with, her husband's drinking. The final analysis was based upon ten of these items which were selected from the total on the basis of an item analysis of data obtained from the first fifty wives. The odd–even split-half reliability coefficient for this 10-item scale, based upon data from the remaining fifty wives, was +0·76. The ten items, along with their frequencies of affirmation by wives at intake are shown in TABLE 22.

Amongst wives whose husbands were subsequently placed in the 'bad' outcome group, a large majority reported relatively many (six or more) of the ten family events contributing to the hardship scale (22/28 wives). The proportion reporting this many events was smaller amongst 'equivocal' group wives (18/33) and smaller still in the 'good' group (9/28). Both the overall chi squared value (12·18, 2 d.f., P < 0·005) and that based on the figures for the two extreme outcome groups only (10·40, 1 d.f., P < 0·002) were significant. Mean 'hardship' scores were calculated for wives in the three outcome groups and these were ordered, from largest to smallest, 'bad', 'equivocal', and 'good'. The difference between the means of the two extreme groups was significant (t = 3·61, P < 0·001). The difference between the equivocal and bad group means was also significant (t = 2·63, P < 0·02).

An inspection of the items constituting the hardship scale (TABLE 22) shows that most of the items are concerned with quarrelling and physical violence to person or property. This definition of 'hardship' is therefore somewhat more narrow than the definition of hardship adopted by Jackson and Kogan (1963), and that of 'deviance' adopted by Haberman (1965). Jackson and Kogan's 'hardship during drinking' score was based upon an assessment of six areas of which 'violence of husband directed at family' was only one. 'Infidelity of husband' and 'job losses' were two areas covered by them and by Haberman and not included in our 'hardship' scale. There is evidence from both these studies, as well as the present one, that the amount of hardship reported by wives of alcoholics is related to 'social class' variables such as occupational status and educational level.

A similar, but slightly less strong, relationship existed between outcome and a third predictive variable, husband's intake self-esteem. Each husband was asked to rate the concept, 'Myself as I have been lately' on each of fourteen semantic differential scales chosen to represent aspects of self-esteem (e.g. miserable–cheerful, relaxed–tense, lacking in confidence–confident, not feeling guilty–feeling guilty, living up to my ideals–letting myself down). The split-half reliability coefficient for this 14-item scale, based on data from the last fifty cases, was +0·80. Group mean self-esteem scores were ordered, high to low, good, equivocal, and bad. The two extreme outcome groups were significantly discriminated (t = 3·31, P < 0·002) as were equivocal and bad outcome groups (t = 2·74, P < 0·01).

By combining these three variables, outcome can be seen to have been highly predictable at least for extreme groups. Husbands whose intake occupational status was relatively low (categories V–VII, i.e. routine non-manual and all manual occupations), and whose wives reported a relatively high degree of hardship, had a particularly poor prognosis. This was specially the case when, in addition, husbands reported a relatively low level of self-esteem. Of twenty-two husbands showing such extreme characteristics, only one subsequently had a 'good' outcome and fifteen had a 'bad' outcome. At the other extreme, good prognosis was associated with relatively high intake occupational status (categories I–IV), a relatively high level of self-esteem, and wives' reports of relatively low levels of hardship. Of eleven couples with such extreme characteristics, six subsequently had a 'good' outcome, and none had a 'bad' outcome.

None of these three predictor variables was independent of 'lack of cohesion', the most predictive of the four marital factors. The mean 'lack of cohesion' score was significantly higher when husbands were of low rather than high intake occupational status ($t = 3.46$, $P < 0.001$); when wives reported high rather than low hardship ($t = 3.78$, $P < 0.001$); and when husbands had self-esteem scores below rather than above the median ($t = 2.61$, $P < 0.02$). It is therefore worth asking how 'lack of cohesion' predicts outcome in combination with each of these three other predictive variables, and in particular whether 'lack of cohesion' remains predictive in its own right when the effects of each is controlled.

FIGURES 1, 2, and 3 show the relationships between 'lack of cohesion' and outcome classification, controlling in turn for intake occupational status, hardship, and self-esteem. In the case of FIGURE 1, it has been necessary to combine 'equivocal' and 'bad' outcome groups in view of the rarity of a 'bad' outcome for husbands of relatively high occupational status.

It can be seen that 'lack of cohesion' remains predictive of outcome for the majority of husbands whose jobs were only of manual or routine non-manual status at intake. However it is not at all predictive for the minority of husbands whose job at intake was of higher status.

From FIGURE 2 it can be seen that the direction of prediction on the basis of 'lack of cohesion' is preserved both for high hardship and low hardship couples, but that the differences between mean scores are no longer significant. However, it should be noted that N's are now rather small in some instances.

FIGURE 3 shows that the direction and significance of prediction on the basis of 'lack of cohesion' is preserved only when husband's self-esteem is low. When that is the case 'good' outcome couples have significantly lower 'lack of cohesion' scores than either 'equivocal' or 'bad' outcome couples. 'Lack of cohesion' is not predictive for husbands with above-median self-esteem.

MARITAL STABILITY AND CHANGE

One of the most important questions bearing on the choice between individual behaviour or social psychological perspectives on alcoholism concerns marital change. Is the state of a marriage simply a reflection of the severity of the husband's drinking problem? And does the marriage improve simply concomitantly with improvement in drinking? To answer these questions requires longitudinal data concerning marital functioning.

With the exception of the standard joint interview procedure and some of the interview questions, marital assessment techniques were repeated at the time of the twelve-month follow-up. This section compares scores at intake and follow-up and in particular relates change to drinking outcome classification. Ns are now rather less than 100 owing to lack of complete information at follow-up. One of the commonest reasons for lack of information was the separation of husband and wife during the intervening year, which made most of the marital techniques inapplicable in such cases.

Marital patterns test

TABLES 23 to 26 show the results for the marital patterns test scales. Each Table includes data only for those subjects who completed the particular scale both at intake and at follow-up. A number of points about the results shown in these Tables can be noted.

Firstly, each table shows the three drinking outcome groups ordered, at follow-up, from 'good' to 'bad', the former group having the highest level of reported affection and the latter group the lowest. In all cases the difference between the two extreme outcome groups is statistically significant, and in the case of husband's affection given and wife's affection received the difference is highly significant.

However, these group differences at follow-up cannot be attributed only to change. There is in fact considerable evidence of stability between intake and follow-up. For one thing, the three groups are almost invariably ordered in the same way *at intake*, showing that some of the difference between groups is to be attributed to predisposition rather than to consequence of change in drinking. Secondly, there are the substantial, and usually highly statistically significant, intake–follow-up correlations both overall and for each outcome group separately. Thirdly, and most importantly, when the difference between intake and follow-up scores is examined directly, only two clearly significant differences are found, and both of these involve husband's affection given (a significant increase from intake to follow-up for subjects overall and for those in the 'good' group alone).

None the less there is some evidence for change in these Tables. The direction of change is as predicted for the 'good' group for all four scales (a reported increase in affection), and the direction of change is opposite for the 'bad' group in three out of four cases. Furthermore, although the three out-come groups were ordered at intake in the same way as at follow-up, only the differences between 'good' and 'bad' groups for the husband's affection given and wife's affection received scales were significant at intake ($P < 0.05$), and between-group differences were much enlarged at follow-up.

WIFE DESCRIPTIONS OF SOBER HUSBANDS

TABLE 27 shows the comparison of intake and follow-up descriptions of sober husbands provided by wives in terms of the adjective check-list. It will be recalled that 'desirability' factor scores for this type of description loaded highly on the 'lack of cohesion' marital factor.

It can be seen that, at follow-up, descriptions giving prominence to 'desira-bility' adjectives or phrases out-number others amongst wives whose hus-bands had a 'good' outcome, whilst descriptions giving prominence to the less desirable 'hostile-dominance', or 'submissiveness' adjectives or phrases outnumber others amongst wives whose husbands had 'equivocal' or 'bad' outcomes. However, in this case it appeared impossible to attribute these group differences to change. The same group differences existed, to a slightly greater degree in fact, at intake. Follow-up group differences must be attri-buted to predisposition rather than consequence. Although the proportion of wives who gave relatively greater prominence to 'desirability' adjectives or phrases at follow-up than at intake was somewhat higher in the 'good' drinking outcome (16/26) than in the 'equivocal' (14/30) or 'bad' groups (10/27), these differences were not significant (this is a slightly more sensitive test of change as the relative prominence of 'desirability' adjectives or phrases might change although the same factor might remain as the factor of rank one).

TASK INVOLVEMENT

TABLES 28 and 29 show the relationship between a couple's task involve-ment category, both at intake and at follow-up, and drinking outcome. It can be seen that there are highly significant differences between 'good' and other groups at follow-up. Wife dominated couples are out-numbered by other types in the 'good' group by 5 to 1 whilst wife dominated couples out-number other types in the 'equivocal' and 'bad' groups by approximately 2 to 1.

Once again, however, these follow-up group differences cannot solely be attributed to change. Group differences are similar, though not as extreme, at intake, and wife domination at intake is predictive of wife domination at follow-up. None the less, it is still the case that there is greater movement towards lesser degrees of wife dominance of task involvement in couples where the drinking has a 'good' outcome at twelve-months follow-up. There was a total of eleven instances of category change towards greater husband partici-pation in the 'good' group and only two and one instances of such change in the 'equivocal' and 'bad' groups respectively (chi squared $= 6.97$, 1 d.f., $P < 0.01$).

DISCUSSION

Reference was made at the beginning of this chapter to two contrasting models of 'alcoholism'. In terms of the first, relatively simple, *individual behaviour*, model, alcoholism in marriage is viewed as a source of stress, or family crisis, with which family members must 'cope' or to which they must react with a characteristic progression of phased behaviours (Jackson, 1954; Lemert, 1960) paralleling the supposed phases of development of the condition alcoholism (Jellinek, 1952). In its purest form, this first model assumes that deterioration in family relationships occurs simply as a *consequence* of the development of alcoholism in one family member; and that in complementary fashion, *improvement* in the state of family relationships occurs when the excessive drinker stops or modifies his drinking behaviour.

The second, or *social psychological*, model supposes that the excessive drinking habit of one family member is simply one aspect of the functioning of the family system, the determinants of which include the 'input' characteristics of the spouses (their social habits, temperaments, expectations, etc.), their early mode of adjustment to marriage, and their continuing readjustments to one another and to fresh external inputs (including children of the marriage as new inputs). Simple assumptions about concomitant changes in drinking habits and family relationships following successful treatment or advice do not follow so inevitably from this second model.

Data on change in marital relationships and drinking outcome, such as those presented in this section of this chapter, are therefore particularly relevant to the debate over the relative appropriateness of these perspectives.

The findings in fact are fairly equivocal. There is plenty of support for an 'individual behaviour' model in the form of evidence that husbands and wives are likely to say more favourable things about their marriages at the end of a year during which the husband's drinking behaviour has 'improved'. This is particularly shown in the results obtained from the application of the marital patterns test (TABLES 23 to 26), and also in the results obtained from the application of the marital role inventories (TABLES 28 and 29).

However, there is as much evidence in support of stability. Even in the case of the marital patterns test, only one scale (husband's affection given) shows a *significant* shift in the direction of greater affection at follow-up, either overall, or for the 'good' outcome group alone. The one-year stability coefficients for these four scales are surprisingly high.

In terms of wives' descriptions of their 'sober' husbands, there is also a surprising absence of change (TABLE 27). The unfavourability of wives' descriptions of their 'sober' husbands appears to be a relatively stable feature of marital interaction in this sample, and the relationship between this feature and outcome categorization is in fact slightly weaker at follow-up than it was at intake. This finding tends to confirm Kogan and Jackson's (1964) supposition that this was an aspect of the marital situation, '. . . which would be little changed by the cessation of drinking'.

Again, in terms of the marital role inventory classification, there is relatively little overall shift in the direction of greater husband participation, and the majority of couples report that the situation is very similar at intake and follow-up. Couples who report wife domination at intake tend to have a 'bad' outcome and report wife domination again at follow-up; on the other hand, couples who report a pattern other than that of wife domination tend to have a 'good' outcome and tend to report a pattern of involvement other than wife domination again at follow-up.

There is therefore a highly significant degree of stability, over a period of one year, in terms of a number of measured aspects of the marital relationship. There appears to be a sort of 'hierarchy' of aspects of the relationship in terms of their modifiability. Opinions about the amount of affection being displayed in the relationship (particularly affection from husbands to wives) appear to be considerably modifiable, despite the overall stability which they display. There is rather less modifiability about the balance of family task participation, and the favourability–unfavourability of wives' descriptions of their sober husbands appears to be scarcely modifiable at all. However, it could be argued that this apparent hierarchy has more to do with the 'speed' of recovery. Some aspects of a relationship may change relatively rapidly, whilst others may take very much longer to change. Only a study which involved follow-up for periods considerably in excess of one year could decide on that point.

Of equal importance and interest is the question of the retrospective stability of aspects of the marital relationship. Are characteristics such as the unfavourability of wives' perceptions enduring attributes of a marriage which have characterized it almost from the beginning? Approximately half the husbands, and an equal proportion of wives, were now of the opinion that the husband had had a drinking problem at or before the time of their marriage. This is a finding very similar to that of Lemert (1962) who reported that 54 per cent of husbands in his sample had a drinking problem at or before marriage. When subjects of the present study were asked to complete the role inventory to indicate the balance of participation during the first year of their marriage, a large minority of couples (23 per cent) reported a 'wife dominated' pattern. It was also found that couples subsequently placed in the 'bad' outcome group were significantly more likely to have recalled a 'wife dominated' or 'wife dominated–egalitarian' pattern of family participation in the first year of marriage than were couples in the 'good' outcome group ($P < 0.01$). The predictive relationship was in fact just as strong as that based upon a classification derived from answers to questions about family task participation in the month preceding intake. Of course, recall of such matters over a number of years cannot be relied upon to give an accurate account of the state of affairs early in marriage, but these results are sufficient to suggest the importance of studies of marriage and deviance which focus upon stability and change from a longitudinal perspective.

WIVES COPING BEHAVIOUR

Finally, in this chapter, we examine the marriage relationship from an altogether different perspective, namely that of behaviour which wives have tried using in order to 'cope' with the circumstances of being married to an excessively drinking husband. What is the range of coping strategies which wives use? Are some more effective? Could all wives be advised, or even trained, to use certain methods?

At intake each wife completed a shortened version of the coping questionnaire developed by Orford and Guthrie (1968, 1976). The fifty-six items retained in this version (see TABLE 30) were those with loadings of at least ± 0·30 on at least one of the five factors identified by them. Wives were asked to indicate for each item whether the behaviour mentioned had been used by them 'often', 'sometimes', 'once or twice', or 'not at all' in the previous twelve months.

An attempt was made to confirm the component structure previously found (Orford and Guthrie, 1968, 1976) by factor analyses and principal component analyses, with and without oblique or orthogonal rotations. In no instance were the same factors or components produced, but in several analyses some of the original five were partly identified. The analysis which produced the most readily interpretable factors or components was a principal component analysis with orthogonal rotation of ten components accounting between them for 55·3 per cent of total variance. It is the latter solution which will be described here.

The predictive utility of the coping questionnaire was examined item by item. The distribution of replies across the four answer categories was examined for each item, and dichotomized as near to the median as possible. The frequencies of above-median responses (e.g. 'yes often' or 'yes sometimes' as opposed to 'yes once or twice' or 'no') were compared in the two groups of wives—those whose husbands were subsequently placed in the 'good' outcome group and those whose husbands were subsequently placed in the 'bad' outcome group. In each case the difference in proportions of wives in the two groups who gave above-median responses was compared with the standard error of the difference in proportions.

ASSOCIATION WITH DRINKING OUTCOME

TABLE 30 shows the ten coping components with a list of those items with loadings greater than ± 0·40, with highest loading items listed first in each case. After each item is given the percentage of wives who gave any response other than 'no' to that item (note that this is not necessarily the same as an 'above median response'). A single word or short phrase has been used to summarize the interpretation given to each component.

Also indicated in TABLE 30 is whether one or other of the groups of wives, defined in terms of the outcome of their husband's drinking, gave a higher frequency of above median responses to the item concerned. Of the fifty-six items, thirty-five were given above median responses more frequently by wives whose husbands subsequently had a 'bad' outcome (items marked B), and only eleven showed a relatively high frequency of above median responses for the 'good' outcome group (marked G). Whereas six of the former showed a *significantly* higher frequency of above median responses for the 'bad' outcome group (marked BB), not a single item showed a significantly higher frequency for the 'good' group (taking a difference in proportions of twice the standard error of the difference as an indication of statistical significance).

Several components of wives' coping behaviour appeared to be associated with a relatively poor prognosis. These are the components which have been labelled 'avoidance' (component 2), 'sexual withdrawal' (component 7), 'fearful withdrawal' (component 8), and 'taking special action' (component 9). Bearing in mind that relatively few items show a higher frequency of above median responses for the 'good' outcome group, three components stand out as containing a relatively high proportion of such items, and a relatively low proportion of B items. These are 'competition' (component 4), 'anti-drink' (component 5), and 'assertion' (component 6). The first of these three components, in particular, is unusual in containing a number of items with a relatively low frequency of endorsement. Other components contain a mixture of items, some associated with good prognosis, others with poor prognosis. Notable amongst these is the first component, 'discord', which contains many items with a very high frequency of endorsement.

CORRELATIONS WITH OTHER VARIABLES

Each item in the coping questionnaire was scored 1 ('no' in the last twelve months) 2, 3, or 4 ('yes often') and ten component scores were computed for each wife. TABLE 31 shows the correlation of each of these scores with each of four other variables: wife's hardship score (see TABLE 22); husband's intake occupational status (Hall-Jones scale, 1950); wife's age; and wife's 'neuroticism' (each wife completed one form of the EPI (Eysenck and Eysenck, 1964). Results from the EPI will be discussed more fully in the following chapter. No single coping component score had a substantial correlation with the extraversion scale of the EPI).

Most apparent from this table is the consistency of the direction of correlations with hardship and neuroticism (all correlations positive), and husband's job status (with one exception all correlations being negative). Many of these correlations are significant. However, only nine correlations are highly significant ($P < 0.001$) and five of these concern the hardship scale. The degree of hardship reported by a wife correlates positively at this level with the amount of discord, avoidance, fearful withdrawal, special action, and marital breakdown which she reports as part of her coping behaviour. Other highly significant correlations are those between wife's neuroticism and both discord and assertion, a negative correlation between husband's job status and assertion, and a positive correlation between wife's age and taking special action.

DISCUSSION

A major purpose in pursuing this line of research was the identification of 'styles' of coping behaviour which might influence the outcome of the husband's drinking in different ways. In this regard, the results are somewhat disappointing. High frequency coping behaviour appears, on the whole, to be associated with a relatively poor outcome, whatever the precise nature of the coping behaviour employed. Only a small minority of individual coping items showed relatively high frequency coping by wives whose husbands subsequently had a good outcome, and in none of these instances was the difference statistically significant.

The commonsense explanation for this overall finding is that wives do more coping when they have more to cope with. Indeed the wives themselves, as a group, gave accounts of themselves which correspond with this commonsense view. Coping behaviour of almost all varieties correlated with the degree of hardship which they reported experiencing through living with drinking husbands. This evidence seems to be in support of James and Goldman's (1971) explanation of coping behaviour as situational responding. In their study wives reported a progressive increase in all five types of coping as drinking progressed from 'social' to 'excessive' to 'alcoholismic'. Furthermore, wives who reported that their husbands became violent and aggressive were more likely to report reacting with quarrelling, avoidance, anger, and helplessness, pretending to be drunk themselves, locking the husband out of the house, and seeking a separation. As the measure of 'hardship' employed here revolved principally around themes of hostility and violence, the present finding linking hardship and nearly all coping components is along the same lines.

The uniformly positive correlations with wife's neuroticism and virtually uniform negative correlations with husband's occupational status could be interpreted in the same way if it is assumed that coping component scores are co-varying with those parts of wife's neuroticism and husband's occupational status which represent the consequences of alcoholism rather than more fundamental aspects of 'personality' or 'social class'.

The relationship between coping and drinking outcome may therefore be misleading, if it is taken to imply that coping is maladaptive, or that it is a causative agent in the drinking change process. What carries a relatively poor prognosis, at least in the short term, is probably not coping behaviour which occurs independently of other events, but rather the whole complex of a family system whose cohesion has deteriorated. Increased hostility and violence in the home, occupational status decline for the husband, and increased tension for the wife and other family members are probably symptoms of this deterioration. This is not to say that family behaviour necessarily runs the course of a predictable sequence divisible into as many as seven stages, as Jackson (1954) suggested. Indeed, Lemert's (1960) study of the progression of family behaviours suggested no more than two broad 'stages'. At a relatively late stage occurred such things as fearful reactions, feelings of hopelessness, sexual withdrawal, and the seeking of outside assistance—a collection of reactions remarkably similar to the avoidance, sexual withdrawal, fearful withdrawal, and taking special action components which we have found to be amongst those carrying the poorest prognosis, and amongst those with the strongest relationship with hardship.

The coping components whose items are most uniformly associated with a relatively poor prognosis are just those that suggest withdrawal or disengagement from the marital bond. The elements are those of avoiding, refusing to talk, feeling hopeless, refusing to sleep together, feeling frightened, making special financial arrangements, seeking outside help, and contemplating terminating the bond altogether. On the other hand, elements such as pleading, rowing, hitting, getting drunk herself, trying to make him jealous or seem ridiculous, and hiding or pouring away his drink are not associated with a relatively poor outcome. Although they do not sound like the sorts of things that go on in the most cohesive marriages, they do suggest a degree of engagement or involvement between wife and husband which is lacking in the bad outcome-related items. The dimension of engagement–disengagement may be crucial in indicating the state of a family system complicated by excessive drinking in the husband, and may give an indication of the potential for immediate change. The importance of this dimension is undoubtedly to be seen in families complicated by conditions other than excessive drinking, and doubtless in non-family social systems as well. Ferreira and Winter (1968) have conceived of a 'family pathology cycle' whereby lack of consensus between family members, reduced communication, and lack of satisfaction in family decisions, feed one another in a vicious circle of ever-decreasing cohesion. Such concepts have obvious application to the specialist field of marriage and excessive drinking.

There remains a very real possibility that the role of individual differences in coping behaviour are being ignored. A hint of this possibility shows in coping component 5, the one which we have labelled 'anti-drink'. Not one of the five items with moderate to high loadings on this component follows the general pattern of association with a poorer outcome. Indeed two of these items display a tendency in the opposite direction. Although, like other components, it is wives who report greater hardship who also more frequently report using these coping behaviours, none the less trying to find her husband's drink, hiding it or pouring it away, and making a firm rule not allowing drink in the house, do not carry the unfavourable prognosis carried by most other coping behaviours. It may be that the execution of this particular coping strategy, despite its active or controlling flavour, carries relatively little risk of reinforcing the family pathology cycle or of adding an increment to the spiral of decreasing family cohesion. Instead of rowing with *him*, avoiding *him*, or refusing to sleep with *him*, it is the bottle that is banned from the home and not the man who has the door locked against him. This differential aspect of coping behaviour could be of the utmost importance if it were coupled with a correspondingly benign system of beliefs about the origins of the husband's excessive drinking and about the appropriate attribution of blame.

CHAPTER VI

PERSONALITY AND ALCOHOLISM-COMPLICATED MARRIAGES

INTRODUCTION

MARRIAGES complicated by excessive drinking raise many questions about individual differences in behaviour. For instance, do excessively drinking husbands and their wives give abnormal accounts of their present personalities? Much previous research (e.g. Hill *et al.*, 1962; Kammeier *et al.*, 1973) leads to the expectation that the husbands would so do, but in the case of their wives clinical accounts and previous research are equivocal (see CHAPTER II, pp. 29–33). Is there evidence for the similarity in the personalities of excessively drinking husbands and their wives as is generally the case for marital pairs, and do husband–wife correlations increase with duration of marriage as has been found in at least one study of men with a diagnosis of neurosis, and their wives (Kreitman, 1964)? Do personality self-accounts return to normal if the husband's excessive drinking is terminated or reduced? Again, research is equivocal with regard to wives and it has even been suggested that some wives, because of their own personality needs, feel more comfortable when their husbands are drinking excessively (CHAPTER II, p. 31). Do the self-descriptions of excessively drinking husbands and their wives correspond well with the descriptions provided by their spouses, or are there some systematic discrepancies as previous research on interperson perception would suggest (CHAPTER II, pp. 28–9). Are husbands' self-descriptions, and descriptions of them by their wives, the same under 'sober' and 'drinking' conditions, or are there systematic discrepancies suggesting the perceived personality-change functions of drinking? (CHAPTER II, p. 28).

The Eysenck Personality Inventory (EPI) (Eysenck and Eysenck, 1964) was used to test the first three of these questions, and the Interpersonal Adjective Check-List (ACL) (Leary, 1957; LaForge and Suczek, 1955) the remaining two questions. Results in this chapter will partly be confined to data from the first fifty couples, which have been analysed in greater detail.

EYSENCK PERSONALITY INVENTORY

This inventory (Eysenck and Eysenck, 1964) consists of two separate parts, forms A and B. Form A, consisting of fifty-seven yes–no questions, was administered to each of the first fifty husbands and to each of their wives. Form B (also fifty-seven items) was administered to each of the remaining husbands and to each of their wives. In each form nine items constitute a 'lie scale'. One purpose of this scale is to detect subjects who are attempting to 'fake good', although it is thought that it may constitute an interesting personality dimension in its own right (Eysenck and Eysenck, 1964). The remaining items of each form are roughly equally divided between those contributing to a *neuroticism* score, and those contributing to an *extraversion* score.

At the twelve-month follow-up each available subject completed the alternative form of the inventory (form B for husbands and wives numbers 1–50, form A for numbers 51–100).

INTERPERSONAL ADJECTIVE CHECK-LIST

The version of the ACL employed was the shortened, forty-item form described in CHAPTER V. The scoring was, however, simpler than that described in CHAPTER V, and was based upon the two supposed major dimensions of the interpersonal behaviour circumplex rather than upon the three factors empirically derived from the data obtained in this study. Thus two scores were derived from each check-list: firstly an *affection–hostility* score computed by subtracting the number of hostility items checked from the number of affection items checked and adding ten to remove negative values; secondly a *dominance–submissiveness* score computed in similar fashion. These discrepancy scores were independent of checking frequency. Data from the following four conditions of administration of the ACL at intake will be reported in this Chapter: Perception of sober husband ('myself as I really am —not when drinking'/'my husband as he really is—not when drinking'); perception of drinking husband ('myself as I am when drinking'/'my husband as he is when drinking'); perception of wife ('my wife'/'myself'); and ideal spouse ('the ideal wife'/'the ideal husband').

RESULTS

A COMPARISON OF INTAKE EPI SCORES WITH EPI NORMS

TABLE 32 shows a comparison of the two halves of the present EPI data with the results for normal subjects reported in the inventory manual (Eysenck and Eysenck, 1964). The results from forms A (couples 1–50) and B (cases 51–100) are consistent. In both cases husbands show highly significantly raised N (neuroticism) scores (P < 0·001), but means for E (extraversion) and L (lie scale) are in neither case significantly different from the published norm.

Both sets of wives also show significantly raised N scores (P < 0·001) but the extent of their departure from normal is less than for husbands. For wives, in addition, there is a tendency towards low E scores which is significant in the case of form A (P < 0·01) and is of borderline significance in the case of form B (P < 0·10). Furthermore, unlike husbands, wives show highly significant raised L scores in both sets of data (P < 0·001).

Inter-scale correlations for husbands are shown in the top left part of

TABLE 33, and those for wives are shown in the bottom right part of the same Table. N and L are significantly negatively correlated both for husbands (P < 0·001) and for wives (P < 0·01), whilst N and E (P < 0·01) and E and L (P < 0·01) are significantly negatively correlated for wives only.

HUSBAND-WIFE EPI CORRELATIONS AND DURATION OF MARRIAGE

In the top right of TABLE 33 are shown husband-wife EPI correlations for the whole sample. Only one of nine correlations is significant (Hs L v. Ws L) and that only at a modest level of significance (P < 0·05). Notable are the near zero husband-wife correlations for N and E.

When the sample is divided as nearly as possible into thirds on the basis of duration of marriage, and husband-wife correlations recalculated for short duration (less than one year to seven years), medium duration (eight to sixteen years) and long duration (seventeen or more years) couples separately, there is a slight trend towards a decrease in size of correlation with increase in duration of marriage for E scores only (+0·18, −0·02, and −0·15 for the three groups respectively), but even here none of the three individual sub-sample correlations reaches a level of statistical significance.

MEAN EPI SCORES AND DURATION OF MARRIAGE

There did emerge, however, a relationship between duration of marriage and wives' N scores. Short duration of marriage wives obtained the highest mean score (15·75) and long duration of marriage wives the lowest (11·65). Medium duration of marriage wives were intermediate (12·54). Means for short and medium groups were significantly different (P < 0·05), as were the means for short and long groups (P < 0·01). In contrast, husbands' mean N scores showed no variation with duration of marriage. As a consequence, the discrepancy between husband and wife means increased with increasing duration of marriage. Over the sample as a whole, husbands obtained a significantly higher mean than wives (P < 0·01). This overall difference was exaggerated for husbands and wives whose marriages were of long duration (P < 0·01), was less marked for those of medium duration (P < 0·05), and was non-existent for those whose marriages were of short duration. This effect is shown graphically in FIGURE 4. No significant between-duration of marriage group mean differences emerged for E scores.

INTAKE-FOLLOW-UP STABILITY OF EPI SCORES AND
DRINKING OUTCOME

TABLE 34 shows intake and follow-up mean scores for husbands who had 'good', 'equivocal', or 'bad' outcomes, and for their wives.

Only in the case of husbands' N scores is there a significant difference, for the sample as a whole, between mean intake and follow-up scores. In this case the two means are highly significantly different (P < 0·001) with husbands showing a much reduced mean N at follow-up. However, TABLE 34 also shows that this reduction is related to drinking outcome; the reduction is manifest for husbands with a 'good' (P < 0·001) or with an 'equivocal' outcome (P < 0·01), but intake and follow-up means are nearly identical for husbands whose outcome is 'bad'. As a consequence, husbands with different drinking outcomes have different levels of N at follow-up, those with a 'good' outcome having the lowest levels and those with a 'bad' having the highest (G *v*. E, not significant; E *v*. B, P < 0·01; G *v*. B, P < 0·001).

However TABLE 34 also shows that the differences between outcome groups are partly a matter of selective recruitment. The three outcome groups are ordered in the same way at intake with husbands whose drinking outcome was subsequently 'bad' having the highest mean N score at that time. None the less, between outcome group differences are less marked at intake and only reach a borderline level of statistical significance in the case of Good *v*. Bad (P < 0·10). The overall intake-follow-up correlation for husbands' N is +0·52 (P < 0·001) and is of a similar order for the three outcome groups separately.

A similar element of selective recruitment is apparent for husbands' E scores. Husbands with a subsequent 'good' outcome have highest E scores and those with a subsequent 'bad' outcome the lowest. However, again intake differences are slight and only reach a borderline level of significance in the case of G *v*. B (P < 0·10). Although changes in E scores between intake and follow-up are not sufficient to produce significant differences, the difference between the two extreme outcome groups is slightly increased by the time of follow-up (P < 0·05). Again the overall intake-follow-up correlation for husbands' E scores is highly significant (r = +0·50, P < 0·001) and is of a similar order for the three outcome groups separately.

TABLE 34 also shows a high overall intake-follow-up correlation for wives' N scores (+0·75, P < 0·001) but an absence of intake-follow-up mean differences or between-outcome group differences. The non-significant trend is towards increased N scores at follow-up and the increase is greatest (but still not significant) for wives whose husbands have a 'good' outcome, and least for those whose husbands have a 'bad' outcome.

TABLE 34 shows a relatively low intake-follow-up overall correlation for wives' E scores (r = +0·25, P < 0·05), but an absence of intake-follow-up mean differences or between-outcome group differences.

A COMPARISON OF SELF AND SPOUSE ACL DESCRIPTIONS

TABLE 35 shows a comparison of husbands' self-descriptions (sober) and wives' descriptions of their husbands (sober), as well as a comparison of wives' descriptions of themselves and their husbands' descriptions of them. Correlations are all positive, but none exceeds +0·46, and the husband–wife correlation for affection–hostility, when sober husbands are the objects of perception, is only of borderline significance. Mean scores are very similar in three out of the four instances in which comparisons have been made. The exception concerns the degree of dominance–submissiveness attributed to wives. Husbands attribute significantly more dominance to their wives than their wives do to themselves (P < 0·001).

THE INTERPERSONAL EFFECTS OF DRINKING

The effects attributed, by husbands and wives, to the husbands' drinking was assessed by comparing 'ideal *spouse*' descriptions, descriptions of husbands sober, and descriptions of husbands when drinking.[1]

Results from Hs and Ws revealed the same general picture. Both considered that the husbands, as a group, were less than ideally dominant (Hs P < 0·01, Ws P < 0·01) and less than ideally affectionate (Hs P < 0·001, Ws P < 0·05) when sober. A comparison of sober and drinking descriptions shows that both husbands and wives considered the husbands to be more dominant when drinking (Hs P < 0·01, Ws P < 0·05) but less affectionate when drinking (Hs P < 0·01, Ws P < 0·001). Finally, a comparison of ideal spouse and husband drinking descriptions shows that both sets of informants considered there to be little difference between ideal and drinking levels of husband dominance, but considered there to be highly significant differences between ideal and drinking levels of affection–hostility (Hs P < 0·001, Ws P < 0·001). These results are shown graphically in FIGURES 5a (dominance–submissiveness) and 5b (affection–hostility).

DISCUSSION

NEUROTICISM, EXTRAVERSION, AND THE ALCOHOLIC HUSBAND

Amongst the most significant findings of this part of the study are the unusually high mean neuroticism scores of the husbands themselves at the time of first presentation at the clinic. Such a result is in line with previous findings (e.g. Hill *et al.*, 1962; Eysenck and Eysenck, 1964; Edwards, 1966; Edwards and Guthrie, 1967; Edwards *et al.*, 1967) but raises as many questions as it answers. It can readily be believed that recent life events associated with problematic consumption of alcohol had been sufficient to alter a previously 'normal' distribution of personality self-accounts in this sample. Alternatively, in line with the long-held assumption about the anxiety-reducing functions of alcohol (e.g. Conger, 1956) it might be supposed that these raised neuroticism scores represent life-long abnormalities, in a proportion of subjects, which predisposed to excessive alcohol use.

---

[1] For this analysis it would have been more satisfactory to compare husbands' descriptions of themselves, sober and drinking, with their descriptions of ideal *selves*, or ideal *husbands*, but these were not available. However, in the event mean 'ideal husband' scores (provided by wives) and mean 'ideal wife' scores (provided by husbands) were not significantly different, and in particular were virtually identical for dominance–submissiveness where differences might have been expected. The ideal descriptions provided by these subjects may therefore be construed as 'ideal person' or 'ideal marriage partner' descriptions irrespective of sex.

Against the latter explanation is the general lack of evidence in support of the supposed anxiety reducing functions of alcohol except in small doses, either for 'normal' or for excessive drinkers (see e.g. Williams, 1966; Mello, 1972), and the results of longitudinal studies of alcoholism and personality (McCord *et al.*, 1960; Robins, 1966; Jones, 1968; Kammeier *et al.*, 1973). These latter studies, usually with admittedly select samples, have not reported that individual differences suggestive of anxiety or neuroticism are associated with a raised probability of later problem drinking, but rather have isolated attributes such as impulsivity and hostility as predisposing. In further support of a reactive hypothesis to explain the anxiety levels of alcoholics is the evidence in these data of a large reduction in neuroticism for those husbands who gave up their excessive drinking in the interval between intake and follow-up. Their follow-up scores were virtually 'normal' whilst husbands who continued to drink excessively retained extremely high scores. However, there was an element of selective recruitment and the latter husbands had somewhat higher intake scores. Amongst this latter group could well be some with life-long problems of coping with unusually high anxiety levels.

A further complicating factor, supporting a reactive explanation, is the direct effect upon arousal or anxiety levels of the regular consumption of high quantities of alcohol. Amongst EPI items contributing to scores on the neuroticism scale are some referring to such things as sleeplessness and tension. Sleep patterns are known to be disturbed during and following excessive drinking by alcoholics but they later return to normal (Mello, 1972). Similarly, tension and mood disturbance are amongst the many 'symptoms' which alcoholics complain of, which they consider are increased during withdrawal from alcohol, and which they believe are relieved by further drinking (Hershon, 1977). These elements of neuroticism are therefore extremely difficult to extricate from alcohol withdrawal effects. The EPI even includes such items as, 'Do you get attacks of shaking or trembling?'.

A further complication is introduced by the significant correlation of husband's intake N score with both recent (-0.25, $P < 0.05$, low status associated with high N) and highest ever (-0.29, $P < 0.01$) occupational status. It will be recalled that a relatively low recent status was associated with a bad one-year outcome (CHAPTER V, p. 75).

WIVES' NEUROTICISM AND 'FAKING GOOD'

Wives also have mean neuroticism scores which are significantly higher than 'normal', although they are less extreme than their husbands'. Again one might suppose that these represent a reaction to the stressful events associated with living with an excessively drinking husband (Jackson, 1954). There are however two additional lines of evidence in these results which are not so easy to incorporate into a reactive explanation.

Firstly there is the evidence of a systematic variation of wives' neuroticism scores with duration of marriage. Wives in the short duration of marriage group, who have the highest neuroticism scores, have been exposed to life with their husbands for a shorter time than wives in medium and long duration groups. Nor is this compensated for by variation in the chronicity of the husbands' drinking problems. Indeed, it is wives in the medium and long duration of marriage groups who (on the basis of the pooled accounts of wives and husbands) are married to husbands with problems of longest duration (averaging twelve years in comparison with eight and a half years for short duration of marriage wives). The argument is of course not fool-proof, but one would, on the face of it, expect wives whose marriages are of the shortest duration to have had the least to react to.

More likely explanations of the duration of marriage effect lie in the realm of mate choice. It is a recurring theme in the literature on alcoholism and marriage that many women consciously or unconsciously choose as mates men who they know to be drinking heavily (e.g. Whalen, 1953; Rae and Forbes, 1966). Amongst couples who served as subjects in this study the frequency with which the husband's drinking was recalled as having been a problem before, or at the time of, the start of marriage varied systematically with the duration of marriage at the time of presentation to the clinic. The majority of couples whose marriages were of short duration (23/32), roughly half in the medium duration group (16/35), and a small minority in the long duration group (5/32) considered the husband's drinking to have been a problem at that time. The suggestion is that pre-marriage anxiety levels of wives-to-be are themselves influential, or are associated with other personal characteristics which are influential, in choosing or avoiding, or settling or not for the bargain of (Murstein, 1970), an excessively drinking mate. Alternatively, the longer duration marriages may be those remaining after many with higher N levels have broken up.

The second line of evidence contrary to a reactive view of wives' anxiety concerns the stability of wives' neuroticism scores over the twelve-month period between intake and follow-up. Despite the dramatic life events to which many wives were exposed during this period, the overall stability was high ($r = +0.75$), and there was an overall increase (but not significant) between intake and follow-up. The increase is in fact greatest (but still not significant) for wives whose husbands had a 'good' outcome and least for those whose husbands had a 'bad' outcome. These results are quite contrary to those that would be expected on the basis of a stress reaction hypothesis. Although the non-significance of these results must be stressed, they are tending in the direction which would be expected on the grounds of the theory that wives have an investment in their husbands' continued drinking and 'decompensate' if they give up their drinking (e.g. Macdonald, 1956). However, such a theory is not the only explanation for illness or emotional disturbance following a relative's recovery. For example, Hansen and Hill (1964) proposed an 'emotional room' theory which supposes that family climate and functioning do not allow room for family members to be ill or disturbed together but necessitate a degree of 'taking it in turns'. It also has to be stressed that in studies where psychiatric or psychosomatic symptomatology has been made the criterion (Bailey, 1967; Haberman, 1964; Kogan and Jackson, 1965), wives recall having more symptoms when their husbands were drinking and fewer symptoms when they weren't (see CHAPTER II, p. 31).

Unlike their husbands, wives had abnormally high lie scale scores. They were more likely than normal subjects to claim, for example, that they would, 'declare everything at the customs', and that, 'all their habits were good and desirable ones'. This result raises interesting questions about the stance which wives adopt towards their own behaviour in comparison with their attitudes towards their husbands' behaviour. It has often been charged, by those involved clinically with alcoholics and their wives (e.g. Gliedman et al., 1956), that wives are frequently resistant to seeing their own involvement in, and responsibility for, family events associated with their husbands' drinking. One interpretation of the high lie scale scores obtained by wives in this study is that they represent a protest of innocence, and a reaction to the suggestion, or suspicion, that they are partially responsible.

Alternatively it could be argued that the lie scale measures a relatively stable propensity towards conscientiousness or conformity. One could speculate on the role which such a propensity might play in the development of a marital system in which non-conforming behaviours, such as excessive drinking, serve a rebellion-like function. In fact, between intake and follow-up there was practically no shift in mean lie scale score for wives, either overall or for any one of the drinking outcome groups separately.

DISAGREEMENT OVER WIVES' DOMINANCE

A highly significant discrepancy emerged in relation to the degree of dominance–submissiveness attributed to wives. The wives' self-description mean was on the submissive side of the 'neutral' point of 10.0, whilst husbands' descriptions of their wives fell on average on the dominance side. Most husbands thought their wives were more dominant than they themselves were, whilst most wives thought the reverse. The importance of dominance–submission conflicts is frequently stressed by marital therapists (e.g. Dicks, 1967) and is a recurrent theme in writings on alcoholism and marriage (e.g. Drewery and Rae, 1969). Whether husbands are exaggerating the degree of their wives' dominance in the interests of providing rationalizations for further excessive drinking, or whether wives are minimizing the degree of their dominance as part of a protestation of innocence, cannot be answered by these data. However, these results are in line with previous reports concerning the unusually 'feminine' self-descriptions of alcoholics' wives (Kogan and Jackson, 1963a; Drewery and Rae, 1969).

THE INTERPERSONAL FUNCTIONS OF DRINKING

Most of these husbands, and most of their wives, viewed the non-drinking husband as insufficiently affectionate, and insufficiently dominant. The reported effects of drinking upon these two dimensions of interpersonal behaviour were in marked contrast. The mean level of dominance attributed to *drinking* husbands was indistinguishable from the ideals, whilst the level of affection attributed to drinking husbands plummeted even further below the already less-than-ideal non-drinking level. By separating out these two components of interpersonal behaviour, some of the ambivalence surrounding the social value of drinking for the excessive drinker may be uncovered. Although we have been discussing average values, it looks as if many of the husbands may have been achieving an increased level of assertiveness at the cost of increased hostility. The interpersonal value of drinking to these men may remain a mystery to the real life actors involved, who may find it difficult to extricate these two dimensions from one another.

CHAPTER VII

ABSTINENCE OR CONTROL: SOME FINDINGS AT TWENTY-FOUR MONTHS

As outlined in CHAPTER III (p. 42), an attempt was made to follow-up the one hundred couples two years after their initial consultation. The aim was to interview each husband and wife separately as soon as possible after the second anniversary of their intake, and in all cases questions were directed at the twelve-month period between the first and second anniversaries of intake. Unlike intake and first anniversary follow-ups, the majority of twenty-four-month follow-ups were conducted in the couple's own home. In all cases an attempt was made to interview husband and wife separately and apart, and in most cases this was possible.

A shortened form of the same inquiry made at twelve months was employed at twenty-four months. Once again this covered husband's and wife's recall of the husband's drinking pattern, details of help-seeking and treatment received, husband's occupational record, and views on marital satisfaction, amongst other areas. However, data on drinking pattern produced the results with the greatest apparent implications for the conduct of alcoholism treatment services, and it is upon these data that this chapter focuses.

The first section of the results describes the cumulative incidence of relapse in the present sample (this section draws upon data for the first anniversary–second anniversary interval as well as upon second year data). The second section compares a classification of drinking outcome at twenty-four months with the classification made at twelve months, and the third section examines the prediction of twenty-four-months outcome from intake data. The remaining sections concern an important treatment issue which has come very much to the forefront of discussions about alcoholism treatment in recent years; namely the question of abstinence or controlled drinking as the more appropriate goal of treatment.

Relapse data, presented in the first section, were very largely obtained during month-by-month contacts with wives during the first year following intake, and this information is available for ninety-five couples. Most of the remainder of the results, however, concerns only sixty-five couples, those for whom complete two-year follow-up data were obtained from *both* marital partners. Occasional reference will also be made to the results for nineteen further couples for whom two-year follow-up data were obtained from one informant only (the husband in thirteen instances, the wife in the remaining six). No two-year follow-up data were obtained for the remaining sixteen couples. It is therefore important to bear in mind the possible biasing effect of this missing data.

RESULTS

CUMULATIVE RELAPSE CURVES

It can be seen from the lower curve in FIGURE 6 that the majority of men, according to their wives, drank within a few weeks of their initial consultation (all but ten of the ninety-five had drunk within the first four months). The curve is strongly negatively accelerated with proportionally fewer and fewer new 'relapses' occurring over time. By the first anniversary all but eight men had drunk and by the second anniversary only two men remained whose wives reported no single instance of drinking since intake. Both men are known to have drunk since the second anniversary.

The slightly higher position of the intermediate curve in FIGURE 6 shows that not all instances of reported drinking are instances of drinking 'unacceptable' to wives. However, all but twenty men were reported to have drunk unacceptably on at least one occasion by four months after intake, all but twelve by the first anniversary, and all but eight by the second anniversary.

Cumulative curves of this nature are of course somewhat misleading, as instances of 'relapse' may be isolated and not necessarily followed by continued drinking or by further instances. A whole variety of possible definitions of 'relapse' would generate a whole family of possible 'relapse' curves, of which the upper curve in FIGURE 6 is only one. To be included as a 'relapse' for purposes of drawing this curve, it was necessary that a total accumulation of ten drinking days 'unacceptable' to a wife be reported since initial consultation. It can be seen that just over half the wives reported such an accumulation by four months after intake, all but twenty-four reported this accumulation by the first anniversary and only eighteen men remained 'non-relapsed', by this definition, at the time of the second anniversary.

A COMPARISON OF DRINKING OUTCOMES AT ONE AND TWO YEARS

On the basis of drinking pattern data, drinking outcome at two years was classified as 'good', 'equivocal', or 'bad' on the following basis: Outcome was considered 'good' if wife reported five or fewer weeks containing any episode of 'unacceptable' drinking and if, in addition, husband reported five or fewer weeks containing any 200 grammes or more per day drinking (of twenty-six men classified as having a 'good' outcome on this basis, all but four would have been similarly classified if the 100 gramme, rather than 200 gramme, criterion had been employed); outcome was considered 'bad' if wife reported twenty-six or more weeks containing an unacceptable drinking episode and if, in addition, the husband reported that twenty-six or more weeks contained any 100 gramme per day drinking; all other cases were considered 'equivocal' in outcome (of twenty such cases, ten were so classified because both husband and wife reported between six and twenty-five unacceptable or 100+ gramme weeks during the year, and the remaining ten were so classified because husbands and wives differed in their estimates of frequency).

FIGURE 7 shows the degree of movement between categories from twelve-months follow-up to twenty-four-months follow-up.[1] The numbers in FIGURE 7 are reduced to sixty-three as two couples who contributed full information at twenty-four months were unclassifiable because of incomplete information at twelve months. A degree of stability in outcome between twelve and twenty-four months is apparent from the fact that just over half the cases (33/63) remained in the same outcome category at two years, and from the highly significant overall chi squared value (21.13, 4 d.f., P < 0·001). Only three men changed from one extreme outcome category to the other extreme and the majority of shifts therefore involved changes to or from 'equivocal' status. Again the possibly biasing effect of the reduced follow-up sample should be noted; shifts in outcome status might conceivably have been disproportionately represented amongst cases without follow-up information.

PREDICTION OF TWO-YEAR OUTCOME FROM INTAKE DATA

A good outcome at one year could have been significantly predicted from a number of intake indicators, particularly high husband job status, high marital cohesion, and a low level of hardship reported by wife (CHAPTER V). In view of the stability of outcome between one and two years, it might be expected that the two-year follow-up outcome could also have been predicted on the basis of the same intake variables.

TABLE 36 shows that the direction of prediction is preserved at two years, but that only the relationship with intake wife *hardship* remained clearly statistically significant. Whilst means for occupational status were significantly different using a one-tailed test, when outcome groups were split at the job status median the resulting chi squared value was quite insignificant. This was because the job status scale appeared to differentiate two-year outcome groups only at the extreme ends of the scale. Men with relatively high status jobs at intake (above the routine non-manual or skilled manual level) had a particularly good two-year prognosis, whilst at the other end of the scale, men with a routine manual job at intake had a relatively poor two-year prognosis. For marital cohesion the chi squared value was of borderline significance only.

Husband's trouble score is included in TABLE 36 as the absence of a significant predictive relationship, either at two years or at one year, is itself of interest. As will be reported below, it appears that trouble score may be more related to *type* of favourable outcome than to the favourability of outcome *per se*.

---

[1] The criteria for classification at twelve months were slightly more complicated as they took account of subjective impressions of problem severity and improvement (CHAPTER IV, p. 49), but the extra complexity makes virtually no difference to the results shown in FIGURE 7.

The nature of good outcome at two years; abstinence or controlled drinking

TABLE 37 shows the complete drinking pattern data for the first anniversary to second anniversary interval for the twenty-six men whose two-year outcome was classified as 'good' according to the rules specified above.[1] In nine cases husband and wife were agreed that the whole year had been spent in total abstinence. In two further cases (cases 02 and 15) husband and wife were agreed that a single 'slip' occurred but that fifty-one weeks out of fifty-two were spent in total abstinence. These eleven men appear to have controlled their former excessive drinking by total, or virtually total, abstinence.[2] On the other hand there are eight men who had not totally abstained during the twelve-month interval but who stated that their drinking had never exceeded 200 grammes of alcohol on any single day (five of these stated that they never or rarely exceeded 100 grammes of alcohol on any day). Each of the wives of these eight men agreed that the husband had not totally abstained but stated that drinking had never been unacceptable to them. In two further cases (cases 30 and 78) the husband reported that all his drinking had been within the 100 grammes a day limit and the wife reported that drinking had been acceptable with the exception of a single week's unacceptable drinking. It appears that these ten men had controlled their former excessive drinking by continuing to drink but in a relatively controlled, acceptable, fashion.[3]

Of the ten controlled drinkers, six had, by their own and by their wives' accounts, drunk during each, or nearly each, of the fifty-two weeks between the first and second anniversaries. The number of days per week, for these six men, varied from approximately two days each week (two men) to every single day of every week (one man). The remaining four controlled drinkers reported varying frequencies of drinking during the year. In one case (case 78) there existed a large and unexplained disparity between husband and wife reports of drinking weeks.

In the remaining five cases disagreement between husband and wife on the details of drinking prevented clear categorization as abstainer or controlled drinker.

Month-by-month follow-up records for the first follow-up year were examined to see if controlled drinking during the second year was preceded by

---

[1] This number includes one husband whose outcome could not be classified at twelve months.

[2] In one of these cases, case 15, the single 'slip' did not involve heavy or 'unacceptable' drinking, but the man concerned, who was a regular AA attender, was dismayed at the occurrence which he hoped not to repeat. He is therefore more appropriately thought of, as he thought of himself, as an abstainer, than as a controlled drinker.

[3] In one further case (case 04), the data appear to suggest controlled drinking, but drinking reported by the husband was confined to the last two weeks of the year and clinical notes indicate a fairly rapid deterioration to uncontrolled drinking thereafter.

lengthy periods of abstinence during the first. The first year pattern for two of the ten second-year controlled drinkers was variable, involving periods of uncontrolled drinking, controlled drinking, and abstinence. The first year pattern was relatively clear cut, according to wives' account, for the remaining eight men. Six had drunk in an acceptable fashion from the very first month after initial consultation, one further man had abstained for a clear four-weeks period but had drunk acceptably from the second month onwards, and one had abstained throughout the first year.

THE PREDICTION OF ABSTINENCE VERSUS CONTROLLED DRINKING FROM INTAKE DATA

It then becomes a matter of great interest to see whether the division of cases into those with a good outcome based upon abstinence and those with a good outcome based upon controlled drinking was predictable at the time of initial consultation. Two variables, age and problem chronicity, which might have been expected to be predictive, were in fact not. Younger men, in their twenties or thirties, were roughly equally represented in the two favourable outcome groups, indeed there was a slight tendency in the direction opposite to that which might have been predicted, the median age for abstainers being just under forty and the median age for controlled drinkers being just over forty. Husbands' and wives' estimates of the chronicity of the husband's drinking problem were treated separately but in neither case was there any very obvious difference between abstainers and controlled drinkers. There were roughly equal numbers of men with problems of short duration (three years or less), and of those with problems of relatively long duration (ten years or more), within the two groups, and the median lay between five and ten years for both sets of informants' data for both groups.

TABLE 38 shows, however, a number of relationships which are statistically significant. It must, though, be heavily stressed that cell numbers at this point are very small and that biases may have been introduced by complete follow-up of only two-thirds of the original sample. Second-year controlled drinkers were more likely to obtain low scores on the 10-item trouble score (described in CHAPTER IV, p. 44). Abstainers at two years were also more likely, at intake, to have been diagnosed by the interviewing psychiatrist as suffering from 'loss of control' alcoholism of Gamma type (Jellinek, 1960), whilst second-year controlled drinkers were more likely to be diagnosed at intake as suffering from alcoholism of one of the other Jellinek types (of these, all but two abstainers and two controlled drinkers were of Alpha type). Trouble score and diagnostic type are not, of course, independent variables, as the diagnosis of Gamma alcoholism was largely based upon the presence of the type of symptom included in the trouble scale.

A number of questions were put to all husbands at their first consultation which were aimed to reveal the extent of their 'motivation' towards abstinence-oriented treatment. In general, men who became successful controlled drinkers were just as well 'motivated' as men who became abstainers, indeed slightly more of the latter gave replies at their first consultation which could have been interpreted as indicating 'denial'. For example, second-year controlled drinkers were just as likely to admit to having a serious drinking problem and were slightly less likely to deny having a drinking problem at all. Although they were a little less likely to give themselves the label 'alcoholic' with certainty, they were more likely to admit that they needed to change their drinking patterns radically (none of these relationships was significant however).[1]

One significant, and surprising, result (shown in TABLE 38) concerns the relationship between level of confidence about abstaining on the one hand, and second-year abstinence versus controlled drinking on the other hand. After being briefly counselled on the need for abstinence (those who were subsequently more intensively treated also received initial brief counselling), those who subsequently controlled their drinking were more likely to express a relatively high level of confidence about *abstaining* than were men who subsequently abstained.

DISCUSSION

Hunt and his colleagues (e.g. Hunt and Matarazzo, 1970) have commented on remarkably similar negatively accelerated relapse curves following treatment for alcoholism, smoking, and heroin addiction. They report, in each case, a rapid resumption of previous behaviour on the part of most of a treated group. Nearly all relapses occur, according to them, within the first three months following treatment after which time an asymptote is reached representing some 20/30 per cent of subjects who are able to make the change to abstinence.

Despite the fact that the period concerned was not a pure 'post-treatment' period, the relapse curves drawn from the present data are similar in shape to those presented by Hunt and support the general thesis that the majority of subjects consulting on account of some drug using behaviour relapse, and that they do so very quickly. Despite the fact that all men in this study were counselled to abstain totally from any further consumption of alcohol, the proportion who followed this advice to the letter had dropped to around 10 per cent after only four months, and although it remained at this level lor most of the first year, had dropped to around 2 per cent after two years and later dropped to zero. Unless wives' accounts are to be disbelieved, it appears that no single man in this sample was totally able to follow the advice upon which this, and most other, alcoholism treatment programmes are based.

[1] Combining abstainers and controlled drinkers, men who had a good two-year outcome were twice as likely to reject the label 'alcoholic' than to accept it at intake. This rate of rejection was higher than for the sample as a whole, so it would appear that, if anything, denial of alcoholism at intake was a favourable prognostic factor.

However, the plotting of a single relapse curve, as Hunt has done, ignores the complexity of appropriate definitions of 'relapse' at least in the context of treatment for excessive drinking. Not all subjects who 'relapse' on one occasion, continue to accumulate further occasions of uncontrolled drinking. At the end of two years there were still nearly 20 per cent of subjects who had not accumulated a total of ten days of drinking unacceptable to their wives, and the latter is probably a rather cautious definition of 'non-relapse'. Follow-up data are rarely presented in this form, but Vallance (1965) is one who has provided cumulative relapse data following alcoholism treatment and his results are remarkably similar. One year after psychiatric treatment for alcoholism around 90 per cent had drunk on at least one occasion, and by two years the figure was 96 per cent. However, using a more relaxed criterion, 19 per cent had remained abstinent for a continuous period of time of at least twelve months sometime during the two-year follow-up interval.

The present results suggest rapid relapse for the majority and relative stability thereafter; a good outcome at the end of the first year is strongly predictive of a good outcome at the end of the second year and the same is true for a bad outcome. These results confirm a variety of previous findings. Data provided by Davies et al. (1956) showed that of twenty men who abstained with at most a brief relapse or who drank lightly during the second year of follow-up after treatment, nineteen had had a similar pattern during the first year. Of fourteen who drank heavily with social incapacity or institutionalization during the second year, twelve had behaved in the same way during the first. There were very few changes of pattern from the first year to the second, and most of these concerned men placed in intermediate categories for the first year (heavy drinking without social incapacity). Similarly, Fox and Smith (1959) showed a high level of stability from the first to the second year of follow-up. The majority of changes again involved the intermediate first year category ('some progress'). Only 1 per cent of 231 subjects changed from 'good progress' at one year to 'little or no progress' at two years, and only 1 per cent changed in the reverse direction.

Amongst possible intake predictor variables, the degree of 'hardship' reported by the wife emerges as the clearest predictor of outcome both at one year and two years. Both Jackson and Kogan (1963) and Haberman (1965) found greater hardship associated with separation or divorce, and Jackson and Kogan found greater hardship associated with more attempts at outside help-seeking. Husbands' violence was particularly associated with divorce. The present findings therefore extend this line of research in demonstrating a connection between greater hardship and a relatively poor outcome as long as two years after first consultation and assessment.

ABSTINENCE AND CONTROLLED DRINKING AS ALTERNATIVE OUTCOMES

Not all drinking behaviour of still-drinking excessive drinkers is necessarily heavy or problematic. While a majority of men continued to drink, by no means all continued to drink in a 'totally uncontrolled' fashion. This confirms the first year follow-up findings (Orford, 1973 and CHAPTER IV, TABLE 7).

When individualized data are examined (as in TABLE 37) it emerges that a number of individual men were drinking in a virtually 'totally controlled' fashion in the second year. Some of these were almost regular weekly drinkers whilst others were more occasional drinkers. This finding just confirms many previous reports that a proportion of excessive drinkers, despite being counselled to abstain, opt for controlled drinking instead (e.g. Selzer and Holloway, 1957; Kendell, 1965). In addition Bailey and Stewart (1967) have reported 'normal drinking' by a proportion of former problem drinkers detected in the course of a community health survey. The future prognoses for controlled drinkers is, of course, as uncertain as it is for former excessive drinkers who are abstaining. In at least one case in the present series (case 98), daily drinking continued during the second year and the psychiatrist thought it likely that the man concerned, '. . . still had a very central relationship with drink', and could very well have further trouble in the future.

As a percentage of the original treatment sample of 100 men, second-year controlled drinkers represent 10 per cent. This figure is in keeping with the range of 5 to 15 per cent within which most reported figures lie. However, this figure probably represents an under-estimate as follow-up information was complete only for 65 of 100. Indeed, if the standard for complete information is relaxed to include cases where a follow-up report is available from one informant but not both (a total of nineteen further cases), five instances of apparent controlled drinking may be added (and no extra cases of total abstinence).

Despite the many reports of this nature, the results are often discounted. One of the arguments is that controlled drinking by former alcoholics is a 'rare phenomenon' and therefore of no clinical importance (e.g. Block, 1963). The evidence is fairly unequivocally contrary to that view. For one thing there are a number of reasons why controlled drinking as an outcome is not reported even more frequently than it is. Firstly, adequate follow-up for a period of at least two years appears to be the circumstance under which controlled drinking is most frequently found (Kendell, 1965) and these circumstances rarely prevail. In this follow-up the number of clearly 'totally controlled' drinkers at one year follow-up was only three, although information was complete on a larger number (eighty-nine) than at two years. More importantly, assumptions about the nature of alcoholism and its treatment frequently result in the use of outcome categories which simply do not allow for the detection of controlled drinking. Abstinence is considered a necessary, although not sufficient, condition for success and any continued drinking results in relegation to a less satisfactory category. For example, Fox and Smith (1959) required that a patient be 'sober' for inclusion in their 'good progress' category and 'resumed drinking' was evidence for placement in the lowest 'little or no progress' category. Even when researchers are alive to the possibility of more moderate drinking by former excessive drinkers they often do not allow for a distinction between 'total control' and 'partial control'. For example, in an early report, Wall and Allen (1944) reported that 19 of 100 ex-patients followed-up between four and ten years were gainfully employed and managing better despite continued drinking. However, the degree of control exercised by this group over their drinking at follow-up was not made clear and the assumption was that they 'continued to struggle' with their drinking problem. There are many other reports about which the same remarks could be made (e.g. Harper and Hickson, 1951; Davies *et al.*, 1956; Mayer and Myerson, 1970).

The strongest argument for rejecting the notion that controlled drinking by former excessive drinkers is a rare and unimportant finding, derives from a consideration of the *relative* frequencies of controlled drinking and abstinence as outcomes. It is rarely explicitly acknowledged that only a minority of treated or untreated uncontrolled drinkers are able to give up their uncontrolled behaviour totally within a period of a few years following treatment or detection. Controlled drinking may be relatively uncommon (to call it 'rare' is misleading) but so too is abstinence. In fact, in these data we found controlled drinking to be equally as likely as abstinence despite the abstinence orientation of the counselling and treatment to which all had been exposed. When previous reports are examined with an eye to the relative frequencies of these two possible outcomes, it is seen to be the case that controlled drinkers represent a substantial minority, and sometimes a majority, *of those who have successfully given up uncontrolled drinking*. For example, Selzer and Holloway (1957) reported that of eighty-three alcoholics followed-up for six years, eighteen had become abstinent and sixteen moderate drinkers. They remark that both showed 'definitely adequate post-hospital adjustment' and that both '. . . may be said to have abandoned their alcoholism'. DeMorsier and Feldman (1952, cited by Pattison *et al.*, 1965) reported that of 500 cases followed-up, 15 per cent were found to be 'social cures' and 31 per cent were 'abstinence cures'. Pattison *et al.* (1965) themselves reported that of thirty-two alcoholics who were discharged from hospital 'improved' and then followed up, eleven were found to be abstinent at follow-up and eleven drinking normally. Gerard and Saenger (1966) reported a one-year follow-up of alcoholics treated in eight geographically and socially disparate alcoholism out-patient clinics in North America. Overall, 12·5 per cent were found to have been successful abstainers for six months or longer during the follow-up year, whilst 5·1 per cent were found to have been successful controlled drinkers for an equivalent period. There was considerable variation between the clinics, however. At one extreme was a clinic with no controlled drinkers at follow-up and another with a ratio of controlled drinkers to abstainers of 1 to 12. At the other extreme was a clinic where controlled drinkers out-numbered abstainers at follow-up by 2 to 1. Goodwin *et al.* (1971) followed-up ninety-three men who had been diagnosed as alcoholics shortly before their release from prison eight years earlier. Thirty-eight were found to be 'in remission' with no problems associated with drinking within the two years prior to the follow-up interview. Of these thirty-eight, seven were total abstainers, seventeen were moderate drinkers (drinking at least once a month but rarely to intoxication) and fourteen were drinking with occasional intoxication but no consequent problems.

It would appear that the present results confirm several previous reports suggesting that controlled drinking amongst former alcoholics or excessive drinkers is far from being an uncommon phenomenon, but is rather one of the major alternative treatment outcomes. Nor does it appear to be the case that a period of several months or even years need necessarily intervene between uncontrolled drinking and later controlled drinking. The present finding that only one of the second-year controlled drinkers abstained throughout the first year confirms what is evident from some of the brief case descriptions provided by such authors as Selzer and Holloway (1957), Kendell (1965), and Bailey and Stewart (1967).

It has occurred to many previous writers that it would be of value to find some way of distinguishing, before the event, those likely to be able to abstain and those likely to be able to control their drinking (e.g. Reinert and Bowen, 1968), but most have reported no clear distinguishing features (e.g. Kendell, 1965; Pattison et al., 1965; Reinert and Bowen, 1968). For example, it seems reasonable to expect that younger people, or people who have had a drinking problem for a shorter time, might be more able to control their drinking, and indeed Gerard and Saenger (1966) found non-significant pointers in this direction. Reinert and Bowen (1968) also suggested that brevity of problem duration might be a predictor of future controlled drinking. Neither variable was predictive in the present investigation.

There were, however, a number of pointers which help towards developing a theory of the circumstances under which excessive drinkers will abstain or control their drinking. Firstly it was found that Gamma alcoholics, or those with a relatively high symptom or trouble score, were more likely to abstain subsequently. On the other hand, non-Gamma alcoholics, or those with relatively low symptom or trouble scores, were more likely to control their drinking in the second year. Although it has been shown that controlled drinking is possible even for people who have shown severe withdrawal symptomatology or alcoholic psychosis (Davies, 1962; Davies et al., 1969), it may none the less be the case that controlled drinking is relatively easier to achieve when these aspects of alcoholism have not been experienced, or have been experienced but less severely. Depending upon how alcoholism is defined, there could even be some truth in the charge that alcoholics who have returned to controlled drinking were not *real* alcoholics in the first place! The breadth of the WHO definition of alcoholism (1952) to include 'habitual symptomatic excessive drinkers' as well as 'alcohol addicts' has often been noted (e.g. Block, 1963; Esser, 1963).

Use of the Jellinek system for sub-classifying excessive drinkers is undoubtedly an operation of very imperfect reliability. Within the present series there were cases who had been previously diagnosed by a different psychiatrist; in some cases there was agreement, in others not. It is our impression that the distinction between the two largest sub-classes, namely Alpha ('psychological dependence' only) and Gamma ('physical dependence' with 'loss of control') can be made fairly reliably but that further distinctions are less reliable. The Alpha–Gamma distinction is clinically important. It is probably the case that a relatively unselected clinic population will contain some excessive drinkers with little or no recent experience of withdrawal symptoms and others with much experience of such symptoms of severe degree. We believe the former are likely to retain the greater degree of capacity to vary their drinking and to exercise some control. They are therefore more likely to be able to ameliorate or limit their drinking in the future, either spontaneously or with help. The matter is complicated by the existence of many borderline cases who show mild, temporary, or only very recent withdrawal symptomatology. Little note should probably be taken of the frequency with which the diagnostic category Gamma is used in any one research report, including the present one. What is involved is undoubtedly a dimension and cut-off points used in practice are almost certainly individual and arbitrary. The development of more objective, reliable, interview procedures for distinguishing sub-types is part of the Addiction Research Unit's current research programme.

CHAPTER VIII

IMPLICATIONS FOR TREATMENT AND RESEARCH

IMPLICATIONS FOR TREATMENT

LIMITATIONS BUT A GENERAL CONCLUSION

There are a number of limitations which it would be wrong to overlook when considering the relevance of the present findings for clinical work. Some of these limitations have already been discussed in relation to the methods of the clinical trial (pp. 51–4), and the conclusions which may be drawn from the trial aspect of the study (pp. 54–7). In particular it should again be stressed that the project concerned only married male alcoholics referred to a single clinic at a single hospital, and extrapolation to a population with very different characteristics treated differently by different personnel would be risky —quite different considerations might for instance operate with unmarried patients of low social stability living in such circumstances that they could not readily begin to use the proferred advice and initiate their own recovery.

The largest difficulty in deciding how the findings of this study are to be interpreted for clinical practice, is however the absence of a 'no treatment' control group. It is important to realize that the Advice offered in the course of the present investigation was particularly *individualized*, offered as *responsible* management and not as second best, and was offered in a spirit of hopeful *expectation* of a good outcome. Furthermore the out-patient setting, with only one family assessed on any one day, kept contact between members of the two treatment groups to a minimum. Hence Emrick's (1975) criticisms of some control groups (p. 19) probably do not apply with much force to the present Advice group. Advice was quite different from No Treatment or Waiting List control. Clinical applications have therefore to be discussed on the evidence of the equal efficacy of Treatment and Advice, but without available research information on what would be achieved with still lesser, or no, treatment intervention.

None the less what can fairly be concluded from the sum of the research literature, including these findings, is that the approach to alcoholism treatment should *in general* be less energetically interventionist than has been the fashion.

Some quotations from an, in many ways interesting, report by the King Edward Fund (James *et al.*, 1972), may illustrate the type of approach which has often over recent years been seen as the desirable level of therapeutic activity:

As soon as alcoholism is detected the patient should be persuaded to see a specialist and advised to enter hospital.

It is vital . . . for the patient to continue with regular A.A. contact.

. . . the tremendous importance of the help and support alcoholics receive from psychiatric social workers, district psychiatric nurses and voluntary agencies, and, perhaps more important than any of these, from the fellowship of A.A.

The manifold purposes of assessment can be listed as follows . . . to see whether he recognises he is extremely unlikely ever to be able to give up drinking unaided . . .

All patients on discharge are advised to attend weekly follow-up groups . . . for from one to two years, and at least one A.A. meeting weekly.

There is today hardly anything in the research literature to support the assumptions that have led to the recommendation of progressively more intensive treatment programmes, and the evolution of the type of programme which these quotations epitomize. On the contrary, what evidence is available largely points in the opposite direction—individual patients and their families should certainly be offered help which is personal to their needs, but the median intensity of intervention should be set very much lower than has become the fashion. This statement would of course have to be revised if future research is able to design more effective treatments than are at present available.

Neither can many of the stereotyped assumptions about the malign role of the spouse, which have fostered the enthusiasm for treating the patient's husband or wife, be seen as well supported by research. Taking again the King Edward's Hospital Fund report as providing an example of an enthusiastic approach to intervention:

Sometimes, the personality disturbance in the spouse is sufficiently great to warrant group treatment in his or her own right, away and above that which can be offered by Al-Anon. . . . Wives of alcoholics quite often have unusual personalities. Many of them have had alcoholic fathers or other key figures with the same problem. Most of them are aware when they marry that the husband has a drinking problem. They initially seem to enjoy trying to manage, mother, and control him.

The background literature on marriages complicated by alcoholism has been reviewed in CHAPTER II, and against that background such a statement as that quoted above can be seen to be based on a too simple reading of the evidence, and potentially to lead to treatment policies for the spouse which are not justified.

The proposals for a basic treatment strategy which are outlined below should therefore be read with all the stated limitations much in mind. The proposed strategy should be seen as based partly on a guarded interpretation of available research findings (the results of the present study and of other relevant work), but also inevitably on untested assumptions which fill in the gaps in the data. Only further research can determine the validity of the series of assumptions which underly this suggested approach. Perhaps the most important conclusion to be drawn from the present study is the folly of accepting any assumptions about alcoholism treatment unless they are rigorously tested, and that must apply as much to the proposals made here as to any other practices.

OUTLINE FOR A BASIC TREATMENT SCHEME: ASSESSMENT AND ONE-SESSION COUNSELLING

1. *Comprehensive assessment.* All patients referred for drinking problems should be comprehensively assessed. The reasons for believing that carefully detailed assessment is still necessary might be placed under three broad headings:

(*a*) *The need to establish a sufficient basis of information to help patients and their families formulate a plan.* Although the extent to which the traditional gathering of information bears on the practical business of decision-making deserves questioning and investigation, it is self evident that plans cannot be formulated without it being known what in the widest sense is the problem. The possible bearing of particular information on aspects of decision-making is made more explicit under later headings.

(*b*) *The need for the patient (and spouse) to engage in a broad review of the situation.* The contention made here is not at present supported by research, and certainly needs to be tested. What is being proposed is that the process of reviewing their own situation may be of therapeutic value to the person or family concerned. A variety of factors may be important—the patient's active engagement in making an inventory of the consequences of his drinking may present him with a picture in the round which he has not previously clearly perceived or cared to face, or he may find that the historical reconstruction of the evolution of his problems may give him a sense of the progressiveness of his condition which has not previously been so apparent. Most important may be the 'set' which the process engenders: the invitation to dispassionate scrutiny, the inference that what has happened is mostly explicable rather than just meaningless chaos, the inherent invitation to see the continuity of past and present and the meanings for the future, the invitation to place one's own behaviour in the context of the behaviour of spouse or others and in its wider social context—this may form an extremely important psychological preparation for active and profitable participation in a counselling session (Section (2) below). Indeed it may be these non-specific elements, which are common to many treatment approaches whatever the intensity of treatment, which are the effective ingredients, and not the specific and supposedly therapeutic elements (Frank, 1961).

(*c*) *The need for the advisory team to establish their credibility and hence their persuasiveness.* Again, what is put forward here is a conjecture which requires testing. However, it seems probable that the perceptions of patient (and spouse) of the status of the advisory team, and their credibility as informants, will be influenced by the belief that these staff are not only generally competent but also very specifically knowledgeable about the life situations of the people engaging in this particular consultation. The ability of the team to display psychological qualities such as warmth and empathy in the relationship engendered during the history taking, might also influence the subsequent persuasiveness of what they say.

2. *A single, detailed counselling session for the patient and, when the patient is married, the spouse.* This might be seen as the basic treatment, replacing currently popular approaches such as routine in-patient admission with subsequent intensive aftercare for the majority of patients, or the present alternative of intensive out-patient care. As has already been stressed, this formulation of a new and much less active general basic treatment policy in no way contradicts the notion that each person requires an individually formulated approach, and there will be circumstances in which clinical judgement leads to the conclusion that more (or very much more) than the basic intervention is needed (see Section (4) below).

What must be resisted however is any tendency to assume that the new formulation is no different from the old, and that for patients who do not immediately respond to counselling there should then routinely be offered treatments of rapidly escalating intensity. This would deny the whole weight of the available research evidence, which suggests that more intensive care is not usually followed by better treatment results.

A number of elements might contribute to such a counselling session:

(*a*) Discussion between patient (and spouse) and staff, with definition of a set of goals which are seen by the people being counselled as logically relating to the perception of their problems which derives from assessment and discussion. Consideration will usually have to be given to:

(i) *Drinking.* Much more information is needed on the matter of drinking goals, but in the meantime the individual drinking plan should be sensitively worked out with each patient and family. Where the patient is showing signs of severe dependence in terms of repeated experience of severe withdrawal symptoms, and is repeatedly relieving withdrawal by further drinking—in other words is showing what Edwards and Gross (1976), have called the alcohol dependence syndrome—many counsellors may well, in the present state of knowledge, prefer to negotiate an abstinence goal. It should be realized that all patients in the Addiction Research Unit study were counselled to abstain, and the results cannot speak confidently to what would have been achieved if controlled drinking had been advised or encouraged, but nevertheless the finding should be noted that patients diagnosed as 'gamma alcoholics' were prospectively less likely than the remainder to have established control over their drinking at twenty-four months (p. 100 and Orford *et al.*, 1976b). The best guide at present may be the close examination with the patient of his ability in the previous year or two to achieve sustained control over his drinking—if such a pattern is to be found within his repertoire it may be reasonable to try to reinforce the circumstances and personal stratagems which make control possible.

The common basis for the treatment contract must then be the therapist giving what advice he honestly believes to be the most responsible, with the patient testing the worth of that advice and resetting drinking goals in the light of continuing experience. The old absolutism and the demand that the patient blindly and unquestioningly accepts the abstinence demand is not a reasonable basis for a treatment which seeks to maximize the patient's self-responsibility.

(ii) *Marriage*. Counselling should emphasize that the behaviour of the marriage partners is interactive, and that it is within their power to aid each other constructively. It should be admitted that the question of how to translate the various findings on marital interaction which come from the present study into immediate application for the counselling of a particular family, is at present very much a matter of guesswork. In general terms, anything which produces a commitment to work toward what, in common sense as well as technical language, may be called greater *marital cohesion*, would seem to be beneficial. A practical pointer from the research might also be the suggestion that if the spouse can employ a coping style which is other than retreatist, the outlook may possibly be improved. Consideration of family role performance provides opportunity for immediate setting of small attainable goals. Quite clearly, within the limits of the sort of brief counselling envisaged none of these aspects of marriage is going to be explored in very great depth, and the marital discussion is not seen as being allowed to escalate into intensive or prolonged marital therapy.

(iii) *Other goals*. The need to set goals for work, leisure, finances, and housing should probably also be discussed.

(b) Counselling should emphasize both the self-responsibility of the patient for working out how goals should be met and, as already discussed, the shared engagement of the spouse. The manner in which such advice is given should reinforce a sense of autonomy and self-direction, rather than its being seen as rejecting or uncaring. As the message may be surprising for those who have come with the expectation of more intensive formal help, its rationale should be discussed and explained, rather than its being given only in terms of an abrupt announcement.

Much support for this approach comes from recent trends in behaviour modification which emphasize personal problem-solving and decision-making (e.g. D'Zurilla and Goldfried, 1971) and self-control (e.g. Premack and Anglin, 1973). Assessment and a single session of counselling may promote these processes by virtue of content, but more particularly because it is made unambiguously clear to all concerned that these are the relevant processes rather than anything resembling the 'treatments' of physical medicine.

It is possible that the counselling will be additionally useful if, before its closure, patient (and spouse) make open and very definite commitment to working towards the agreed goals. The view is widely held, if not fully validated by research, that statements of intention made publicly are more likely to be followed by satisfactory execution of those intentions than if resolutions are made privately (e.g. Kanfer and Karoly, 1972).

3. *Some follow-up system to check on progress.* Reference has already been made to the possible therapeutic influence on the Advice group of the monthly information gathering from wives. Apart from the research value of some sort of routine monitoring, it is certainly possible that the evidence of a clinic's continued friendly interest, even if in no way interventionist, may enhance the determination of patient (and spouse) to work towards the committed goals. The monitoring also reassures the staff that some sort of safety net is operating for patients who may well develop further serious or life threatening problems. It should though be noted that in the present study it was only thought necessary to remove two Advice patients from the experiment. The exact manner in which progress should be checked would be open to experiment, and would obviously depend on whether or not patients were married. An invitation to write or telephone might substitute for hospital visits or home calls. What has to be guarded against is the possibility of such a checking system again accidentally escalating into a system which reinstates the old notion of active community care.

4. *Common reasons for going beyond the basic approach.* What has been outlined in the three preceding numbered sections is a basic framework for treatment. However this research showed, as have many previous reports, the heterogeneity of a patient population referred for reasons of drinking. To take as examples only two relevant dimensions, present results revealed wide variation in drink-related variables (level of drinking, adverse consequences of drinking, degree of dependence), and also in marital interactions. If the potential range is then seen as extending from the homeless skid-row population to alcoholics seen in private practice, or from patients with an early drinking problem to those who may be referred from a general hospital with advanced liver disease, the absurdity becomes very apparent of any attempt to design treatment in terms of one rigid formula for all patients. There must therefore still be an element of clinical judgement in deciding, after due assessment, on the immediate programme for helping the particular patient. The existing research literature cannot possibly be interpreted as giving such confident pointers to the individual case as to propose eliminating clinical judgement altogether.

It is not necessary here to enter into any extended discussion of the likely exceptions to the basic formulation, for this would lead to speculative consideration of a great range of familiar clinical judgements. However a few common circumstances where it may be appropriate to go beyond the basic counselling approach may be listed:

(i) Brief admission for detoxification may sometimes be indicated, especially when there is a previous history of delirium tremens or withdrawal fits and the patient is again heavily dependent, when there is concomitant sedative misuse, or where there is very poor social support.

(ii) Underlying or concomitant psychological illness or distress may require special treatment, possibly as an inpatient. Depressive illness, and phobic disorder may provide important examples.

(iii) Similarly, physical illness may require referral or admission.

(iv) Immediate admission may be indicated for any life threatening situation, or where there is acute danger to the family.

(v) For the homeless alcoholic, hostel care and a range of social provisions may be necessary.

The Way Ahead

The significance must be faced of proposing a basic treatment which is much at variance with what is today considered in many parts of the world to be the best practice. Resistance to the ideas which have been developed here might have a number of origins. The first and most important criticism might be that the formulation builds on a very insubstantial research foundation. Such an objection certainly deserves examination in terms of specific detailed points, and it has already been conceded that much of what is being put forward is conjecture which has to be tested. We are however standing on fairly firm ground in suggesting that the present formulation is more generally in accord with the broad message which comes from research, than is the case with the energetic approaches which have entrenched acceptance.

A further important source of resistance may be the humane fear that what is being proposed, with many caveats, may be misread and the caveats forgotten. In particular there may be a fear that the arguments will be used destructively to attack the work of many devoted individuals and organizations (including AA), which have striven to make society's response to the alcoholic more compassionate. Such need not be the case, and it would be grossly improper reading of what is being said in this book to extract from it the message that the alcoholic is undeserving of help. The only question is how best to design that help. It could be considerably more humane, and cost-effective, to redeploy present services so as to offer much less intensive help to many more people.

Yet another reason for questioning the proposals which are being made here is that staff pursuing existing policies are happy and confident in the intensive treatments they offer, and will plead that their daily experience shows the worth of what they are doing. That there is now in many countries a sizable and in some instances (such as America) an enormous investment in an attempt to provide care in terms of intensive models, is not to be doubted. It would certainly be reasonable to expect those responsible for such programmes to question the evidence closely before accepting the necessity for a change in direction. Of course what is being proposed here is not an overthrow or negation of all the established effort, the compassion which it witnesses, and the community support which it has won. What is proposed is only that, in terms of what should be seen as a process of evolution rather than a static treatment model, there is now need for further evolution. And what is now put forward should itself be only a passing phase in yet further development, as more is learnt about the helping processes.

IMPLICATIONS FOR ORGANIZATION OF TREATMENT SERVICES

The evolution of services in this country for the treatment of alcoholism has been reviewed in CHAPTER I, but the immediate focus of the research reported in this book is simply treatment of the individual family where drinking has presented as a problem. It would indeed be going too far beyond the proper remit of the present study to enter here into an extended discussion of the wider question of comprehensive service planning, or the details of manpower requirements and costing. Without taking discussion too far in that direction, it does though seem useful to consider briefly some of the more immediate organizational implications which might result from the rather different basic treatment model proposed earlier in this chapter.

Firstly, the implication of proposals for basic individual treatment would entail a considerable lessening in the occupancy of specialized in-patient places by patients receiving prolonged group therapy. These centres would therefore have the opportunity to explore other functions, including the usefulness of brief detoxification, or admissions for any of the reasons briefly listed on pp. 112–13. Indeed it will become an open question whether the specialism of in-patient units needs to be retained at all.

The type of basic approach envisaged might be managed by a team drawing from a variety of professions such as clinical psychology, nursing, occupational therapy, general practice, psychiatry, and social work. Whether such a group has to be considered a whole-time specialist team devoting its energies only to alcoholism, may depend on local options. The skills required do not necessarily propose a high degree of specialism, and the rather over-specialized view, which has for instance been taken of alcoholism and marriage (see CHAPTER II), might suggest that there would be some benefit in bringing into alcoholism work more people who were able to take a less specialized view of the processes involved. If the basic service pattern were seen as involving assessment, one-session counselling, and rather loose supervision, rather than specialized in-patient care and intensive follow-up, there would certainly be a much better chance of organizing the specialized element in the services on a scale which met the potential community need, and without long waiting lists.

So little is known about what constitute effective elements in the therapeutic interventions practised by the supposedly specialized services, that it is certainly not at all easy to discover a basis on which the specialists are to become teachers of the non-specialist. It might be supposed that the roles of, say, the family practitioner, the borough's social worker, and the probation officer attached to the local Court, will usefully include early case detection, the ability to give sensible advice, and a role in the monitoring of progress. Perhaps the expectation will now have to be reversed that it is the function of such agencies to refer alcoholics to specialists, who will then take these patients off their hands. It is exactly into this area of investigating the role of community agencies and the relationship with hospital services, that the work of the Maudsley Alcohol Pilot Project (Cartwright et al., 1975) has more lately extended. Furthermore, the role of non-professional volunteer counsellors whether they be alcohol specialists or not, is one that will certainly be explored more fully in the future.

IMPLICATIONS FOR THE BALANCE OF NATIONAL STRATEGIES

In the first chapter of this book, a brief account was given of the recent historical development of the nation's response to drinking problems. A trend was identified toward a dominant official emphasis on a response conceived in terms of treatment and rehabilitation of the *individual*. The DHSS has heavily invested cash and manpower over the last two decades in the expansion of NHS alcoholism treatment services, and there now promises to be a drive toward establishment of detoxification centres, and the provision of an increasing number of hostel places for the homeless alcoholic. The DHSS has produced a 'long term strategic document' (DHSS, 1975) which gives careful thought to the future design of health care for the individual alcoholic.

In contrast, it is impossible to discover evidence of anything which could be described as an official strategy for prevention. The single paragraph devoted to that topic in the recent DHSS strategy document is remarkably lacking in content. Recent efforts by the Health Education Council though commendable, certainly do nothing to substitute for sustained preventive endeavour. Significantly, a large part of the Health Education Council's effort seems to have been directed toward secondary prevention, and getting more people into treatment.

If the research evidence given in this book is taken as requiring a revision of present common appraisal of the efficacy of current alcoholism treatments, by implication there should be a re-examination of the balance of national strategies on alcohol. The invitation is certainly not toward a new imbalance—no suggestion is being made here that treatment strategies should be relegated to the sort of limbo which prevention has suffered for the last sixty years. The plea is wholly that thought should be given to design of a balanced and total strategy rather than any one element being irrationally advanced.

The treatment dominance in Britain's recent national strategy toward alcohol problems must though now be seen as an absurdly dysfunctional imbalance in response to a range of behaviours which often cannot properly be conceived as illnesses or conditions residing within the individual, behaviours which are not necessarily susceptible to medical or social work intervention or which may respond to much less costly interventions than have usually been employed, and behaviours for which moreover the individual may be entirely resistant to the notion that he should seek professional help. Why this imbalance should ever have come about cannot be analysed here at length but a provisional guess might be that there exists here a particular example of the general tendency of society conveniently to hand over awkward problems to psychiatry for *personal* solutions, rather than persevering with the quest for *social* solutions. The personal solutions can be based on the assumption that there is a delimited class of ill or deviant people, and the solutions need not affect the rest of us. The social and preventive solutions which less comfortingly conceive of 'the problem' as graded, various, and widely disseminated rather than as the 'illness' of the few, may in contrast impinge on all our lives. The Temperance campaigner epitomized that latter approach, and hence his inevitable unpopularity and the eclipse of an at one time very powerful expression of preventive endeavour, which has not since found other expression.

The argument that a new balance should be found between treatment and prevention strategies would of course be empty, if there were no effective technology available for prevention. In fact, there is persuasive evidence that pricing of alcohol and in some circumstances licensing, may influence alcohol-related problems (Bruun *et al.*, 1975). This knowledge is however at present in no way assimilated into the design of the British government response to alcohol problems—and the indicated social and preventive responses would very evidently make less comfortable demands on society that the formula which proposes only that we 'treat alcoholism', or run the occasional campaign to persuade more people to come forward for treatment.

Thus the argument developed here is essentially that a balanced and total strategy needs to be designed rather than our continuing with a lop-sided approach to alcohol problems which is witness to historical accident and society's self-comfort, rather than to present understanding of the nature of the problems on the respective powers and limitations of available therapeutic and preventive technologies.

IMPLICATIONS FOR RESEARCH

Rather than elaborating an extensive list of all possible investigations which could lead from this study, it may be more useful to identify simply the *broad research direction* which seem to be evolving. The discussion which follows therefore considers general themes and largely avoids great detail.

ALCOHOLISM TREATMENT RESEARCH

By far the greater weight of evidence suggests that the active ingredients of existing therapeutic approaches to alcoholism are those that are common to nearly all these approaches. These non-specific factors include the reinforcing of motivation for change, the clarifying of behavioural options, and the enhancing of self-determination and adaptive problem-solving. Almost all effort has been devoted to the design and testing of specific elements of therapeutic approaches which have later turned out to have no special effectiveness. Non-specific factors have been relatively ignored and it is in this direction that alcoholism treatment should move.

Of course, the possibility cannot be ruled out that future research will reveal specially successful specific forms of therapeutic approach. What seems almost certain, however, is that such research should design and test radically new approaches rather than minor modifications of existing treatment. Alcoholism treatment research now badly needs an injection of inventiveness and daring. Some new approaches might operate within the prevailing 'referral' and 'treatment' of 'cases' model of intervention, whilst others should begin to explore variations in the manner of recruiting or selecting subjects and should experiment with forms of intervention which best fit other models (e.g. education, preventive medicine), than the prevailing medical treatment model.

The movement which currently offers greatest hope of an overall improvement in success rates concerns *treatment goals* rather than specific methods. However, opinions differ on the subject of the possibility of alcoholics resuming some form of controlled drinking. Some see the acceptance of this possibility as nothing less than a liberation of clinical practice, whilst others see it as dangerous and irresponsible. The careful collecting of the facts on this matter is now badly needed. There is a variety of research questions here. We require to know who, with what size and sort of drinking problem, can resume what kind of drinking, after what interval of time, and by what means? It is of course important to bear in mind that a change in drinking habits is not the only, nor necessarily always the most important, criterion of outcome following intervention, even when consideration is confined to the individual drinker. When consideration is expanded to include the spouse, and further to include children, then there is clearly room for study of goals for intervention which may leave drinking habits untouched and yet in other important ways be successful.

Data from the present study, and from others, show that some degree of 'relapse' into uncontrolled drinking is the rule rather than the exception following treatment or advice. Further knowledge is needed about the precipitants, the forms and consequences of relapse, and study should be made of factors which prevent relapse or lessen its consequences. Indeed much treatment research effort might be redirected towards the anticipation of further episodes of uncontrolled drinking and finding the means of shortening the duration, or reducing the effects, of such episodes.

Whatever the content of alcoholism treatment research, there is a need for the use of a wider variety of research designs. The type of controlled trial employed in this study is a lengthy and costly enterprise. Indeed, an N of more than 100, although highly desirable, is rarely attained in this sort of research. Furthermore the controlled trial design is rarely feasible in most clinical settings, and is not without the sorts of problems of interpretation which have been discussed here (pp. 51–4). There should be much wider knowledge, and use made, of the various quasi-experimental designs which are available (Campbell and Stanley, 1963; Riecken and Boruch, 1974, Chapter IV), and individual case research methods (Leitenberg, 1973).

FAMILY AND OTHER NATURAL INFLUENCES

The influences, whether non-specific or specific, which go under the heading of 'treatment' do not impinge on an individual who is isolated from all other influence. On the contrary, treatment or advice should be seen as elements added to, and inter-reacting with, a continuously evolving field of what might be termed *natural influences*. It seems likely that treatment may often be quite puny in its powers in comparison to the sum of these background forces. Further understanding of natural influences on drinking behaviours might none the less allow the planning of strategies which exploited natural forces. Therapy may not in itself be a particularly powerful force, but if we understand the natural balance of forces, the balance could be favourably tipped.

A hint of the potential importance of extra-treatment factors comes from the frequent mention made of change in the environment as helpful influence, both by the Advice and Treatment groups (TABLE 15). Much more precise analysis needs to be made of these influences, both conceptually and in field studies. A further hint of the importance of this general line of investigation comes from the demonstrated relationship in this study between socio-economic status and outcome (p. 75): The challenge is to analyse the precise nature of the influences which lie behind the relationship between factors which are broadly subsumed in the idea of status or class, and the individual's chances of recovery.

Of course, to describe influences as 'natural' begs many questions which ought to be further pursued. For instance, an improvement in housing might be a life-event of an arbitrary and almost accidental nature—a name unexpectedly comes up on a housing list after a ten-year wait. Alternatively, finding a better house might be a direct consequence of a person's energetic and purposeful striving. And thirdly, the new house might have been found not by the householder but by a social worker. Without taking this example further it must be obvious that 'natural influence' is simply a convenient but very broad term which puts together a wide variety of complex influences which can occur outside of, or in the absence of, 'treatment'.

This line of study should obviously draw upon previous research in alcoholism and other fields which focuses upon stress, *life events* and psychological disorder (e.g. Brown *et al.*, 1975; Hore, 1971). The concepts of natural history and the alcoholic's career (Edwards, 1975) may also potentially bear on issues of natural influence.

Of paramount importance for future research on natural influence are all the influences of marriage and the family, some of which have been a major focus of the present study. The present finding, linking marital cohesion and favourable outcome, requires replication, and if confirmed calls for more detailed process studies to try and throw light upon the intervening causal process. There is a need to complement the present study with investigations of family processes and outcome where it is the wife/mother who is the identified problem drinker. The general hypothesis put forward here (p. 74) linking a breakdown in family cohesion and a poor outcome following treatment or consultation for any psychological disorder, should be tested using samples of people with diagnoses other than alcoholism or schizophrenia. Other researchers have recently reported work using a sample for whom depression is the diagnosis (Vaughn and Leff, 1976). A sample of men or women complaining principally of anxiety or obsessional-compulsive symptoms might provide a further test of this hypothesis.

As has already been stated in CHAPTER II, theories of alcoholism and the family should be more sophisticated than hitherto, and in particular should acknowledge that the family is an interpersonal network or social 'system' (Steinglass et al., 1971). In the meantime there is need for better and fuller descriptive information on the stresses to which family members living with a drinking problem are exposed, and the ways in which they react or attempt to cope. In particular we require much better research than has been carried out to date on children of alcoholic parents.

Study of the disturbances suffered by the children in such families, and the remission in their disturbance when drinking behaviour of a parent ameliorates, might provide a useful opportunity for exploring general questions related to the influence of parental disturbance on children. Very long term follow-up might give critical information on factors related to the processes of non-genetic transmission of problem behaviour.

DEGREE OF DEPENDENCE AND OTHER INDIVIDUAL DIFFERENCES

Amongst extra-treatment factors which may operate independently of treatment factors, or may interact with them, are a number which may be understood as sources of individual difference residing within the alcoholic drinker him/herself. Still too little is known about the meanings, or functional significance, of alcohol for the individual. Two potentially important leads emerged from this study. Firstly, the clear ideas which husbands and wives held collectively about the impact of drinking upon the drinker's affectionate and dominant behaviours (FIGURE 5). Secondly, findings emerged which suggested that the individual's degree of dependence on alcohol, a variable relatively neglected in recent research and thinking on the subject, affected the desire or the capacity to resume controlled drinking, at least under the conditions of this trial. Research on this topic could lead to valuable knowledge concerning the type of goal to be recommended for different drinkers.

Study of 'the alcoholic personality' has over recent years become rather unrewarding. The idea that patients with drinking problems have a stereotyped personality defect is now seen as much too simple. In the present study only a very small selection of personality attributes were measured, but there was sufficient indication of a number of research leads which might profitably be followed. For instance, the reduction in N (neuroticism) score over the twelve months following intake for men with a good outcome (TABLE 34) emphasizes the need for long-term study of the stability of supposed personality traits: without such information it is hazardous to form conclusions about what is cause, and what is consequence, of drinking. The non-significant rise in their wives' N scores, and the high intake level of wives' L (lie) scores raise many questions also.

A FINAL CONCLUSION

It is worth repeating, finally, a plea that has been made at various points in this book—namely that alcohol and alcoholism studies should not be allowed to become too great a specialism, isolated from the study of other aspects of psychosocial disorder, or indeed from the general scientific study of behaviour. There are obvious parallels between excessive drinking or alcoholism and their traditional bed-fellow, drug addiction. There are however equally obvious parallels with other forms of excessive behaviour, such as excessive gambling and over-eating, as well as with most other forms of disorder or deviance which are a source of distress for the individual or for others. There are shared questions of family and marital interaction, of treatment response and treatment organization, and indeed of definition—*what is alcoholism*, what *is* neurosis, what *is* schizophrenia? Making a specialty of alcoholism can have the effect of cutting its students adrift from developments, often more advanced, in related fields. Isolation also carries with it increased danger of too unchallenged an investment of the therapist in his own activities, too confident pronouncements on treatment effectiveness, and too great a ritualization of therapeutic methods.

TABLES

TABLE 1

ADMISSIONS TO MENTAL ILLNESS HOSPITALS AND UNITS UNDER REGIONAL HOSPITAL BOARDS AND TEACHING HOSPITALS IN ENGLAND OR WALES, WHERE PRIMARY OR SECONDARY DIAGNOSIS WAS ALCOHOLISM OR ALCOHOLIC PSYCHOSIS, 1949–74

| YEAR | PRIMARY DIAGNOSIS | | | SECONDARY DIAGNOSIS | TOTAL ADMISSIONS |
	Alcoholic Psychosis	Alcoholism	Total	Alcoholism Only	(Primary or Secondary Diagnosis)
1949	214	225	439		
1950					
1951	195	326	512		
1952	204	464	668		
1953	233	542	775		
1954	253	546	799		
1955	393	660	1,053		
1956	551	834	1,385		
1957	531	1,004	1,535		
1958	478	1,117	1,595		
1959	532	1,512	2,044		
1960	609	1,870	2,479		
1961					
1962					
1963					
1964	448	4,975	5,423	1,160	6,583
1965	457	5,317	5,774	1,102	6,876
1966	461	5,627	6,088	1,268	7,356
1967	396	5,836	6,232	1,409	7,641
1968	353	6,038	6,391	1,425	7,816
1969	360	6,329	6,689	1,376	8,065
1970	917	7,174	8,091	617	8,708
1971	1,353	7,877	9,230	671	9,901
1972	1,514	8,653	10,167	683	10,850
1973	1,714	9,851	11,565	693	12,258
1974	1,750	10,745	12,495	689	13,184

Source: DHSS (personal communication). Since 1970 'depressives not otherwise stated' have been shown in the figures for primary diagnosis, whereas previously they were included in the secondary diagnosis figures. This means that when divided into primary and secondary diagnosis the pre-1970 figures are not comparable with post-1970 figures. The totals are of course comparable.

TABLE 2
OFFENCES FOR DRUNKENNESS PROVED IN ENGLAND AND WALES 1950–74

YEAR	NUMBERS OF OFFENCES	NUMBER PER 10,000 POPULATION AGED 15 YEARS AND OVER (1950–68) OR 14 YEARS AND OVER (1970 FORWARD)
1950	47,717	14·0
1951	53,676	15·8
1952	53,888	15·8
1953	53,574	15·7
1954	53,277	15·5
1955	54,210	15·8
1956	60,182	17·4
1957	67,002	19·3
1958	65,058	18·7
1959	65,187	18·6
1960	68,109	19·3
1961	74,694	21·0
1962	83,992	23·3
1963	83,007	22·8
1964	76,842	21·0
1965	72,980	19·8
1966	70,499	19·0
1967	75,544	20·3
1968	79,070	21·2
1969	80,502	21·2
1970	82,374	21·6
1971	86,735	22·9
1972	90,198	23·7
1973	99,274	25·9
1974	103,203	26·8

Source: Annual Home Office Reports (Offences for Drunkenness, HMSO).

TABLE 3
CIRRHOSIS DEATHS RECORDED AS ALCOHOLIC OR OTHER CAUSE, ENGLAND AND WALES

YEAR	TOTAL DEATHS DUE TO CIRRHOSIS	DEATH RATES PER MILLION ALL PERSONS
1950	1,016	23
1951	1,117	25
1952	1,124	26
1953	1,155	26
1954	1,168	26
1955	1,159	26
1956	1,153	26
1957	1,206	27
1958	1,146	26
1959	1,203	27
1960	1,272	28
1961	1,370	30
1962	1,302	28
1963	1,325	28
1964	1,309	28
1965	1,384	29
1966	1,366	29
1967	1,350	28
1968	1,462	30
1969	1,578	32
1970	1,387	28
1971	1,570	32
1972	1,662	34
1973	1,804	37
1974	1,754	36

Source: Registrar General's Annual Statistical Reviews (London: HMSO).

TABLE 4

UNITED KINGDOM HOME CONSUMPTION OF ALCOHOLIC
BEVERAGES 1950–74

YEAR	BEER Million Bulk Barrels	SPIRITS Million Proof Gallons	WINE (BRITISH AND IMPORTED) Million Gallons	ANNUAL PER CAPITA CONSUMPTION Persons aged 15 years and over Litres of absolute alcohol
1950	26	10	13	5·2
1951	26	10	15	5·3
1952	26	10	14	5·3
1953	25	10	15	5·1
1954	25	11	17	5·2
1955	25	12	18	5·3
1956	25	12	19	5·3
1957	25	13	20	5·3
1958	25	13	20	5·3
1959	26	14	23	5·6
1960	27	15	27	5·8
1961	29	16	28	6·2
1962	29	16	30	6·1
1963	29	17	33	6·2
1964	30	18	37	6·5
1965	30	18	36	6·5
1966	30	18	38	6·5
1967	31	18	42	6·7
1968	31	19	46	7·0
1969	33	18	45	7·0
1970	34	20	46	7·3
1971	35	21	54	7·7
1972	35	24	62	7·7
1973	37	30	78	7·9
1974	39	33	83	8·9

Source: HM Customs and Excise Annual Reports (London: HMSO) for data in first three columns. The *per capita* consumption (fourth column) is based on the assumption that beer on average contains 4 per cent alcohol, spirits 39·9 per cent alcohol, and wine 16 per cent: these figures can only be approximate. The relevant population base for each year was gained from the series Annual Abstract of Statistics (London: HMSO), and between Censuses involves projections.

TABLE 5

MATCHING OF INTAKE SAMPLES ON DEMOGRAPHIC
AND SOCIAL CHARACTERISTICS

	GROUPS ADVICE n = 50	TREATMENT n = 50
Present age: mean years	40·9 ± 1·3	40·9 ± 1·3
Best ever Occupational Status: % I–IV	44	46
% V–VII	56	54
Duration of present marriage: mean years	12·1 ± 1·2	13·7 ± 1·1
Time at present address: mean years	3·0 ± 0·2	3·0 ± 0·2
Number of jobs last 36 months: mean number	2·4 ± 1·6	2·6 ± 1·7
Time off work previous 12 months: mean weeks	12·4 ± 2·1	16·2 ± 2·4

All data based on husband's report. No significant differences between groups.

TABLE 6

MATCHING OF INTAKE SAMPLES ON DRINK RELATED VARIABLES

INFORMANT	GROUPS	
	ADVICE n = 50	TREATMENT n = 50
H. Age first experienced damage: mean years	28·1 ± 1·3	28·7 ± 1·3
H. Age first realized problem: mean years	30·7 ± 1·3	31·3 ± 1·9
H. Previous IP treatment for alcoholism ever:		
% NO	78	68
% YES	22	32
H. Weeks heavy drinking in previous 12 months: mean weeks	24·9 ± 2·5	22·8 ± 2·6
W. As above	32·7 ± 2·5	31·2 ± 2·3
H. Longest abstinence previous 12 months:		
% −1 month	74	76
1–2 months	18	16
>2 months	8	8
W. As above % −1 month	64	70
1–2 months	20	20
>2 months	10	10
N.K.	6	0
H. 'Trouble score' for previous 12 months: mean score	5·2 ± 0·4	5·1 ± 0·4
W. 'Hardship score' for previous 12 months: mean score	5·4 ± 0·4	6·0 ± 0·4

Data based on husband's (H) or wife's (W) report as indicated in left hand column. See text for item definitions. No significant differences between groups.

TABLE 7

OUTCOME: HUSBAND'S DRINKING BEHAVIOUR DURING 12 MONTHS TO INTAKE ANNIVERSARY AS REPORTED BY H (HUSBAND) OR W (WIFE)

INFORMANT	GROUPS	
	ADVICE n = 46	TREATMENT n = 48
H. Longest period of continuous abstinence during previous 52 weeks: mean weeks	15·3 ± 2·6	15·3 ± 2·3
W. Longest period of continuous abstinence during previous 52 weeks: mean weeks	14·6 ± 2·5	15·9 ± 2·4
H. 10+ pints beer (or equivalent) on any day of the given week: mean number of such weeks during previous 52 weeks	14·7 ± 2·8	12·7 ± 2·2
H. 5–10 pints beer ...... mean weeks	7·7 ± 2·2	6·3 ± 1·4
H. −5 pints beer ...... mean weeks	8·4 ± 2·3	10·2 ± 2·3
H. Totally abstinent ...... mean weeks	21·2 ± 2·9	23·1 ± 2·5
W. Drinking 'unacceptable' on any day of given week: mean number of such weeks during previous 52 weeks	20·7 ± 2·6	22·9 ± 2·6
W. Drinking 'acceptable' ...... mean weeks	11·2 ± 2·3	8·3 ± 2·0
W. Totally abstinent ...... mean weeks	20·0 ± 2·9	20·6 ± 2·6
H. Mean 'Trouble Score', previous 12 months	3·2 ± 0·4	3·1 ± 0·4
W. Mean 'Hardship Score', 4 weeks prior to anniversary	2·8 ± 0·4	3·0 ± 0·4

Rounding errors account for the sum of reported categories not totalling 52 weeks in each instance. No significant differences between groups.

TABLE 8

OUTCOME: HUSBAND'S REPORT OF HUSBAND'S DRINKING
BEHAVIOUR DURING 12 MONTHS TO INTAKE ANNIVERSARY,
CORRECTED TO A NOTIONAL YEAR SO AS TO CONTROL
OUT BETWEEN-GROUP DIFFERENCES IN DURATION
OF HOSPITALIZATION

| INFORMANT | GROUPS | |
	ADVICE n = 44	TREATMENT n = 48
10+ pints beer (or equivalent) on any day of the given week: mean number of *corrected* weeks during previous 52 weeks	15·5 ± 3·2	13·9 ± 2·5
10–5 pints beer . . . . . . mean weeks	8·6 ± 2·3	7·0 ± 1·4
Sum: 5+ pints beer . . . . . . mean weeks	24·1 ± 3·3	20·9 ± 2·6
−5 pints beer . . . . . . mean weeks	8·5 ± 2·4	10·9 ± 2·3
Totally abstinent . . . . . . mean weeks	19·0 ± 3·0	20·4 ± 2·7

No significant differences between groups.

TABLE 9

OUTCOME: SUBJECTIVE RATINGS OF HUSBAND'S DRINKING
PROBLEM AT 12 MONTHS ANNIVERSARY OF INTAKE,
AS REPORTED BY H (HUSBAND) OR W (WIFE)

| INFORMANT | GROUPS | |
	ADVICE n = 46	TREATMENT n = 48
	%	%
H. Self-rating of current drinking problem at anniversary:		
Slight or no problem	57	65
Moderate or serious problem	37	33
Other, N.K.	6	2
W. Rating of H's current drinking problem at anniversary:		
Slight or no problem	37	38
Moderate or serious problem	52	60
Other, N.K.	11	2
H. Self-rating of improvement in drinking problem at anniversary:		
Moderately or distinctly improved	59	63
No, or slight, improvement	35	35
Other, N.K.	6	2
W. Rating of H's improvement in drinking problem at anniversary:		
Moderately or distinctly improved	39	50
No, or slight, improvement	48	48
Other, N.K.	13	2

No significant differences between groups.

TABLE 10

OUTCOME: ASPECTS OF SOCIAL ADJUSTMENT AT 12 MONTH ANNIVERSARY OF INTAKE, AS REPORTED BY H (HUSBAND) OR W (WIFE)

INFORMANT	GROUPS	
	ADVICE n = 46	TREATMENT n = 48
H. Time off work (sick or unemployed) during previous 12 months: mean working days	$63 \cdot 4 \pm 12 \cdot 7$	$84 \cdot 0 \pm 12 \cdot 8$
H. Improvement in marital problem at anniversary:		
Living together, moderately or distinctly improved	39%	42%
Living together, slight or no improvement	41%	44%
Separated/divorced	17%	15%
Other, N.K.	2%	0%
W. Improvement in marital problem at anniversary:		
Living together, moderately or distinctly improved	32%	35%
Living together, slight or no improvement	46%	46%
Separated/divorced	15%	15%
Other, N.K.	7%	4%

No significant differences between groups.

TABLE 11

HUSBAND'S TOTAL TIME SPENT IN PSYCHIATRIC HOSPITAL DURING 12 MONTHS AFTER STUDY INTAKE

TOTAL DURATION OF TIME SPENT IN PSYCHIATRIC HOSPITALS	GROUPS			
	ADVICE n = 44		TREATMENT n = 48	
	n	%	n	%
No such admission	35	80	34	71
—1 week total admission	2		0	
—2 weeks	1		1	
—3 weeks	1		1	
—4 weeks	4		0	
—1 month (summation)	8	18	2	4
—8 weeks	1		2	
—12 weeks	0		4	
12+ weeks	0		6	
1+ month (summation)	1	2	12	25
Husband's total period of psychiatric admission: mean days	$5 \cdot 2^{a} \pm 1 \cdot 7$		$23 \cdot 9^{a} \pm 5 \cdot 4$	

Husband's report to doctor at 12 month anniversary, with information then checked against hospital notes and data revised if necessary.
    a: $P < 0 \cdot 01$.

TABLE 12

HUSBAND'S CONTACT WITH HELPING AGENCIES OTHER THAN ALCOHOLISM FAMILY CLINIC DURING 12 MONTHS AFTER INTAKE

INFORMANT	GROUPS	
	ADVICE n = 45	TREATMENT n = 47
W. Alcoholics Anonymous:		
number of meetings attended: 0	67%	40·5%
1–6	4%	19%
7–12	16%	17%
13+	13%	23·5%
Mean number	4·8 ± 1·3	7·2 ± 1·4
W. Visits to General Practitioner,		
Mean number	8·1 ± 1·0	6·7 ± 1·1
W. O.P. psychiatric attendances,		
Mean number	2·2 ± 0·6	1·2 ± 0·4
W. O.P. General Hospital attendances,		
Mean number	3·5 ± 0·7	3·9 ± 0·9
H. Days General Hospital In-patient treatment during 12 months	0·6 ± 0·4	1·3 ± 0·8

Summation of wife's four weekly report to research social worker and (bottom line) husband's report on IP (general) treatment. No significant differences between groups.

TABLE 13

TREATMENT GROUP: DETAILS OF ALCOHOLISM FAMILY CLINIC O.P. CARE

(1) Appointments kept during 12 months:

	0–6 appointments	35%
	7–12 appointments	34%
	13+ appointments	31%

Mean appointments kept 9·7 ± 0·79
(2) Appointments failed during 12 months:

	0–6 appointments	55%
	7+ appointments	45%

Mean appointments failed 8·0 ± 1·6
(3) Summated individual interview time during 12 months:

	−3 hours	37%
	−6 hours	28%
	>6 hours	35%

Mean summated interview time 5·3 ± 0·63 hours
Mean duration of individual interview 32·6 minutes
(4) Out-patient prescription of drugs, at any time during 12 months:

Psycho-active drug at any time:	35%
Citrated calcium carbimide at any time:	61%

Summation of doctor's monthly records for 12 months to anniversary study intake. N = 48.

TABLE 14

HELP-SEEKING ENGAGEMENT OF PATIENTS BY OUTCOME CATEGORIES, FOR ADVICE AND TREATMENT GROUPS SEPARATELY

A

SUBJECTIVE IMPROVEMENT IN DRINKING PROBLEM
(PATIENT'S REPORT)

		ADVICE		TREATMENT	
		None or little $n = 15$	Some $n = 28$	None or little $n = 17$	Some $n = 30$
Proportion having psychiatric admission for number of weeks	0	12/15 (80%)	23/27 (85%)	12/17 (70%)	21/30 (70%)
	1–3	1/15 (7%)	3/27 (11%)	1/17 (6%)	1/30 (3%)
	4+	2/15 (13%)	1/27 (4%)	4/17 (24%)	8/30 (27%)
Proportion having AA attendances by number of attendances	0	12/14 (86%)	20/25 (80%)	7/16 (44%)	15/29 (52%)
	1–5	2/14 (14%)	0/25 (0%)	3/16 (19%)	3/29 (10%)
	6+	0/14 (0%)	5/25 (20%)	6/16 (37%)	11/29 (38%)
Number of G.P. visits		8·7 ± 2·3	6·0 ± 0·9	3·1[a] ± 0·6	6·1[a] ± 1·0
Number of psychiatric O.P. visits		1·5 ± 0·9	0·7 ± 0·4	0·3 ± 0·2	0·2 ± 0·2
Number of O.P. general visits		3·3 ± 2·6	1·5 ± 0·5	0·5[b] ± 0·4	2·0[b] ± 0·
Number of other agency contacts per month		2·8 ± 0·6	1·5 ± 0·4	3·1 ± 0·8	2·3 ± 0·6
Treatment Groups Only Number of appointments kept		—	—	10·6 ± 1·1	8·7 ± 1·1
Number of social worker contacts with family		—	—	15·9 ± 1·7	17·9 ± 2·0
Number of social worker contacts with patient		—	—	4·3 ± 1·0	4·1 ± 1·0
Citrated calcium carbimide prescribed		—	—	12/17 (71%)	17/30 (57%)

B

COMPOSITE OUTCOME CATEGORIES

	ADVICE			TREATMENT		
	Bad n = 13	Equivocal n = 12	Good n = 16	Bad n = 15	Equivocal n = 20	Good n = 12
/13 (77%)	10/11 (91%)	15/16 (94%)	9/15 (60%)	14/20 (70%)	10/12 (83%)
/13 (15%)	1/11 (9%)	1/16 (6%)	2/15 (13%)	—	—
/13 (7%)	0/11 (0%)	0/16 (0%)	4/15 (27%)	6/20 (30%)	2/12 (17%)
/12 (92%)	8/10 (80%)	12/15 (80%)	7/14 (50%)	9/20 (45%)	6/11 (55%)
/12 (8%)	—	1/15 (7%)	1/14 (7%)	4/20 (20%)	1/11 (9%)
—	2/10 (20%)	2/15 (13%)	6/14 (43%)	7/20 (35%)	4/11 (36%)
2 ± 1·8	5·5 ± 1·6	7·9 ± 1·9	4·1 ± 0·8	5·3 ± 2·3	5·7 ± 1·5
·0 ± 0·9	0·3 ± 0·3	0·6 ± 0·6	0·6 ± 0·6	0·0	0·4 ± 0·4
4 ± 0·3	1·1 ± 0·5	4·3 ± 2·5	1·0 ± 0·6	0·9 ± 0·4	3·0 ± 1·0
7 ± 0·8	2·2 ± 0·8	2·2 ± 0·6	3·2 ± 0·6	2·8 ± 0·8	2·1 ± 0·7
—	—	—	9·7 ± 1·4	9·5 ± 1·4	9·5 ± 1·5
—	—	—	17·1[c] ± 2·0	20·6[d] ± 2·4	11·8[cd] ± 2·5
—	—	—	4·5 ± 1·1	4·8 ± 1·3	2·8 ± 1·1
—	—	—	10/15 (67%)	14/20 (68%)	6/12 (50%)

utcome categories defined in terms of (A) patients subjective assessment of improvement in king problem and (B) composite criteria (see text for explanation).
b, c, and d indicate differences between corresponding means significant beyond the 5 per cent

TABLE 15

SUBJECTIVE JUDGEMENT BY PATIENTS AT 12-MONTH
FOLLOW-UP AS TO WHICH FACTORS HAD AIDED THEIR
IMPROVEMENT DURING THE PREVIOUS YEAR

	PERCENTAGE OF PATIENTS IN EACH GROUP ANSWERING AFFIRMATIVELY		
	ADVICE n = 46 %	TREATMENT n = 48 %	TOTAL n = 94 %
Change in external realities (e.g. work, housing)	54[a]	27[a]	40
Family clinic 'intake' advice	41	29	35
Internal psychic change (e.g. mood, self-appraisal)	37	27	32
Improvement in marital relationship	31	33	32
Other or Family Clinic In-patient care	17	19	18
Other or Family Clinic Out-patient care	11	19	15
Alcoholics Anonymous	7	8	7
Other helping agencies	9	2	5
Change in physical health	4	6	5
Social pressures to stop drinking	4	2	5

Percentages given separately for Advice, Treatment, and Total groups, and ranked according to percentages in last column.

a: difference between distribution, $P < 0.01$. No other significant differences between groups.

TABLE 16

CORRELATIONS BETWEEN INTAKE TROUBLE SCORES
AND MEASURES OF 12 MONTHS OUTCOME

	GROUPS	
OUTCOME MEASURE	ADVICE	TREATMENT
3 category Outcome Categories	0·04	—0·20
0–6 Improvement Score	0·21	—0·21

The figures are Kendall's Tau coefficients. No significant between-group differences.

TABLE 17

INTAKE MARITAL PATTERNS TEST SCORES: RANGES, MEANS, AND STANDARD DEVIATIONS

	N	RANGE	MEAN	STANDARD DEVIATION
Husbands'				
Affection Given (AG)	99	0–10	4·25	2·76
Affection Received (AR)	99	0–10	6·23	2·75
Total Affection (AG + AR)	99	0–20	10·48	4·61
	(AG v. AR, t = −6·42, p < 0·001)			
Wives'				
Affection Given	98	0–10	5·79	2·72
Affection Received	98	0–10	4·44	2·78
Total Affection	98	0–20	10·22	4·88
	(AG v. AR, t = +5·23, p < 0·001)			

TABLE 18

FREQUENCIES OF ADJECTIVE CHECK-LIST FACTOR RANKS FOR TEN DIFFERENT CONDITIONS OF ADMINISTRATION

	FACTOR OF RANK I			
	Factor 1	Factor 2	Factor 3	Others*
	(desirability)	(hostile-dominance)	(submissiveness)	
H → W†	68	15	14	3
H → W (Ideal)	98	0	0	2
H → H (Sober)	45	28	24	3
H → W → H (Sober)	22	55	13	10
H → H (Drinking)	23	65	7	5
W → H (Sober)	38	38	20	4
W → H (Ideal)	98	1	1	0
W → H (Drinking)	6	88	6	0
W → W	54	10	25	11
W → H → W	37	34	19	10

* Ties and Missing Data.

† Letter at head of arrow indicates object of description; letter at tail indicates source of description. e.g. W → W, wife describes self; H → W → H, husband describes how he thinks wife describes him.

TABLE 19

REPORTED ACTUAL AND IDEAL MARITAL ROLE PERFORMANCE

	LAST MONTH				IDEAL			
	H		W		H		W	
	x	s.d.	x	s.d.	x	s.d.	x	s.d.
1. Who decides (should decide) what should be bought for the home apart from necessities?	2·30†	0·99	2·25†	1·04	2·90	0·75	2·96	0·45
2. Who does (should do) necessary repairs around the house?	3·73*†	1·19	3·16†	1·42	4·40*	0·82	4·16	0·55
3. Who looks after (should look after) the family's money matters, paying bills and keeping accounts?	2·04*†	1·36	1·82†	1·20	3·07	1·39	3·52*	1·08
4. Who decides (should decide) how the family spends its spare time?	2·85†	0·94	2·78	1·06	3·07	0·61	2·95	0·44
5. Who does (should do) the housework?	1·89*	0·88	1·53†	0·75	1·90	0·74	1·87	0·71
6. Who decides (should decide) which friends and relatives the family sees most of?	2·68†	0·99	2·76	1·08	3·03	0·52	2·97	0·39
7. Who tries (should try) to keep the family together, trying to keep up companionship and understanding?	2·35*†	0·92	2·01†	0·82	3·02	0·65	2·92	0·53
8. Who earns or provides (should earn or provide) the money for the family's needs?	3·65†	1·04	3·46†	1·27	4·48*	0·76	3·99	0·83
9. Who decides (should decide) how often you have sexual relations together?	3·36	0·98	3·39	0·98	3·12†	0·61	3·05†	0·46
10. Who is (should be) 'at hand' when needed by the family?	2·29*†	0·96	1·95†	0·83	3·23*	0·92	2·91	0·82

High scores indicate greater relative husband actual or ideal involvement; 1·00 represents 'W does all'; 3·00 represents the mid-point, or 'H and W equally'; and 5·00 represents 'H does all'.
* Significantly higher (p < 0·05) than corresponding mean for informants of other sex.
† Significantly lower (p < 0·05) than corresponding 'LAST MONTH' or 'IDEAL' mean from same set of informants.

TABLE 20

A CLASSIFICATION OF THE TASK PARTICIPATION BALANCE
REPORTED BY HUSBANDS AND WIVES FOR THE MONTH
PRIOR TO INTAKE AND THE FIRST YEAR OF MARRIAGE
(BASED ON SIX TASK PARTICIPATION ITEMS)

	IDEAL	MONTH BEFORE INTAKE	FIRST YEAR OF MARRIAGE
W dominated (H and W 8–12)	I	52	23
W dominated-egalitarian (H or W 8–9, W or H 5–7)	5	15	14
Egalitarian (H and W 5–7)	33	12	14
H dominated-egalitarian (H or W 3–4, W or H 5–7)	33	6	19
H dominated (H and W 0–4)	12	0	8
Disputed-egalitarian (H or W 0–2 or 10–12, W or H 5–7)	10	9	10
Disputed (H or W 8–12, W or H 0–4)	4	5	6
N	98	99	94
r H–W	+0·16 (N.S.)	+0·50 (p < 0·001)	+0·51 (p < 0·001)
t H–W	3·52 (p < 0·001)	−2·81 (p < 0·01)	−2·66 (p < 0·01)

TABLE 21

THE RELATIONSHIP BETWEEN MARITAL FACTOR
SCORES AND OUTCOME

	OUTCOME			
	Good	Equivocal	Bad	
Factor 2—'Open hostility'*				
Above median (0 to 5)	11	22	16	Chi squared (2 d.f.) = 4·65
Below median (−5 to −1)	16	10	12	p < 0·10
Mean	−1·22	+0·37	0·00	G v. E, t = 2·17
Standard deviation	2·80	2·81	2·84	p < 0·05
Factor 4—'Wife's submissiveness'				
Above median (2 to 6)	14	15	13	
Below median (−3 to 1)	14	18	15	N.S.
Mean	+1·39	+1·03	+1·28	N.S.
Standard deviation	1·79	2·27	2·08	
Factor 5—'Hostile-dominance balance'				
Above median (1 to 5)	11	15	12	
Below median (−4 to 0)	17	18	16	N.S.
Mean	+0·10	−0·12	+0·57	N.S.
Standard deviation	2·07	2·39	2·13	
Factor 6—'Lack of cohesion'				
Above median (0 to 3)	6	13	20	Chi squared (2 d.f.) = 14·63
Below median (−6 to −1)	22	20	8	p < 0·001
Mean	−1·96	−1·15	−0·03	G v. B, t = 3·26
Standard deviation	2·30	2·59	2·11	p < 0·002

* Factor 2 scores could not be calculated due to missing information in two cases.

TABLE 22

ITEMS INCLUDED IN THE HARDSHIP SCALE

	FREQUENCY OF AFFIRMATIVES (N = 100)
Is he restless at night, or does he wake up with bad dreams?	74
Does he let himself get dirty, unkempt, or smelly?	61
Does he fail to join in family activities?	65
Does he pick quarrels with you?	76
Has he sometimes threatened you?	72
Has he beaten you?	45
Has he ever attempted to injure you seriously, even kill you?	27
Does he sometimes go on and on for hours rowing with you?	57
Does he, when he's like this, break furniture (or windows or doors or china)?	49
Is he very possessive and jealous towards you, asking questions about everyone you meet?	49

TABLE 23

MARITAL PATTERNS TEST—HUSBAND, AFFECTION GIVEN—A COMPARISON OF SCORES AT INTAKE AND FOLLOW-UP FOR THREE OUTCOME GROUPS, AND OVERALL

OUTCOME GROUP		INTAKE	F.U.		
'Good'	Mean	4.78^{ab}	6.03^{de}	$t = 2.55$	$r = 0.34$
	s.d.	2.43	2.04	(p < 0.02)	(p < 0.10)
	N	28	28		
'Equivocal'	Mean	4.43^{ac}	4.96^{df}	$t = 1.15$	$r = 0.47$
	s.d.	2.62	2.29	(N.S.)	(p < 0.01)
	N	30	30		
'Bad'	Mean	3.09^{bc}	3.47^{ef}	$t = 1.75$	$r = 0.90$
	s.d.	3.09	2.95	(p < 0.10)	(p < 0.001)
	N	19	19		
Overall	Mean	4.27	5.05	$t = 2.95$	$r = 0.63$
	s.d.	2.79	2.60	(p < 0.01)	(p < 0.001)
	N	80*	80*		

[a]—t = 0.52 (N.S.). [d]—t = 1.86 (p < 0.10).
[b]—t = 2.27 (p < 0.05). [e]—t = 3.52 (p < 0.001).
[c]—t = 1.80 (p < 0.10). [f]—t = 1.98 (p < 0.10).
 * Including some cases whose drinking outcome could not be classified because of incomplete information.

TABLE 24

MARITAL PATTERNS TEST—HUSBAND, AFFECTION RECEIVED—A COMPARISON OF SCORES AT INTAKE AND FOLLOW-UP FOR THREE OUTCOME GROUPS, AND OVERALL

OUTCOME GROUP		INTAKE	F.U.		
'Good'	Mean	6.46^{ab}	7.17^{de}	$t = 1.63$	$r = 0.53$
	s.d.	2.39	2.37	(N.S.)	$(p < 0.01)$
	N	28	28		
'Equivocal'	Mean	6.36^{ac}	5.96^{df}	$t = -0.80$	$r = 0.49$
	s.d.	2.61	3.17	(N.S.)	$(p < 0.01)$
	N	30	30		
'Bad'	Mean	5.31^{bc}	5.21^{ef}	$t = -0.31$	$r = 0.90$
	s.d.	3.41	3.06	(N.S.)	$(p < 0.001)$
	N	19	19		
Overall	Mean	6.23	6.31	$t = 0.27$	$r = 0.64$
	s.d.	2.76	2.95	(N.S.)	$(p < 0.001)$
	N	80*	80*		

[a]—$t = 0.14$ (N.S.).   [d]—$t = 1.63$ (N.S.).
[b]—$t = 1.35$ (N.S.).   [e]—$t = 2.47$ $(p < 0.02)$.
[c]—$t = 1.21$ (N.S.).   [f]—$t = 0.82$ (N.S.).
* Including some cases whose drinking outcome could not be classified because of incomplete information.

TABLE 25

MARITAL PATTERNS TEST—WIFE, AFFECTION GIVEN—A COMPARISON OF SCORES AT INTAKE AND FOLLOW-UP FOR THREE OUTCOME GROUPS, AND OVERALL

OUTCOME GROUP		INTAKE	F.U.		
'Good'	Mean	6.16^{ab}	6.58^{de}	$t = 0.93$	$r = 0.68$
	s.d.	2.77	2.68	(N.S.)	$(p < 0.001)$
	N	24	24		
'Equivocal'	Mean	5.32^{ac}	5.35^{df}	$t = 0.06$	$r = 0.54$
	s.d.	3.07	2.98	(N.S.)	$(p < 0.002)$
	N	31	31		
'Bad'	Mean	5.40^{bc}	4.68^{ef}	$t = -1.63$	$r = 0.69$
	s.d.	2.72	2.89	(N.S.)	$(p < 0.001)$
	N	25	25		
Overall	Mean	5.55	5.46	$t = -0.35$	$r = 0.62$
	s.d.	2.85	2.93	(N.S.)	$(p < 0.001)$
	N	84*	84*		

[a]—$t = 1.05$ (N.S.).   [d]—$t = 1.58$ (N.S.).
[b]—$t = 0.97$ (N.S.).   [e]—$t = 2.38$ $(p < 0.05)$.
[c]—$t = -0.09$ (N.S.).   [f]—$t = 0.85$ (N.S.).
* Including some cases whose drinking outcome could not be classified because of incomplete information.

TABLE 26

MARITAL PATTERNS TEST—WIFE, AFFECTION
RECEIVED—A COMPARISON OF SCORES AT INTAKE AND
FOLLOW-UP FOR THREE OUTCOME GROUPS, AND OVERALL

OUTCOME GROUP		INTAKE	F.U.		
'Good'	Mean s.d. N	5·29[ab] 2·57 24	6·33[de] 2·80 24	t = 2·03 (p < 0·10)	r = 0·56 (p < 0·01)
'Equivocal'	Mean s.d. N	4·12[ac] 2·98 31	4·03[df] 2·66 31	t = −0·18 (N.S.)	r = 0·48 (p < 0·01)
'Bad'	Mean s.d. N	3·60[bc] 2·67 25	3·04[ef] 2·38 25	t = −1·39 (N.S.)	r = 0·59 (p < 0·002)
Overall	Mean s.d. N	4·37 2·81 84*	4·42 2·92 84*	t = 0·16 (N.S.)	r = 0·57 (p < 0·001)

[a]—t = 1·51 (N.S.).   [d]—t = 3·07 (p < 0·01).
[b]—t = 2·25 (p < 0·05).   [e]—t = 4·38 (p < 0·001).
[c]—t = 0·68 (N.S.).   [f]—t = 1·45 (N.S.).
* Including some cases whose drinking outcome could not be classified because of incomplete information.

TABLE 27

ADJECTIVE CHECK-LIST WIFE DESCRIPTIONS OF SOBER
HUSBANDS, BOTH AT INTAKE AND FOLLOW-UP,
FOR THREE OUTCOME GROUPS

ACL	OUTCOME					
	'Good'		'Equivocal'		'Bad'	
W → H (Sober) FACTOR OF RANK ONE	Intake	F.U.	Intake	F.U.	Intake	F.U.
F1 Desirability	17[ab]	16[cd]	8[b]	10[d]	6[ab]	9[cd]
F2 Hostile Dominance	6 ⎫	5 ⎫	16 ⎫	15 ⎫	11 ⎫	13 ⎫
F3 Submissiveness	2 ⎬9[ab]	2 ⎬10[cd]	5 ⎬22[b]	3 ⎬20[d]	8 ⎬21[ab]	4 ⎬18[cd]
Ties	1 ⎭	3 ⎭	1 ⎭	2 ⎭	2 ⎭	1 ⎭
	26	26	30	30	27	27

[a]—Chi squared (1 d.f.) = 8·36 (p < 0·005).
[b]—Chi squared (1 d.f.; combining 'Equivocal' and 'Bad' groups) = 11·03 (p < 0·001).
[c]—Chi squared (1 d.f.) = 3·17 (p < 0·10).
[d]—Chi squared (1 d.f.; combining 'Equivocal' and 'Bad' groups) = 4·73 (p < 0·05).

TABLE 28

INTAKE AND FOLLOW-UP TASK-INVOLVEMENT CLASSIFICATIONS FOR THREE OUTCOME GROUPS

	OUTCOME					
	'Good'		'Equivocal'		'Bad'	
	Intake	F.U.	Intake	F.U.	Intake	F.U.
W Dominated	9^{ab}	4^{cd}	13^{b}	10^{d}	15^{ab}	12^{cd}
W Dominated-egalitarian	5	8	3	5	2	3
Egalitarian	6 ⎱ 15^{ab}	8 ⎱ 20^{cd}	2 ⎱ 6^{b}	2 ⎱ 7^{d}	0 ⎱ 3^{ab}	1 ⎱ 4^{cd}
H Dominated-egalitarian	4	1	1	0	1	0
H Dominated	0	3	0	0	0	0
Disputed-egalitarian	1	2	3	5	0	2
Disputed	1	0	2	2	0	0
	26	26	24	24	18	18

[a]—Chi squared (1 d.f.) = 7·05 (p < 0·01).
[b]—Chi squared (1 d.f.; combining 'Equivocal' and 'Bad' groups) = 7·36 (p < 0·01).
[c]—Chi squared (1 d.f.) = 11·28 (p < 0·001).
[d]—Chi squared (1 d.f.; combining 'Equivocal' and 'Bad' groups) = 12·06 (p < 0·001).

TABLE 29

THE RELATIONSHIP BETWEEN INTAKE AND FOLLOW-UP TASK-PARTICIPATION BALANCE, FOR THREE OUTCOME GROUPS SEPARATELY AND OVERALL

	FOLLOW-UP	INTAKE	
		W Dominated	Others (non-disputed)
'Good'	W Dominated	3	1
	Others	5	14
'Equivocal'	W Dominated	7	2
	Others	2	2
'Bad'	W Dominated	12	0
	Others	1	2
Overall	W Dominated	22^{a}	3^{a}
	Others	8^{a}	18^{a}

[a]—Chi squared (1 d.f.) = 14·95 (p < 0·001).

TABLE 30

INTAKE 'COPING' ITEMS WITH LOADINGS ABOVE ±0·40 ON EACH OF 10 ROTATED PRINCIPAL COMPONENTS

G —Items with a higher frequency of above median responses by wives in the subsequent 'Good' outcome group.
B —Items with a higher frequency of above median responses by wives in the subsequent 'Bad' outcome group.
BB —Items with a *significantly* higher frequency (difference in proportions 2·0 × s.e.) of above median responses by wives in the subsequent 'Bad' outcome group.
( )+—Figures in brackets are the nos. of Ws. endorsing each item.

Component 1—'Discord'

		Item No.*	
		41	Have you had rows with him about the drinking itself? (91)+
G		12	Do you plead with him to stop drinking? (92)
	B	4	Have you threatened to leave him? (88)
	BB	13	Do you have rows with him about problems *related to* his drinking? (91)
G		3	Have you shown him that his drinking is making you ill? (93)
		1	Have you tried to stop him drinking too much by having a row about it before he goes out? (74)
	BB	47	Have you told him he must leave? (66)
	B	55	Have you suggested all the good things he could have if he would stop? (91)
	BB	34	Have you felt you could not face going home? (77)
	B	54	Have you tried to show him how you feel by threatening to kill yourself? (45)
	B	42	When he gets drunk do you feel too hopeless yourself to do anything? (83)
G		16	When he gets drunk, do you start a row with him about it? (62)
G		46	Have you tried to stop him drinking too much by making him feel small or ridiculous in public? (24)

Component 2—'Avoidance'

	B	7	When he gets drunk, do you keep out of the way? (70)
	B	53	Do you avoid him? (55)
	B	15	When he gets drunk, do you refuse to talk to him while he is in that frame of mind? (73)
	B	42	When he gets drunk, do you feel too hopeless yourself to do anything? (83)
	B	32	When he gets drunk, do you leave him to it? (74)
		38	When he brings drink home, do you seem not to mind but take the first chance to get rid of it? (45)
	B	27	When he gets drunk, do you feel too angry yourself to do anything? (80)
	B	48	When he gets drunk do you feel too frightened to do anything? (70)
	B	6	Have you told him the children will lose their respect for him? (71)

Component 3—'Indulgence'

	B	2	When he is sobering up, have you given him a drink to help with the hangover? (25)
	B	45	Have you yourself gone without to give him the money he asks for? (54)
G		30	Have you poured some of it away? (59)

Component 4—'Competition'

G		28	Have you tried to stop him drinking too much by actually getting drunk yourself? (12)
	B	5	Have you tried to stop him drinking too much by pretending to be drunk yourself? (14)
G		24	Have you tried to make him jealous? (6)
		50	Have you tried to stop him drinking too much by trying to keep up with him when he drinks? (15)
G		29	When he brings drink home with him, have you drunk some of it yourself? (41)
		49	Have you gone out by yourself (or with others) and pretended you were having a whale of a time? (26)

TABLE 30 (Continued)

Component 5—'Anti-drink'

	Item No.	
	19	When he brings drink home with him, have you tried to find where it is hidden? (38)
G	56	When he brings drink home with him do you hide it? (30)
	43	Have you made a firm rule that you do not allow drink in the house? (22)
	38	When he brings drink home, do you seem not to mind but take the first chance to get rid of it? (45)
G	30	Have you poured some of it away? (59)

Component 6—'Assertion'

G	33	Have you hit him, or tried to hurt him physically? (54)
B	35	Have you paid his debts or bills? (70)
G	46	Have you tried to stop him drinking too much by making him feel small or ridiculous in public? (24)
G	16	When he gets drunk, do you start a row with him about it? (62)
B	−8	When he gets drunk, do you make him comfortable, perhaps by giving him something to eat? (81)

Component 7—'Sexual withdrawal'

B	25	Have you refused to share the same room with him? (52)
B	36	Have you refused to sleep with him? (58)
BB	52	When he is drunk, do you refuse to share the bed with him? (57)

Component 8—'Fearful withdrawal'

B	39	Do you pretend to everyone that all is well? (83)
B	48	When he gets drunk do you feel too frightened to do anything? (70)
B	40	Do you keep the children out of his way? (57)

Component 9—'Taking special action'

B	14	Have you made special arrangements about money matters? (36)
B	9	Have you been out to work, or used your own income, to keep the family going? (73)
B	37	Have you arranged special treats for him? (56)
B	11	Have you been yourself to the doctor about his drinking problem? (71)
B	20	Have you had contact with Alcoholics Anonymous? (20)
B	26	Have you tried to stop him drinking too much by inviting friends or relatives in? (22)
B	35	Have you paid his debts or bills? (70)

Component 10—'Marital breakdown'

BB	22	Have you consulted a solicitor or advice bureau about getting legal separation or divorce? (36)
	23	Have you left home, even for one day? (36)
B	−51	When he gets drunk, do you get him to bed? (60)
B	17	Have you locked him out of the house? (19)

The following items did not load ±0·40 or above on any of the above components:

B	10	Have you threatened to contact someone to try to stop him? (63)
	18	Have you asked his employer to step in? (2)
BB	21	Have you hidden valuables or household things so that he cannot pawn or sell them? (26)
	31	Have you been legally separated? (2)
G	44	Have you been out to fetch him home? (48)

* Items are listed in order of magnitude of their loadings with highest loadings given first. One item listed under Component 6, and one under Component 10, loaded negatively and is shown with a minus sign.

TABLE 31

THE CORRELATES OF TEN VARIETIES OF WIVES' COPING BEHAVIOUR (SPEARMAN RANK ORDER CORRELATIONS)

COPING COMPONENT	Wife's Hardship	Husband's Job Status	Wife's Age	Wife's Neuroticism
1. Discord	0·35[a]	−0·31[b]	−0·05	0·39[a]
2. Avoidance	0·37[a]	−0·28[b]	0·16	0·25[b]
3. Indulgence	0·28[b]	−0·24[c]	0·15	0·09
4. Competition	0·09	0·04	−0·29[b]	0·19[c]
5. Anti-drink	0·29[b]	−0·18[c]	0·21[c]	0·22[c]
6. Assertion	0·17[c]	−0·34[a]	−0·11	0·36[a]
7. Sexual withdrawal	0·27[b]	−0·21[c]	0·21[c]	0·16
8. Fearful withdrawal	0·32[a]	−0·10	−0·13	0·18[c]
9. Special action	0·32[a]	−0·11	0·31[a]	0·08
10. Marital breakdown	0·37[a]	−0·19[c]	0·02	0·12

[a]—$p < 0.001$.   [b]—$p < 0.01$.   [c]—$p < 0.05$.

TABLE 32

A COMPARISON OF INTAKE EPI SCORES AND PUBLISHED NORMS

	FORM A				FORM B			
	No.	X	s.d.	t	No.	X	s.d.	t
Neuroticism (N)								
Norms	2000	9·07	4·78		2000	10·52	4·71	
Excessive Drinkers	50	15·34	5·20	9·22[a]	50	16·06	4·61	8·26[a]
Wives	50	12·84	5·75	5·54[a]	49	13·75	5·43	4·82[a]
Extraversion (E)								
Norms	2000	12·07	4·37		2000	14·15	3·92	
Excessive Drinkers	50	12·42	3·71	0·56	50	13·28	4·25	−1·55
Wives	50	10·28	3·13	−2·88[b]	49	13·06	3·89	−1·94
Lie Scale (L)								
Norms	651	2·26	1·57		329	1·38	1·35	
Excessive Drinkers	50	2·52	1·75	1·18	50	1·58	1·37	1·00
Wives	50	4·28	1·69	8·78[a]	49	2·28	1·64	4·28[a]

[a] $= p < 0.001$.   [b] $= p < 0.01$.   [c] $= p < 0.05$.

TABLE 33

INTAKE EPI INTER-SCALE CORRELATIONS

	Hs E	Hs L	Ws N	Ws E	Ws L
Hs N	0·04	−0·45[a]	0·03	−0·09	−0·09
Hs E		−0·14	−0·02	0·01	0·03
Hs L			−0·02	0·05	0·23[c]
Ws N				−0·31[b]	−0·29[b]
Ws E					−0·26[b]

[a] = p < 0·001.   [b] = p < 0·01.   [c] = p < 0·05.

TABLE 34

EPI INTAKE-FOLLOW-UP MEANS, MEAN DIFFERENCES AND CORRELATIONS BY DRINKING OUTCOME

	HUSBANDS							
OUTCOME	NEUROTICISM				EXTRAVERSION			
	IN	F.U.	t	r	IN	F.U.	t	r
'Good' N = 27	14·40	10·00	−4·00[a]	0·46[b]	13·77	14·03	0·33	0·54[b]
'Equivocal' N = 32	15·09	12·09	−3·24[b]	0·55[b]	12·63	12·63	−0·00	0·41[c]
'Bad' N = 26	16·96	16·88	−0·08	0·49[b]	11·64	11·56	−0·10	0·47[b]
'Overall' N = 85	15·54	12·83	−4·56[a]	0·52[a]	12·70	12·76	0·13	0·50[a]
t G v. E	0·48	1·40			−1·08	−1·33		
t G v. B	1·82	4·61[a]			−1·96	−2·25[c]		
t E v. B	1·41	3·25[b]			−0·95	−1·12		

	WIVES							
	NEUROTICISM				EXTRAVERSION			
	IN	F.U.	t	r	IN	F.U.	t	r
'Good' N = 26	12·80	13·73	1·30	0·81[a]	11·15	12·00	0·93	0·38
'Equivocal' N = 29	13·76	14·23	0·65	0·76[a]	11·56	11·16	−0·41	0·12
'Bad' N = 28	14·03	14·03	0·00	0·70[a]	12·03	11·40	−0·72	0·30
'Overall' N = 83	13·55	14·01	1·07	0·75[a]	11·59	11·50	−0·15	0·25[c]
t G v. E	0·65	0·31			0·37	−0·77		
t G v. B	0·76	0·19			0·81	−0·53		
t E v. B	0·18	−0·13			0·46	0·22		

[a] = p < 0·001.   [b] = p < 0·01.   [c] = p < 0·05.

TABLE 35

ACL SELF-DESCRIPTION AND SPOUSE-DESCRIPTION CORRELATIONS AND DISCREPANCIES (N = 50)

Descriptions by	DESCRIPTIONS OF HS (Sober)		DESCRIPTIONS OF WS	
	Dom.–Sub.	Affect.–Host.	Dom.–Sub.	Affect.–Host.
Hs	10·00	10·78	11·24	10·34
Ws	10·22	10·40	9·30	10·40
t	0·46	−0·59	−4·76[a]	0·11
r	0·46[a]	0·23	0·43[b]	0·43[b]

[a]—p < 0·001.   [b]—p < 0·01.

TABLE 36

THE PREDICTION OF EXTREME OUTCOME GROUP MEMBERSHIP AT 24 MONTHS FOLLOW-UP FROM EACH OF FOUR INTAKE VARIABLES

	t (1-tailed tests)	CHI SQUARED (Median split)	DIRECTION (Good outcome associated with:)
Husband's job status	1·86 p < 0·05	0·15 N.S.	High job status
Wife's hardship	2·48 p < 0·01	5·74 p < 0·02	Low hardship
Marital cohesion	1·05 N.S.	3·44 p < 0·10	High cohesion
Husband's trouble score	0·93 N.S.	0·32 N.S.	Low trouble score

TABLE 37

THE NATURE OF DRINKING 12 TO 24 MONTHS AFTER INTAKE FOR 26 MEN WITH A 'GOOD' OUTCOME AT 24 MONTHS

Case no.		HUSBAND REPORTS: Weeks out of 52 containing:				WIFE REPORTS: Weeks out of 52 containing:		
		Any 200+ gms days	No 200+ but any 100+ day	No 100+ but any drinking day	only abstinent days	Any unacceptable (UA) days	No UA days but any acceptable drinking days	only abstinent days
02	A	0	1	0	51	1	0	51
03		0	2	0	50	0	0	52
04		0	0	2	50	0	6	46
07	A	0	0	0	52	0	0	52
08	CD	0	2	50	0	0	52	0
10	A	0	0	0	52	0	0	52
13		2	0	0	50	0	0	52
15	A	0	0	1	51	0	1	51
16	A	0	0	0	52	0	0	52
21	CD	0	40	12	0	0	50	2
26	CD	0	7	10	35	0	16	36
29	CD	0	5	45	2	0	52	0
30	CD	0	0	8	44	1	5	46
31	A	0	0	0	52	0	0	52
46	A	0	0	0	52	0	0	52
49	CD	0	0	52	0	0	52	0
53		0	0	6	46	3	1	48
65	CD	0	52	0	0	0	52	0
69	CD	0	0	24	28	0	12	40
73	A	0	0	0	52	0	0	52
78	CD	0	0	4	48	1	25	26
81		0	0	0	52	0	8	44
83	A	0	0	0	52	0	0	52
92	A	0	0	0	52	0	0	52
95	A	0	0	0	52	0	0	52
98	CD	0	2	50	0	0	52	0

A—Abstainer.   CD—Controlled drinker.

King

TABLE 38

THE PREDICTION FROM INTAKE VARIABLES OF SECOND YEAR ABSTINENCE VERSUS CONTROLLED DRINKING

	ABSTAINERS	CONTROLLED DRINKERS	PROBABILITY LEVEL (Fisher exact test)
5+/10 troubles	7	2	<0.05
4-/10 troubles	4	8	
Gamma alcoholism	6	0	<0.025
Non-Gamma alcoholism	5	10	
Unconfident about+ abstaining	8	2	<0.025
Confident about abstaining	2	7	

+ Numbers reduced due to missing information.

APPENDICES

Marital patterns test (adapted from Ryle, 1966)

	SCORING WEIGHTS		
	True	Uncertain	Not true
1. (a) I am usually very patient with her	1	0	0
(b) She is usually very patient with me	1	0	0
2. (a) I am very warm-natured and affectionate to her	1	0	0
(b) She is very warm-natured and affectionate to me	1	0	0
3. (a) I wish I could be more affectionate	0	1	1
(b) She wishes she could be more affectionate	0	1	1
4. (a) I give a lot of time to her	1	0	0
(b) She gives a lot of time to me	1	0	0
5. (a) I seldom express affection for her	0	1	1
(b) She seldom expresses affection for me	0	1	1
6. (a) I am quick to criticize and slow to praise her	0	1	1
(b) She is quick to criticize and slow to praise me	0	1	1
7. (a) I am nearly always prepared to do what she says	1	0	0
(b) She is nearly always prepared to do what I say	1	0	0
8. (a) I make her feel more confident	1	0	0
(b) She makes me feel more confident	1	0	0
9. (a) I find it easy to forgive her for her faults	1	0	0
(b) She finds it easy to forgive me for my faults	1	0	0
10. (a) I am considerate of her feelings	1	0	0
(b) She is considerate of my feelings	1	0	0

Only affection scales of Ryle's original MPT were used; domination items were excluded. Ryle's affection scales contained 14 items. Of these, 4 were excluded before scoring, on the basis of an item analysis. The item analysis was carried out by cross-tabulating total scores (grouped in thirds of the distribution of total scores) against scores on each of the 14 items taken in turn. The 10 items retained were those showing a significant chi squared value when the association between total score and item score was tested, and which showed a linear increase in individual item responses weighted 1 across the 3 total score groups.

The version given to husbands is shown above; the version for wives was the same with the appropriate alteration of pronouns.

APPENDIX 2

Adjective check-list items and factor weights

	OCTANT	FACTOR 1 'Desirability'	FACTOR 2 'Hostile-dominance'	FACTOR 3 'Sub-missiveness'
Sarcastic	DE	−1	2	0
Shy	HI	0	−1	2
Always pleasant and agreeable	LM	2	−1	1
Hard hearted	DE	0	1	0
Often admired	AP	2	1	0
Fond of everyone	LM	2	0	2
Usually gives in	HI	0	−1	2
Lacks self confidence	HI	−1	1	2
Manages others	AP	2	1	−1
Stern but fair	DE	2	1	0
Wants everyone to like him/her	LM	1	2	1
Frequently angry	DE	0	2	1
Firm but just	DE	2	1	0
Cruel and unkind	DE	0	2	1
Respected by others	AP	2	0	0
Outspoken	DE	1	1	0
Affectionate and understanding	LM	2	−1	1
Meek	HI	0	0	2
Always ashamed of self	HI	0	1	2
Acts important	AP	1	2	0
Bossy	AP	0	2	0
Dictatorial	AP	1	2	0
Always giving advice	AP	1	2	0
Modest	HI	1	−1	1
Agrees with everyone	LM	1	0	2
Too easily influenced by friends	LM	0	1	2
Impatient with others mistakes	DE	−1	2	0
Warm	LM	2	−1	0
Apologetic	HI	1	0	2
Critical of others	DE	0	2	0
Likes responsibility	AP	2	1	−1
Spineless	HI	0	1	1
Friendly all the time	LM	2	−1	1
Obeys too willingly	HI	1	0	2
Irritable	DE	−1	2	1
Forceful	AP	1	2	−1
Expects everyone to admire him/her	AP	1	2	1
Timid	HI	0	0	2
Loves everyone	LM	2	0	2
Will confide in anyone	LM	1	1	2

This scoring system is based upon the results of the four separate multi-variate analyses described in Chapter 5 (analyses of self-descriptions and spouse-descriptions for husband and wife separately). In each case the inter-item correlation matrix was factor analysed, using a principal components factor analysis (i.e. a principal components analysis carried out on a matrix with estimates of communalities in the diagonals, as in factor analysis), BMDO3M, using a standard program available on the ULCC CDC 6600 computer.

To facilitate the determination of suitable item weights, husband and wife data were then combined and two separate factor analyses carried out—one for self-descriptions and one for spouse-descriptions (each with $N = 198$, as two wives did not supply complete data). Three factors were rotated orthogonally, using the Varimax method. Item weights were then assigned in the following manner: for each of the three rotated factors, each item was given a weight of 2 if one loading exceeded +0·40 and the other exceeded +0·12, a weight of 1 if one loading was greater than +0·12, so long as the other was greater than −0·12, a weight of 0, or a weight of −1 if both loadings were −0·12 or below, or if one loading was −0·20 or below and the other loading was negative.

APPENDIX 3

Intake marriage variables; loadings on six rotated factors

			FACTOR LOADINGS					
			F1	F2	F3	F4	F5	F6
1.	MPT	Affection Given (H)	0·23	−0·24	0·12	−0·07	−0·33	−0·42
2.		Affection Received (H)	0·00	−0·70	0·00	−0·02	0·14	−0·23
3.		Affection Given (W)	0·04	−0·38	−0·01	−0·17	0·20	−0·65
4.		Affection Received (W)	−0·12	−0·39	0·08	0·02	−0·11	−0·69
5.	ACL	H → W F1	0·71	−0·25	0·14	−0·35	0·06	0·08
6.		H → W F2	0·30	0·56	0·01	−0·30	−0·23	0·15
7.		H → W F3	0·50	0·07	0·08	0·43	−0·07	−0·07
8.		H ↑↑ H (Sober) F1	0·72	0·12	0·02	−0·18	0·18	−0·29
9.		H ↑↑ H (Sober) F2	0·29	0·06	0·02	0·18	0·64	0·12
10.		H ↑↑ H (Sober) F3	0·60	−0·08	0·04	0·29	−0·07	0·33
11.		H → W ↑↑ H (Sober) F1	0·65	−0·10	−0·06	−0·00	−0·06	−0·38
12.		H ↑↑ W ↑↑ H (Sober) F2	0·37	0·32	−0·07	0·22	0·51	0·27
13.		H ↑↑ W ↑↑ H (Sober) F3	0·72	−0·04	0·06	0·14	−0·17	0·24
14.		W ↑↑ H (Sober) F1	0·10	−0·17	0·38	0·13	0·15	−0·61
15.		W ↑↑ H (Sober) F2	0·30	0·36	0·23	0·31	0·26	0·24
16.		W ↑↑ H (Sober) F3	0·09	0·15	0·56	0·09	−0·29	−0·02
17.		W ↑↑ W F1	0·16	−0·05	0·75	−0·22	0·23	−0·10
18.		W ↑↑ W F2	0·08	0·02	0·20	0·13	−0·57	0·16
19.		W ↑↑ W F3	0·09	0·17	0·38	0·64	−0·08	−0·10
20.		W ↑↑ H F1	−0·03	−0·25	0·75	−0·02	0·05	−0·17
21.		W ↑↑ H F2	0·14	0·12	0·36	0·03	−0·34	0·47
22.		W ↑↑ H F3	0·08	0·16	0·36	0·70	−0·04	−0·14
23.		H ↑↑ W Frequency of checking	0·83	0·17	0·13	−0·12	−0·13	0·08
24.		H ↑↑ H (Sober) Frequency of checking	0·85	0·06	0·04	0·10	0·32	0·06
25.		H → W ↑↑ H (Sober) Frequency of checking	0·90	0·09	−0·04	0·17	0·13	0·04
26.		W ↑↑ H (Sober) Frequency of checking	0·24	0·18	0·65	0·30	0·11	−0·25
27.		W ↑↑ W Frequency of checking	0·17	0·06	0·82	0·23	−0·08	−0·02
28.		W → H ↑↑ W Frequency of checking	0·05	−0·00	0·79	0·29	−0·17	0·10

Intake History						
29. W ever left home (H or W)	0·02	0·11	−0·07	−0·05	−0·08	0·20
30. Frequency of recent intercourse (average of H and W)	−0·02	0·26	0·32	−0·11	0·04	0·21
31. Likelihood of future marital breakdown (average of H and W)	−0·14	0·29	−0·04	0·10	0·02	0·38
32. Age discrepancy (H minus W)	0·11	−0·01	−0·20	−0·04	0·02	−0·07
33. Status background discrepancy (H's father minus W's father)	−0·10	−0·04	0·14	−0·06	−0·09	−0·02
34. Education discrepancy (H minus W)	−0·08	−0·00	−0·02	0·13	−0·12	0·35
35. Wife's work status (W)	−0·02	−0·09	0·30	−0·14	0·44	0·19
Joint-interview						
36. Speaks first	0·05	0·24	0·10	−0·53	−0·04	0·01
37. H → W Warmth	0·02	−0·69	0·09	0·04	0·17	−0·12
38. H → W Dominance	0·05	0·61	−0·05	0·17	0·35	−0·12
39. H → W Hostility	−0·02	0·82	0·04	0·02	0·20	0·04
40. W → H Warmth	−0·05	−0·53	0·02	−0·09	0·23	−0·33
41. W → H Dominance	0·02	0·56	0·13	−0·46	0·13	0·08
42. W → H Hostility	−0·03	0·74	0·15	−0·09	0·07	0·23
Role Inventories						
43. Participation departure from ideal (W)	0·16	0·15	0·27	−0·29	0·18	0·47
44. Participation departure from ideal (H)	0·04	−0·16	0·05	−0·03	0·25	0·51
45. Socio-sexual decision-making (W)	0·07	−0·10	0·08	0·40	0·18	0·02
46. Socio-sexual decision-making (H)	0·08	0·35	0·05	−0·19	−0·37	−0·08

FIGURES

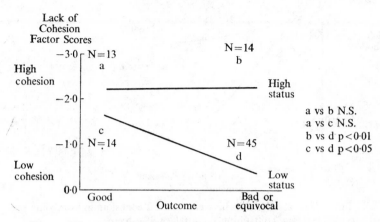

FIG. 1. The relationship between marital cohesion and outcome
controlling for intake occupational status

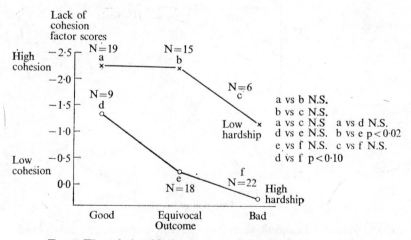

FIG. 2 The relationship between marital cohesion and outcome
controlling for intake hardship

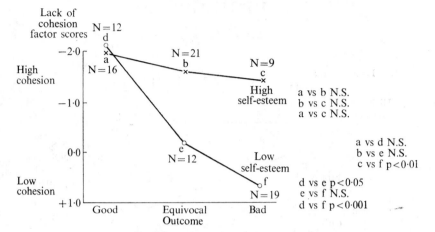

FIG. 3 The relationship between marital cohesion and outcome controlling for intake self-esteem

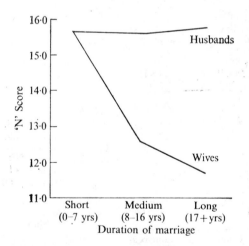

FIG. 4 Mean EPI neuroticism (N) scores of husbands and wives who had been married for short, medium and long periods of time

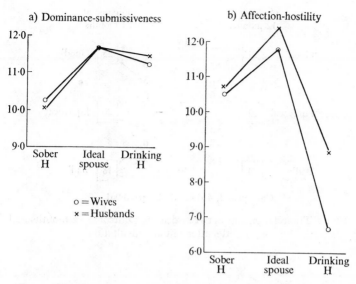

FIG. 5 The interpersonal functions attributed to the husbands'
drinking by themselves and their wives

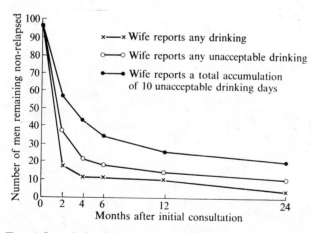

FIG. 6 Cumulative 'relapse' curves of 95 men for two years
following intake

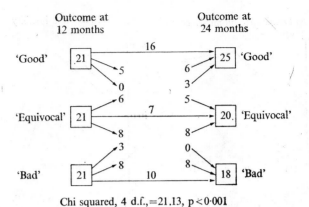

Chi squared, 4 d.f.,=21.13, p < 0·001

Fig. 7 The relationship between drinking outcome 12 months and 24 months after initial consultation

REFERENCES

AGULNIK, P. L. (1970) The spouse of the phobic patient, *Brit. J. Psychiat.* **117**, 59–67.

ANGELL, R. C. (1936) *The Family Encounters the Depression*, New York.

BAEKLAND, F., LUNDWALL, L., and KISSIN, B. (1975) Methods for the Treatment of Chronic Alcoholism: a Critical Appraisal, In *Research Advances in Alcohol and Drug Problems*, Vol. 2., Chapter 7, R. J. Gibbins, Y. Israel, H. Kalant, R. E. Popham, W. Schmidt, and R. G. Smart, eds., London.

BAILEY, M. B. (1967) Psychophysiological Impairment in Wives of Alcoholics as Related to Their Husbands' Drinking and Sobriety, In *Alcoholism; Behavioral Research, Therapeutic Approaches*, p. 134–44, R. Fox, ed., New York.

BAILEY, M. B., HABERMAN, P. W., and ALKSNE, H. (1962) Outcomes of alcoholic marriages; endurance, termination or recovery, *Quart. J. Stud. Alc.*, **23**, 610–23.

BAILEY, M. B. and STEWART, J. (1967) Normal drinking by persons reporting previous problem drinking, *Quart. J. Stud. Alc.*, **28**, 305–15.

BELASCO, J. A. (1971) The criterion question revisited, *Brit. J. Addict.*, **66**, 39–44.

BERNE, E. (1964) *Games People Play; the Psychology of Human Relationships*, New York.

BERTALANFFY, L., VON. (1966) General System Theory and Psychiatry, In *American Handbook of Psychiatry*, Vol. 3, S. Arieti, ed., New York.

BLOCK, M. A. (1963) Normal drinking in recovered alcohol addicts: comment on the article by D. L. Davies, *Quart. J. Stud. Alc.*, **24**, 114–17.

BLOOD, R. W. and WOLFE, B. M. (1960) *Husbands and Wives: the Dynamics of Married Living*, New York.

BOYD, W. H. and BOLEN, D. W. (1970) The compulsive gambler and spouse in group psychotherapy, *Int. J. group Psychother.*, **20**, 77–90.

BRITISH MEDICAL ASSOCIATION AND THE MAGISTRATES ASSOCIATION (1961) Memorandum on Alcoholism, *Brit. med. J.*, **1**, Supplement, 190–3.

BRODERICK, C. B. (1971) Beyond the five conceptual frameworks; a decade of development in family theory, *J. Marriage Fam.*, **33**, 139–59.

BROWN, G. W., BHROLCHAIN, M. N., and HARRIS, T. (1975) Social class and psychiatric disturbance among women in an urban population, *Sociology*, **9**, 225–54.

BROWN, G. W., BIRLEY, J. L. T., and WING, J. K. (1972) Influence of family life on the course of schizophrenic disorders; a replication, *Brit. J. Psychiat.*, **121**, 241–58.

BROWN, G. W., MONCK, E. M., CARSTAIRS, G. M., and WING, J. K. (1962) Influence of family life on the course of schizophrenic illness, *Brit. J. prev. social Med.*, **16**, 55–68.

BRUUN, K., EDWARDS, G., LUMIO, M., MAKELA, K., PAN, L., POPHAM, R. E., ROOM, R., SCHMIDT, W., SKOG, O-J., SULKUNEN, P., and OSTERBERG, E. (1975) *Alcohol Control Policies in Public Health Perspective*, Helsinki.

BULLOCK, S. C. and MUDD, E. H. (1959) The inter-relatedness of alcoholism and marital conflict. Symposium, 2. The interaction of alcoholic husbands and their non-alcoholic wives during counselling. *Amer. J. Orthopsychiat.*, **29**, 519–27.

BURGESS, E. W. and COTTRELL, L. S. (1939) *Predicting Success or Failure in Marriage*, New York.

BURGESS, E. W. and WALLIN, P. (1943) Homogamy in social characteristics, *Amer. J. Sociol.*, **49**, 109–24.

BURR, W. R. (1970) Satisfaction with various aspects of marriage over the life cycle; a random middle-class sample, *J. Marriage Fam.*, **32**, 28–37.

BURTON, G. and KAPLAN, H. M. (1968) Sexual behaviour and adjustment of married alcoholics, *Quart. J. Stud. Alc.*, **29**, 603–9.

CAMPBELL, D. T. and STANLEY, J. C. (1963) Experimental and Quasi-experimental designs for research, In *Handbook of Research on Teaching*, N. L. Gage, ed., Chicago.

CARTWRIGHT, A. K. J., SHAW, S. J., and SPRATLEY, T. A. (1975) *Designing a comprehensive community response to problems of alcohol abuse: Report to the Department of Health and Social Security by the Maudsley Alcohol Pilot Project.* Mimeographed.

CATTELL, R. B. and NESSELROADE, J. R. (1967) Likeness and completeness theories examined by sixteen personality factor measures on stably and unstably married couples, *J. Personality social Psychol.*, **7**, 351–61.

CHEEK, F. E. (1965) Family interaction patterns and convalescent adjustment of the schizophrenic, *Arch. gen. Psychiatry*, **13**, 138–47.

CLARK, W. (1966) Operational definitions of drinking problems and associated prevalence rates, *Quart. J. Stud. Alc.*, **27**, 648–68.

CLAUSEN, J. A. and YARROW, M. R. (1955) The impact of mental illness on the family, *J. social Issues*, **11**, 3–65.

COLLINS, J., KREITMAN, N., NELSON, B., and TROOP, J. (1971) Neurosis and marital interaction. III. Family roles and function, *Brit. J. Psychiat.*, **119**, 233–42.

CONGER, J. J. (1956) Alcoholism: Theory, problem and challenge. II, Reinforcement theory and the dynamics of alcoholism, *Quart. J. Stud. Alc.*, **17**, 296–305.

COOK, T. (1975) *Vagrant Alcoholics*, London.

COOK, T., MORGAN, H. G., and POLLAK, B. (1968) The Rathcoole Experiment: First year at a hostel for vagrant alcoholics, *Brit. med. J.*, **1**, 240–2.

COOK, T. and POLLAK, B. (1970) In place of Skid Row: the first three years of the Rathcoole Experiment, May 1966–May 1969, *NACRO paper, No. 4.* London: National Association for Care and Rehabilitation of Offenders.

COPPEN, A., COWIE, V., and SLATER, E. (1965) Familial aspects of neuroticism and extraversion, *Brit. J. Psychiat.*, **111**, 70–83.

CORSINI, R. J. (1956) Understanding and similarity in marriage, *J. abnorm. social Psychol.*, **52**, 327–32.

CRONBACH, L. J. (1955) Processes affecting scores on understanding of others and assumed similarity, *Psychol. Bull.*, **52**, 177–93.

D'ZURILLA, T. J. and GOLDFRIED, M. R. (1971) Problem solving and behaviour modification, *J. abnorm. Psychol.*, **78**, 107–26.

DAVIES, D. L. (1962) Normal drinking in recovered alcohol addicts, *Quart. J. Stud. Alc.*, **23**, 94–104.

DAVIES, D. L., SCOTT, D. F., and MALHERBE, M. E. L. (1969) Resumed normal drinking in recovered psychotic alcoholics, *Int. J. Addict.*, **4**, 187–94.

DAVIES, D. L., SHEPHERD, M., and MYERS, E. (1956) The two-year prognosis of 50 alcohol addicts after treatment in hospital, *Quart. J. Stud. Alc.*, **17**, 485–502.

DEMORSIER, G. and FELDMAN, H. (1952) Le traitement de l'alcoolisme par l'apomorphine; étude 500 cas, *Schweiz. Arch. Neurol. Psychiat.*, **70**, 434–40.

DHSS (1973a) *Community Services for Alcoholics*, Department of Health and Social Security, Circular 21/73.

DHSS (1973b) *Alcoholism*. Report Prepared by the Standing Medical Advisory

Committee for the Central Health Services Council, the Secretary of State for Social Services and the Secretary of State for Wales, London: Department of Health and Social Security.

DHSS (1975) *Better Services for the Mentally Ill*, London.

DHSS (1976) Personal Communication.

DICKS, H. (1967) *Marital Tensions; Clinical Studies Towards a Psychological Theory of Interaction*, London.

DREWERY, J. and RAE, J. B. (1969) A group comparison of alcoholic and non-alcoholic marriages using the interpersonal perception technique, *Brit. J. Psychiat.*, **115**, 287–300.

EDWARDS, G. (1966) Hypnotic treatment of alcohol addiction, *Quart. J. Stud. Alc.*, **27**, 221.

EDWARDS, G. (1970) The place of treatment professions in society's response to chemical abuse, *Brit. Med. J.*, **2**, 195–9.

EDWARDS, G. (1973) Epidemiology applied to alcoholism. A review and an examination of purposes, *Quart. J. Stud. Alc.*, **34**, 28–56.

EDWARDS, G. (1975) Epidemiology of What? Anglo-French Symposium on Alcoholism, *INSERM/MRC. 27–28 novembre 1975*, Vol. **54**, 13–22.

EDWARDS, G., CHANDLER, J., HENSMAN, C., and PETO, J. (1972) Drinking in a London suburb. II. Correlates of trouble with drinking among men, *Quart. J. Stud. Alc.*, Suppl. **6**, 94–119.

EDWARDS, G. and GROSS, M. M. (1976) Alcohol dependence: Provisional description of a clinical syndrome, *Brit. med. J.*, **1**, 1058–61.

EDWARDS, G., GROSS, M., KELLER, M., and MOSER, M. eds. (1976) Alcohol-related problems in the disability perspective. A summary of the consensus of the WHO Group of Investigators on Criteria for identifying and classifying disabilities related to alcohol consumption, *J. Stud. Alc.*, **37**, 1360–82.

EDWARDS, G. and GUTHRIE, S. (1966) A comparison of in-patient and out-patient treatment of alcohol dependence, *Lancet* **1**, 467–8.

EDWARDS, G. and GUTHRIE, S. (1967) A controlled trial of in-patient and out-patient treatment of alcohol dependence, *Lancet* **1**, 555–9.

EDWARDS, G., HAWKER, A., and HENSMAN, C. (1966) Setting up a therapeutic community, *Lancet* **2**, 1407–8.

EDWARDS, G., HAWKER, A., WILLIAMSON, V., and HENSMAN, C. (1966) London's Skid Row, *Lancet* **1**, 249–52.

EDWARDS, G., HAWKER, A., HENSMAN, C., PETO, J., and WILLIAMSON, V. (1973) Alcoholics known or unknown to agencies: Epidemiological studies in a London suburb, *Brit. J. Psychiat.*, **123**, 169–83.

EDWARDS, G., HENSMAN, C., and PETO, J. (1971) Drinking problems amongst recidivist prisoners, *Psychol. Med.*, **115**, 388–99.

EDWARDS, G., HENSMAN, C., and PETO, J. (1972) Drinking in a London suburb. III. Comparisons of drinking troubles among men and women, *Quart. J. Stud. Alc.*, Suppl. **6**, 120–8.

EDWARDS, G., KELLOG-FISHER, M., HAWKER, A., and HENSMAN, C. (1967) Clients of Alcoholism Information Centres, *Brit. med. J.*, **4**, 346–9.

EDWARDS, G., KYLE, E., and NICHOLLS, P. (1974) A study of alcoholics admitted to four hospitals: 1. Social class and the interaction of the alcoholic with the treatment system, *Quart. J. Stud. Alc.*, **35**, 499–522.

EDWARDS, G., WILLIAMSON, V., HAWKER, A., HENSMAN, C., and POSTOYAN, S. (1968) Census of a reception centre, *Brit. J. Psychiat.*, **114**, 1031–9.

EDWARDS, P., HARVEY, C., and WHITEHEAD, P. C. (1973) Wives of alcoholics; a critical review and analysis, *Quart. J. Stud. Alc.*, **34**, 112–32.

EHRENWALD, J. (1963) *Neurosis in the Family and Patterns of Psychosocial Defense; A Study of Psychiatric Epidemiology*, New York.

ELIOT, P. D. (1948) Bereavement; Inevitable but not Insurmountable. In *Family, Marriage and Parenthood*, H. Becker and R. Hill eds., Boston.

EMRICK, C. D. (1974) A review of psychologically oriented treatment of alcoholism. I. The use and inter-relationships of outcome criteria and drinking behaviour following treatment, *Quart. J. Stud. Alc.*, **35**, 523–49.

EMRICK, C. D. (1975) A review of psychologically oriented treatment of alcoholism. II. The relative effectiveness of different treatment approaches and the effectiveness of treatment versus no treatment, *J. Stud. Alc.*, **36**, 88–109.

ENDS, E. J. and PAGE, C. W. (1957) A study of three types of group psychotherapy with hospitalised male inebriates, *Quart. J. Stud. Alc.*, **18**, 263–77.

ESSER, P. H. (1963) Normal drinking in recovered alcohol addicts: a comment on the article by D. L. Davies, *Quart. J. Stud. Alc.*, **24**, 119–21.

EVANS, M. (1970) Integrated hospital and community care for alcohol dependents and their families, Chapter 9. In *Modern Trends in Drug Dependence and Alcoholism*, R. V. Phillipson, ed., London.

EYSENCK, H. J. and EYSENCK, S. B. G. (1964) *Manual of the Eysenck Personality Inventory*, London.

FERREIRA, A. J. and WINTER, W. D. (1968) Decision making in normal and abnormal two-child families, *Fam. Process*, Basel **7**, 17–36.

FOX, V. and SMITH, M. A. (1959) Evaluation of a chemopsychotherapeutic program for the rehabilitation of alcoholics: observations over a two-year period, *Quart. J. Stud. Alc.*, **20**, 767–80.

FRANK, J. D. (1961) *Persuasion and Healing: A Comparative Study of Psychotherapy*, London.

FREEMAN, H. E. and SIMMONS, O. G. (1963) *The Mental Patient Comes Home*, New York.

FUTTERMAN, S. (1953) Personality trends in wives of alcoholics, *J. psychiat. social Work*, **23**, 37–41.

GATH, D., HENSMAN, C., HAWKER, A., KELLY, M., and EDWARDS, G. (1968) The drunk in court: A survey of drunkenness offenders from two London courts, *Brit. med. J.*, **4**, 808–11.

GERARD, D. L. and SAENGER, G. (1959) Interval between intake and follow-up as a factor in the evaluation of patients with a drinking problem, *Quart. J. Stud. Alc.*, **20**, 620–30.

GERARD, D. L., SAENGER, G., and WILE, R. (1962) The abstinent alcoholic, *Arch. gen. Psychiat.*, **6**, 83–95.

GERARD, D. L. and SAENGER, G. (1966) *Out-patient Treatment of Alcoholism: A Study of Outcome and its Determinants*, Brookside Monograph No. 4. Toronto.

GILLESPIE, D. F. (1967) The fate of alcoholics: an evaluation of alcoholism follow-up studies, In *Alcoholism*, D. J. Pittman ed., New York.

GLATT, M. M. (1955) A treatment centre for alcoholics in a public mental hospital; its establishment and its working, *Brit. J. Addict.*, **52**, 55–92.

GLATT, M. M. (1961a) Drinking habits of English (middle class) alcoholics, *Acta psychiat. scand.*, **37**, 88–113.

GLATT, M. M. (1961b) Treatment results in an English mental hospital alcoholic unit, *Acta psychiat. scand.*, **37**, 143–68.

GLATT, M. M. (1975) *Alcoholism: A Social Disease*, London.

GLATT, M. M. and WHITELY, J. S. (1956) Problems of alcoholics at different social levels, *Mschr. Psychiat. Neurol.*, **132**, 1–12.

GLIEDMAN, L. H., ROSENTHAL, D., FRANK, J. D., and NASH, H. T. (1956)

Group therapy of alcoholics with concurrent group meetings of their wives, *Quart. J. Stud. Alc.*, **17**, 655–70.

GOODWIN, D. W., CRANE, J. B., and GUZE, S. B. (1971) Felons who drink: An 8-year follow-up, *Quart. J. Stud. Alc.*, **32**, 136–47.

GORAD, S. L. (1971) Communicational styles and interaction of alcoholics and their wives, *Fam. Process*, Balt., **10**, 475–89.

GREGORY, I. (1959) Husbands and wives admitted to mental hospitals, *J. ment. Sci.*, **105**, 457–62.

HABERMAN, P. W. (1964) Psychological test score changes for wives of alcoholics during periods of drinking and sobriety, *J. clin. Psychol.*, **20**, 230–2.

HABERMAN, P. W. (1965) Some characteristics of alcoholic marriages differentiated by level of deviance, *J. Marriage Fam.*, **27**, 34–6.

HAGNELL, O. and KREITMAN, N. (1974) Mental illness in married pairs in a total population, *Brit. J. Psychiat.*, **125**, 293–302.

HALD, J., JACOBSEN, E., and LARSEN, V. (1948) The sensitizing effect of tetraethylthiuram-disulphide (Antabuse) to ethyl alcohol, *Acta pharmacol. toxicol.*, **4**, 285–96.

HALL, J. and JONES, D. C. (1950) Social grading of occupations, *Brit. J. Sociol.*, **1**, 31–55.

HAMBURG, S. (1975) Behaviour therapy in alcoholism: a critical review of broad-spectrum approaches, *J. Stud. Alc.*, **36**, 69–87.

HANSEN, D. A. and HILL, R. (1964) Families under Stress, In *Handbook of Marriage and the Family*, pp. 782–819, H. T. Christensen, ed., Chicago.

HARE, E. H. and SHAW, G. K. (1965) A study in family health. 2. A comparison of health of the fathers, mothers and children, *Brit. J. Psychiat.*, **111**, 467–71.

HARPER, J. and HICKSON, B. (1951) The results of hospital treatment of chronic alcoholism, *Lancet* **2**, 1057–9.

HAWKINS, J. L. (1968) Associations between companionship, hostility and marital satisfaction, *J. Marriage Fam.*, **30**, 647–50.

HAWKS, D. (1976) Social research as a determinant of social policy, In *Alcohol Dependence and Smoking Behaviour*, Chapter 31, G. Edwards, M. A. H. Russell, D. Hawks, and M. MacCafferty, eds., Farnborough.

HERBST, P. G. (1954) Conceptual framework for studying the family, In *Social Structure and Personality in a City*, O. A. Oeser and S. B. Hammond, eds., London.

HERSHON, H. (1977) Withdrawal symptoms: Clinical study of 100 male alcoholics, *Brit. J. Addict.*, (in press).

HICKS, M. W. and PLATT, N. (1970) Marital happiness and stability: A review of the research in the 1960's, *J. Marriage Fam.*, **32**, 553–74.

HILL, M. J. and BLANE, H. T. (1966) Evaluation of psychotherapy with alcoholics: A critical review, *Quart. J. Stud. Alc.*, **27**, 76–104.

HILL, H. E., HAERTZEN, C. A., and DAVIS, H. (1962) An MMPI factor analytic study of alcoholics, narcotic addicts and criminals, *Quart. J. Stud. Alc.*, **23**, 411–31.

HILL, R. (1949) *Families Under Stress; Adjustment to the Crisis of War Separation and Reunion*, New York.

HOME OFFICE (1971) *Habitual Drunken Offenders: Report of the Working Party*, London, HMSO.

HORE, B. D. (1971) Life events and alcoholic relapse, *Brit. J. Addict.*, **66**, 83–8.

HORE, B. D. and SMITH, E. (1975) Who goes to Alcoholic Units, *Brit. J. Addict.*, **70**, 263–70.

HUNT, W. A. and MATARAZZO, J. D. (1970) Habit mechanisms in smoking, In *Learning Mechanism in Smoking*, W. A. Hunt, ed., Chicago.

HURVITZ, N. (1965) Control roles, marital strain, role deviation, and marital adjustment, *J. Marriage Fam.*, **27**, 29–31.

JACKSON, J. K. (1954) The adjustment of the family to the crisis of alcoholism, *Quart.J. Stud. Alc.*, **15**, 562–86.

JACKSON, J. K. and KOGAN, K. L. (1963) The search for solutions; help-seeking patterns of families of active and inactive alcoholics, *Quart. J. Stud. Alc.*, **24**, 449–72.

–JAMES, J. E. and GOLDMAN, M. (1971) Behavior trends of wives of alcoholics, *Quart.J. Stud. Alc.*, **32**, 373–81.

JAMES, W. P., SALTER, C. E., and THOMAS, H. G. (1972) *Alcohol and Drug Dependence—Treatment and Rehabilitation*, King Edward's Hospital Fund: London.

JELLINEK, E. M. (1952) Phases of alcohol addiction, *Quart. J. Stud. Alc.*, **13**, 673–84.

JELLINEK, E. M. (1960) *The Disease Concept of Alcoholism*, New Haven, Connecticut.

JONES, M. C. (1968) Personality correlates and antecedents of drinking patterns in adult males, *J. cons. clin. Psychol.*, **32**, 2–12.

KAMMEIER, M. L., HOFFMAN, H., and LOPER, R. G. (1973) Personality characteristics of alcoholics as college freshmen and at time of treatment, *Quart. J. Stud. Alc.*, **34**, 390–9.

KANFER, F. H. and KAROLY, P. (1972) Some additional conceptualizations, In *Conscience, Contract and Social Reality: Theory and Research in Behavioural Science*, R. C. Johnson, P. R. Dokecki, and O. H. Mowrer, eds., New York.

KARP, E. S., JACKSON, J. H., and LESTER, D. (1970) Ideal-self fulfilment in mate selection; a corollary to the complementary need theory of mate selection, *J. Marriage Fam.*, **32**, 269–72.

KENDELL, R. E. (1965) Normal drinking by former alcohol addicts, *Quart.J. Stud. Alc.*, **26**, 247–57.

KEPHART, W. M. (1954) Drinking and marital disruption; a research note, *Quart. J. Stud. Alc.*, **15**, 63–73.

KERCKHOFF, A. and DAVIS, K. A. (1962) Value consensus and need complementarity in mate selection, *Amer. sociol. Rev.*, **27**, 295–303.

KINSEY, A. C., POMEROY, W. B., and MARTIN, C. E. (1948) *Sexual Behaviour in the Human Male*, Philadelphia.

KINSEY, A. C., POMEROY, W. B., MARTIN, C. E., and GEBHARD, P. H. (1953) *Sexual Behaviour in the Human Female*, Philadelphia.

KIRKPATRICK, C. (1967) Familial development, selective needs, and predictive theory, *J. Marriage Fam.*, **29**, 229–36.

KOGAN, K. L., FORDYCE, W. E., and JACKSON, J. K. (1963) Personality disturbances of wives of alcoholics, *Quart.J. Stud. Alc.*, **24**, 227–38.

KOGAN, K. L. and JACKSON, J. K. (1961) Some role perceptions of wives of alcoholics, *Psychol. Rep.*, **9**, 119–24.

KOGAN, K. L. and JACKSON, J. K. (1963a) Conventional sex role stereotypes and actual perceptions, *Psychol. Rep.*, **13**, 27–30.

KOGAN, K. L. and JACKSON, J. K. (1963b) Role perceptions in wives of alcoholics and of nonalcoholics, *Quart.J. Stud. Alc.*, **24**, 627–39.

KOGAN, K. L. and JACKSON, J. K. (1964) Patterns of atypical perceptions of self and spouse in wives of alcoholics, *Quart.J. Stud. Alc.*, **25**, 555–7.

KOGAN, K. L. and JACKSON, J. K. (1965) Some concomitants of personal difficulties in wives of alcoholics and nonalcoholics, *Quart. J. Stud. Alc.*, **26**, 595–604.

KREITMAN, N. (1964) The patient's spouse, *Brit. J. Psychiat.*, **110**, 159–73.

KREITMAN, N. (1968) Married couples admitted to mental hospitals. I. Diagnostic similarity and the relation of illness to marriage. II. Family history, age and duration of marriage, *Brit. J. Psychiat.*, **114**, 699–718.

KUDER, G. F. and RICHARDSON, M. W. (1937) The theory of the estimation of test reliability, *Psychometrika*, **2**, 151–60.

LA FORGE, R. and SUCZEK, R. F. (1955) The interpersonal dimensions of personality: an interpersonal check-list, *Journal of Personality*, **24**, 94.

LEARY, T. (1957) *Interpersonal Diagnoses of Personality; a Functional Therapy and Methodology for Personality Evaluation*, New York.

LEDERMANN, S. (1956) *Alcool, Alcoolisme, Alcoolisation. Donnés Scientifiques de Caractère Physiologique, Économique et Social.* (Institut National d'Études Démographiques Travaux et Documents, Cahier No. 29), Paris.

LEITENBERG, H. (1973) The use of single-case methodology in psychotherapy research, *J. abnorm. Psychol.*, **82**, 87–101.

LEMERT, E. M. (1960) The occurrence and sequence of events in the adjustment of families to alcoholism, *Quart. J. Stud. Alc.*, **21**, 679–97.

LEMERT, E. M. (1962) Dependency in married alcoholics, *Quart. J. Stud. Alc.*, **23**, 590–609.

LEVINGER, G. (1965) Marital cohesiveness and dissolution; an integrative review, *J. Marriage Fam.*, **27**, 19–28.

LEVINGER, G. (1966) Sources of marital dissatisfaction among applicants for divorce, *Amer. J. Orthopsychiat.*, **36**, 803–7.

LEVINSON, T. and SERENY, G. (1969) An experimental evaluation of 'Insight Therapy' for the chronic alcoholic, *Canad. psychiat. Ass. J.*, **14**, 143–6.

LEWIS, M. L. (1954) The initial contact with wives of alcoholics, *Social Casework*, **35**, 8–14.

LIVELY, E. L. (1969) Towards concept clarification; the case of marital interaction, *J. Marriage Fam.*, **31**, 108–14.

LUCKEY, E. B. (1960) Marital satisfaction and its association with congruence of perception, *J. Marriage Fam.*, **22**, 49–54.

LUCKEY, E. B. (1964) Marital satisfaction and its concomitant perceptions of self and spouse, *J. counsel. Psychol.*, **11**, 136–45.

MCCANCE, C. and MCCANCE, P. F. (1969) Alcoholism in north-east Scotland: its treatment and outcome, *Brit. J. Psychiat.*, **115**, 189–98.

MCCORD, W., MCCORD, J., and GUDEMAN, J. (1960) *Origins of Alcoholism.* (Stanford Studies in Sociology, No. 1), Stanford.

MACDONALD, D. E. (1956) Mental disorders in wives of alcoholics, *Quart. J. Stud. Alc.*, **17**, 282–7.

MAYER, J. and MYERSON, D. J. (1970) Characteristics of outpatient alcoholics in relation to change in drinking, work and marital status during treatment, *Quart. J. Stud. Alc.*, **31**, 889–97.

MELLO, N. K. (1972) Behavioural Studies of Alcoholism, In *The Biology of Alcoholism*, Vol. 2, Chapter 9, 219–91, B. Kissin and H. Begleiter, eds. New York.

MERRILL, G. (1969) How fathers manage when wives are hospitalized for schizophrenia; an exploratory study, *Soc. Psychiat.*, Berl. **4**, 26–32.

MINISTRY OF HEALTH (1962) *National Health Service: Hospital Treatment of Alcoholism*, H M (62) 43.

MINISTRY OF HEALTH (1968) *National Health Service: The Treatment of Alcoholism*, H M (68) 37.

MITCHELL, H. E. (1959) The interrelatedness of alcoholism and marital conflict.

Symposium, 1958. 4. Interpersonal perception theory applied to conflicted marriages in which alcoholism is and is not a problem, *Amer. J. Orthopsychiat.*, **29**, 547–59.

MORROW, W. R. and ROBINS, A. J. (1964) Family relations and social recovery of psychotic mothers, *J. Hlth. hum. Behav.*, **5**, 14–24.

MOSS, M. C. and DAVIES, E. B. (1967) *A Survey of Alcoholism in an English County*, London.

MURSTEIN, B. I. (1970) Stimulus-Value-Role; a theory of marital choice, *J. Marriage Fam.*, **32**, 465–81.

MURSTEIN, B. I. and GLAUDIN, V. (1966) The relationship of marital adjustment to personality; a factor analysis of the interpersonal check list, *J. Marriage Fam.*, **28**, 37–43.

NICHOLLS, P., EDWARDS, G., and KYLE, E. (1974) A study of alcoholics admitted to four hospitals: II, General and cause-specific mortality during follow-up, *Quart. J. Stud. Alc.*, **35**, 841–55.

NIELSEN, J. (1964) Mental disorders in married couples (assortative mating), *Brit. J. Psychiat.*, **110**, 683–97.

OLSON, D. H. (1969) The measurement of family power by self report and behavioural methods, *J. Marriage Fam.*, **31**, 545–50.

OLSON, D. H. and RABUNSKY, C. (1972) Validity of four measures of family power, *J. Marriage Fam.*, **34**, 224–34.

OPPENHEIM, A. N. (1966) *Questionnaire Design and Attitude Measurement*, New York.

ORFORD, J. (1973) A comparison of alcoholics whose drinking is totally uncontrolled and those whose drinking is mainly controlled, *Behav. Res. & Therapy*, **11**, 565–76.

ORFORD, J. (1974) *A prospective study of the relationship between marital factors and the outcome of treatment for alcoholism*, Ph.D. Thesis, London University.

ORFORD, J. and GUTHRIE, S. (1968) Coping behavior used by wives of alcoholics; a preliminary investigation, *Int. Congr. Alc. Alcsm. Abst.* 28th. p. 97.

ORFORD, J. and GUTHRIE, S. (1976) Coping behaviour used by wives of alcoholics: a preliminary investigation, In *Alcohol Dependence and Smoking Behaviour*, Chapter 21, 136–43, G. Edwards, M. A. H. Russell, D. Hawks, and M. MacCafferty, eds., Farnborough.

ORFORD, J. and HAWKER, A. (1974) An investigation of an Alcoholism Rehabilitation Halfway House: II. The complex question of client motivation, *Brit. J. Addict.*, **69**, 315–23.

ORFORD, J., HAWKER, A., and NICHOLLS, P. (1974) An investigation of an Alcoholism Rehabilitation Halfway House: I. Types of client and modes of discharge, *Brit. J. Addict.*, **69**, 213–24.

ORFORD, J., HAWKER, A., and NICHOLLS, P. (1975a) An investigation of an Alcoholism Rehabilitation Halfway House: III. Reciprocal staff-resident evaluations, *Brit. J. Addict.*, **70**, 55–64.

ORFORD, J., HAWKER, A., and NICHOLLS, P. (1975b) An investigation of an Alcoholism Rehabilitation Halfway House: IV. Attractions of the Halfway House for residents, *Brit. J. Addict.*, **70**, 179–86.

ORFORD, J., OPPENHEIMER, E., EGERT, S., HENSMAN, C., and GUTHRIE, S. (1976a) The cohesiveness of alcoholism-complicated marriages and its influence on treatment outcome, *Brit. J. Psychiat.*, **128**, 318–39.

ORFORD, J., OPPENHEIMER, E., EGERT, S., and HENSMAN, C. (1976b) The role of excessive drinking in alcoholism-complicated marriages: a study of stability and change over a one-year period, *Int. J. Addict.*, (in press).

ORT, R. S. (1950) A study of role-conflicts as related to happiness in marriage, *J. abnorm. social Psychol.*, **45**, 691–9.

OTTO, S. and ORFORD, J. (1977) *Not Quite like Home: Small hostels for alchololics and others.* Chichester (in press).

OVENSTONE, I. M. K. (1973) The development of neurosis in the wives of neurotic men. II. Marital role functions and marital tension, *Brit. J. Psychiat.*, **122**, 35–45.

PATTISON, E. M. (1968) A critique of abstinence criteria in the treatment of alcoholism, *Int. J. social Psychiat.*, **14**, 268–76.

PATTISON, E. M., HEADLEY, E. B., GLESER, G. C., and GOTTSCHALK, L. A. (1968) Abstinence and normal drinking: an assessment of changes in drinking patterns in alcoholics after treatment, *Quart. J. Stud. Alc.*, **29**, 610–33.

PATTISON, E. M., HEADLEY, E. B., GLESER, G. C., and GOTTSCHALK, L. A. (1965) *Abstinence and Normal Drinking: The relation of drinking patterns to overall health in successfully treated alcoholics.* Paper read at the 121st Annual Meeting of the American Psychiatric Association, May 3–7, 1965, New York.

PITTMAN, D. J. and TATE, R. C. (1972) A comparison of two treatment programs for alcoholics, *Int. J. social Psychiat.*, **18**, 183–93.

PIXLEY, J. M. and STIEFEL, J. R. (1963) Group therapy designed to meet the needs of the alcoholic's wife, *Quart. J. Stud. Alc.*, **24**, 304–14.

PREMACK, D. and ANGLIN, B. (1973) On the possibilities of self-control in man and animals, *J. abnorm. Psychol.*, **81**, 137–51.

RAE, J. B. (1972) The influence of the wives on the treatment of alcoholics; follow-up study at two years, *Brit. J. Psychiat.*, **120**, 601–13.

RAE, J. B. and DREWERY, J. (1972) Interpersonal patterns in alcoholic marriages, *Brit. J. Psychiat.*, **120**, 615–21.

RAE, J. B. and FORBES, A. R. (1966) Clinical and psychometric characteristics of wives of alcoholics, *Brit. J. Psychiat.*, **112**, 197–200.

RATHOD, N. M., GREGORY, E., BLOWS, D., and THOMAS, G. H. (1966) A two year follow-up study of alcoholic patients, *Brit. J. Psychiat.*, **112**, 683–92.

REINERT, R. E. and BOWEN, W. T. (1968) Social drinking following treatment for alcoholism, *Bull. Menn. Clin.*, **32**, 280–90.

RICHARDSON, H. M. (1939) Studies of mental resemblance between husbands and wives and between friends, *Psychol. Bull.*, **36**, 104.

RIECKEN, H. W. and BORUCH, R. F. (1974) *Social Experimentation: A method for planning and evaluating social interaction*, London.

RITSON, B. (1968) The prognosis of alcohol addicts treated by a specialised unit, *Brit. J. Psychiat.*, **114**, 1019–29.

ROBINS, L. N. (1966) *Deviant Children Grown Up; a sociological and psychiatric study of sociopathic personality*, Baltimore.

RYLE, A. (1966) A marital patterns test for use in psychiatric research, *Brit. J. Psychiat.*, **112**, 285–93.

SELECT COMMITTEE (1834) *House of Commons Select Committee on Intoxication*, London: Parliamentary Papers.

SELZER, M. L. and HOLLOWAY, W. H. (1957) A follow-up of alcoholics committed to a State hospital, *Quart. J. Stud. Alc.*, **18**, 98–120.

SHANNON, J. and GUERNEY, B. (1973) Interpersonal effects of interpersonal behaviour, *J. Person. soc. Psychol.*, **26**, 142–50.

SLATER, E. and WOODSIDE, M. (1951) *Patterns of Marriage; a study of marriage relationships in the urban working classes*, London.

SMART, R. G. (1974) The effect of licensing restrictions during 1914–1918 on drunkenness and liver cirrhosis deaths in Britain, *Brit. J. Addict.*, **69**, 109–21.

SMITH, C. G. (1967) Marital influences on treatment outcome in alcoholism, *J. Irish med. Ass.*, **60**, 433–4.

SOBELL, M. B. and SOBELL, L. C. (1973) Alcoholics treated by individualized behaviour therapy; one-year treatment outcome, *Behav. Res. Ther.*, **11**, 599–618.

STEINER, C. M. (1969) The alcoholic game, *Quart. J. Stud. Alc.*, **30**, 920–38.

STEINGLASS, P., WEINER, S., and MENDELSON, J. H. (1971) A systems approach to alcoholism: a model and its clinical application, *Arch. Gen. Psychiat.*, **24**, 401–8.

TAYLOR, S. D., WILBUR, M., and OSNOS, R. (1966) The wives of drug addicts, *Amer. J. Psychol.*, **123**, 585–91.

TERMAN, L. M. (1938) *Psychological Factors in Marital Happiness*, New York.

THARP, R. G. (1963) Psychological patterning in marriage, *Psychol. Bull.*, **60**, 97–117.

TOMSOVIC, M. and EDWARDS, R. V. (1970) Lysergide treatment of schizophrenic and non-schizophrenic alcoholics: a controlled evaluation, *Quart. J. Stud. Alc.*, **31**, 932–49.

TROTTER, T. (1804) *Drunkenness, and its Effects on the Human Body*, London.

TURK, J. L. and BELL, M. W. (1972) Measuring power in families, *J. Marriage Fam.*, **34**, 215–22.

VALLANCE, M. (1965) A two-year follow-up study of patients admitted to the psychiatric department of a general hospital, *Brit. J. Psychiat.*, **111**, 348–56.

VAUGHN, C. E. and LEFF, J. P. (1976) The influence of family and social factors on the course of psychiatric illness, *Brit. J. Psychiat.*, **129**, 125–37.

VOEGTLIN, W. L. and BROZ, W. R. (1949) The conditional reflex treatment of chronic alcoholism. X. An analysis of 3125 admissions over a period of ten and a half years, *Ann. Intern. Med.*, **30**, 580–97.

VOGLER, R. E., LUNDE, S. E., JOHNSON, G. R. and MARTIN, P. L. (1970) Electrical aversion conditioning with chronic alcoholics, *J. cons. clin. Psychol.*, **34**, 302–7.

WALL, J. H. and ALLEN, E. B. (1944) Results of Hospital treatment of alcoholism, *Amer. J. Psychiat.*, **100**, 474–9.

WALTON, H. J., RITSON, E. B., and KENNEDY, R. I. (1966) Response of alcoholics to clinical treatment, *Brit. med. J.*, **2**, 1171–4.

WATZLAWICK, P., BEAVIN, J. H. and JACKSON, B. D. (1968) *Pragmatics of Human Communication; a Study of Interactional Patterns, Pathologies and Paradoxes*, London.

WELSH, G. S. and DAHLSTROM, W. G. (1956) *Basic Readings on the MMPI in Psychology and Medicine*, New York.

WHALEN, R. (1953) Wives of alcoholics: four types observed in a family service agency, *Quart. J. Stud. Alc.*, **14**, 632–41.

WILKINS, R. H. (1974) *The Hidden Alcoholic in General Practice*, London.

WILLEMS, P. J. A., LETEMENDIA, F. J. J., and ARROYAVE, F. (1973a) A two-year follow-up study comparing short- with long-stay in-patient treatment of alcoholics, *Brit. J. Psychiat.*, **122**, 637–48.

WILLEMS, P. J. A., LETEMENDIA, F. J. J., and ARROYAVE, F. (1973b) A categorization for the assessment of prognosis and outcome in the treatment of alcoholism, *Brit. J. Psychiat.*, **122**, 649–54.

WILLIAMS, A. F. (1966) Social drinking, anxiety and depression, *J. Personality soc. Psychol.*, **3**, 689–93.

WILSON, G. B. (1940) *Alcohol and the Nation*, London.

WINCH, R. S. (1958) *Mate selection; A Study of Complementary Needs*, New York.

WORLD HEALTH ORGANISATION (1951) *Expert Committee on Mental Health,*

Report of the First Session of the Alcoholism Sub-Committee. Techn. Rep. Ser. No. 42. Geneva: WHO.

WORLD HEALTH ORGANISATION (1952) *Expert Committee on Mental Health, Alcoholism Sub-Committee, Second Report,* Techn. Rep. Ser. No. 48. Geneva: WHO.

WORLD HEALTH ORGANISATION (1970) *Expert Committee on Drug Dependence, Eighteenth Report,* Techn. Rep. Ser. No. 437. Geneva: WHO.

WRIGHT, P. H. (1968) Need similarity, need complementarity and the place of personality in interpersonal attraction, *J. exp. Res. Personality,* 3, 128–35.

INDEXES

A. SUBJECT

B. AUTHOR

Agulnik, P. L. (1970), 71
Angell, R. C. (1936), 23

Baekland, F.
— *et al.* (1975), 19
Bailey, M. B. (1967), 31, 32, 35, 94
— *et al.* (1962), 23, 26, 31, 32, 35
— and Stewart, J. (1967), 103, 105
Belasco, J. A. (1971), 52
Berne, E. (1964), 36
Block, M. A. (1963), 105
Blood, R. W.
— and Wolfe, B. M. (1960), 25, 63, 64
Boyd, W. H.
— and Bolen, D. W. (1970), 31
Broderick, C. B. (1971), 24
Brown, G. W.
— *et al.* (1962), 34, 36, 59, 74
— *et al.* (1972), 34, 74
— *et al.* (1975), 118
Bruun, K.
— *et al.* (1975), 17, 116
Bullock, S. C.
— and Mudd, E. H. (1959), 26, 71
Burgess, E. W.
— and Cottrell, L. S. (1939), 27
— and Wallin, P. (1943), 27, 30

Burr, W. R. (1970), 24
Burton, G.
— and Kaplan, H. M. (1968), 23

Campbell, D. T.
— and Stanley, J. C. (1963), 118
Cartwright, A. K. J.
— *et al.* (1975), 2, 12, 115
Cattell, R. B.
— and Nesselroade, J. R. (1967), 30
Cheek, F. E. (1965), 74
Clark, W. (1966), 2
Clausen, J. A.
— and Yarrow, M. R. (1955), 23, 24, 26
Collins, J.
— *et al.* (1971), 25, 65
Conger, J. J. (1956), 91
Cook, T. (1975), 15
— *et al.* (1968), 11, 15
— and Pollak, B. (1970), 15
Coppen, A.
— *et al.* (1965), 31
Corsini, R. J. (1956), 28–9
Cronbach, L. J. (1955), 28

D'Zurilla, T. J.
— and Goldfried, M. R. (1971), 111